Making US Foreign Policy

SECOND EDITION

Making US Foreign Policy

The Essentials

Ralph G. Carter

LYNNE
RIENNER
PUBLISHERS

BOULDER
LONDON

Published in the United States of America in 2020 by
Lynne Rienner Publishers, Inc.
1800 30th Street, Boulder, Colorado 80301
www.rienner.com

and in the United Kingdom by
Lynne Rienner Publishers, Inc.
Gray's Inn House, 127 Clerkenwell Road, London EC1 5DB

The first edition of this book was published by Pearson Education, Inc.

Library of Congress Cataloging-in-Publication Data
Names: Carter, Ralph G., author.
Title: Making US foreign policy : the essentials / Ralph G. Carter.
Other titles: Essentials of U.S. foreign policy making | Making U.S. foreign
  policy | Making United States foreign policy
Description: 2nd edition. | Boulder, Colorado : Lynne Rienner Publishers,
  Inc., 2019. | Revised edition of: Essentials of U.S. foreign policy
  making. Boston : Pearson, 2015. | Includes bibliographical references and
  index.
Identifiers: LCCN 2019009924 | ISBN 9781626378131 (pbk. : alk. paper)
Subjects: LCSH: United States—Foreign relations—Decision making.
Classification: LCC JZ1480 .C374 2019 | DDC 327.73—dc23
LC record available at https://lccn.loc.gov/2019009924

British Cataloguing in Publication Data
A Cataloguing in Publication record for this book
is available from the British Library.

Printed and bound in the United States of America

 The paper used in this publication meets the requirements
of the American National Standard for Permanence of
Paper for Printed Library Materials Z39.48-1992.

5 4 3 2 1

To Nita

Contents

1

Making US Foreign Policy

Learning Objectives

- Define "foreign policy."
- Describe the five stages of the foreign policy input-output process. Explain the formal foreign policy powers of the three main branches of the US government.
- Differentiate between the concentric circles approach and the shifting constellations approach to foreign policy making.

On January 20, 2017, President Donald J. Trump took the oath of office, vowing to protect the United States from all enemies, foreign and domestic. In his inaugural speech, he stressed that Americans were threatened by terrorists and criminals. One week later, he issued an executive order banning travel to the United States by people from a number of Muslim-majority countries. Chaos ensued as officials tried to determine if those already in the air bound for the United States with valid visas would be admitted, if those with permanent residency status were included in the ban, and so on. Critics demonstrated across the country, and many called the ban an unconstitutional religious test. Ultimately, it took the administration three tries to produce a travel ban that the Supreme Court would accept as constitutional. Then in early 2018,

1

the Justice Department announced a "zero tolerance" policy toward illegal immigrants, a policy whose consequence was the separation of children from their parents, who would be prosecuted. The outrage created by family separations and the impounding of children—which critics called "kids in cages"—was overwhelming. After denying that he could change the policy, President Trump signed an executive order doing so.

Both these examples demonstrate problematic foreign policy making. Were they just bad ideas? Were they policy options that had not been carefully considered through a good vetting process that included all of the agencies involved? Were they the result of an inexperienced administration and a passive Congress controlled by the president's own political party? If nothing else, these examples show that foreign policy making is rarely simple or easy, and the challenge of making foreign policy is nothing new. From the earliest days of the republic, international events and US responses to them affected where Americans could travel, the safety risks to which they were exposed, the availability and prices of goods, and the quality of life they could expect. Like other countries, the United States has to adapt to events beyond its borders, as these events present either challenges to be solved or opportunities to be exploited. That adaptation process involves making foreign policy.

Simply defined, **foreign policy**** refers to the goals and actions of the US government in the international system. Thus, foreign policy may be what the US government wants to achieve, and the steps taken in that regard toward other international actors (for example, North Korea, the United Nations [UN], or Hezbollah) and issues (such as foreign trade, genocide, or global climate change). The overarching thesis of this book is this: *how policies are made, and by whom, affects the substance of the resulting policies.* That means the actors (the individuals, groups, and organizations) involved in making the policies, their motivations, their differing amounts of power or influence, and the processes by which they make foreign policy decisions combine to shape the resulting policy outputs, and ultimately their overall outcomes. These actors, motivations, processes, outputs, and outcomes are the focus of this book.

---

* Terms that are defined in the glossary appear in **boldface** on first substantive use.

How Is Foreign Policy Made and by Whom?

In the United States, foreign policy making is very much like domestic policy making. Although there are some differences, overall the similarities between the two basic processes outweigh those differences. At its most fundamental level, policy making is a five-stage process involving inputs, decision making, outputs, outcomes, and feedback. As shown in Figure 1.1, the first stage begins with **inputs**—things that stimulate policy makers to act. Such inputs could be international events that seem to require or invite a response, or they might be domestic pressures by those who seek a foreign policy change. In the second stage, policy makers make decisions about whether to address these inputs, and if so, how. There are many different ways to make such decisions, as will be discussed in the pages to follow. In stage three, the results of the decision are foreign policy **outputs**. They are the response by the foreign policy makers to the inputs. Sometimes outputs are words—signals that convey what the United States is willing to do—or broader policy declarations; other times they are more assertive actions on the part of the government. In stage four, these outputs produce results called **outcomes**, which answer the "so what?" question: once policy makers choose a course of action, what happens next? The "what happens next" is the outcome. Finally, in stage five, outcomes can create a feedback loop: based on the outcomes, new inputs may arise.

Some foreign policies are the results of decisions made in the executive branch; others are the result of interactions between a number of interested governmental and nongovernmental actors—such as presidents, other administration officials, formal and informal presidential advisers, Congress or its individual members, representatives of relevant interest groups, the broader public, concerned foreign leaders, and at times the federal courts. All these interactions are reported by the various elements of the national media, which may also become a factor in determining whether policies get made and how. Compared to many other countries, the United States has processes that are extremely open to inputs from numerous participants who may become significantly involved in foreign policy making.

In the crucial decision-making phase of any foreign policy process, the amount of influence these actors wield is a unique blend of the intersection of the nature of the issue, the political

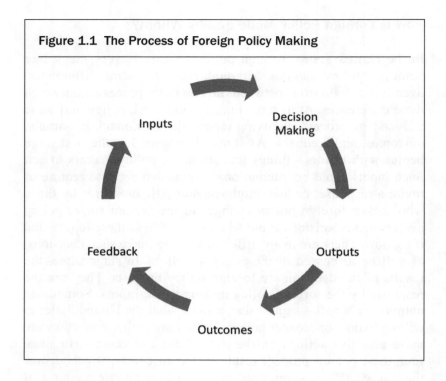

Figure 1.1 The Process of Foreign Policy Making

Inputs

Decision Making

Outputs

Outcomes

Feedback

context involved, the timing, the actors' positions in government or politics, and so on. However, presidents and members of Congress have important foreign policy advantages in terms of powers granted to them by the Constitution, and that should be noted from the outset.

Let's begin with presidents. The constitutional powers presidents have in foreign policy making are significant. Presidents serve as the commander in chief of the nation's military. This power allows them to order troops into conflict and determine military strategies. Presidents also have other constitutional roles that allow them to serve essentially as the nation's chief diplomat. For example, the role of sending and receiving ambassadors gives presidents the sole power to recognize diplomatically other regimes as being legitimate representatives of their population. Presidents often attend summit conferences where they meet with other countries' leaders to discuss issues of mutual concern. Presidents have the power to negotiate treaties with other countries, but the Senate must approve such treaties by a two-thirds vote of those present. Presidents can also make personal commitments in the form of executive agreements with other world leaders, and those do not require Senate approval. Like other handshake agreements, executive agreements are only as good as the word of the leaders who made them. At least while those leaders are in office, their executive agreements are normally seen as the functional equivalent of treaties. Of course, subsequent presidents are under no obligation to adhere to executive agreements they did not make, and presidents may later change their minds about their own prior agreements with others.

As the nation's chief executive, presidents appoint (with Senate approval) a number of other foreign policy officials. These officials range from cabinet officers (for example, secretaries of state, defense, treasury, or homeland security, and diplomats given cabinet rank such as the US trade representative or ambassador to the United Nations) to the directors of national intelligence and central intelligence and to the different ambassadors who represent the United States in foreign capitals. Presidents also appoint some other influential foreign policy officials without Senate confirmation. A good example is the post of national security adviser. The Constitution further gives presidents the power to see that the nation's laws are faithfully executed, a power that provides presidents with considerable authority to conduct the nation's foreign affairs. Finally, because presidents, along with their vice presidents, are the only nationally elected officials in the country, they are uniquely situated to speak for the entire nation when dealing with other international actors or issues.

Surprisingly, Congress—the legislative branch—actually has more enumerated constitutional foreign policy powers than do presidents. These include the specific powers to:

- Declare war
- Raise, support, and regulate the nation's military
- Make rules regarding piracy and its punishment
- Regulate international commerce
- Regulate immigration
- Make any other laws "necessary and proper" for carrying out the above powers

When they are not willing to wait for an administration to act, some individual members of Congress will take these powers and push and prod the US government into making new policies; these legislators will use whatever political leverage is available to put their imprint on foreign policy.

More generally, as a collective body, Congress has the power to pass whatever legislation its members desire—such as imposing economic sanctions on Russia or reaffirming the US commitment to defend North Atlantic Treaty Organization (**NATO**) allies, to name two recent examples. Presidents have the right to veto such legislation, but Congress can override presidential vetoes by a two-thirds vote of each chamber. Finally, virtually everything done by the US government requires money, and the Constitution provides Congress the sole power to authorize and appropriate funds. Put another way, every part of a presidential administration is dependent on Congress for its annual budget. Just like parents dealing with their children's allowances, Congress can provide or withhold funds to reward or punish the administration for its policy actions.

Long ago, these overlapping foreign policy powers were described as an "invitation . . . to struggle," and that depiction remains appropriate.[1] When their policy preferences diverge, the presidential administration and Congress struggle for control of the policy-making process, because *the actor who controls the process will have the best chance of influencing the resulting policy output.* Some situations favor presidential control, such as decisions to send US troops into harm's way, recognize a foreign regime, undertake a covert operation abroad, or make an executive agreement with another country's leadership. In the case of the **presidential preeminence model**, the foreign policy process can be seen as a series of concentric circles, as illustrated in Figure 1.2. The innermost and most important circle is dominated by presidents and their advisers and top political appointees. Other executive branch departments and agencies play a secondary role and are therefore in the second circle. Finally, the least significant actors are in the outermost circle of influence. These include Congress, interest groups, public opinion, and the mass media.[2]

The fact that presidents are undoubtedly the single-most-important foreign policy makers in most cases does not mean other actors are without significant influence. At times, foreign policy bureaucracies or Congress dominates foreign policy mak-

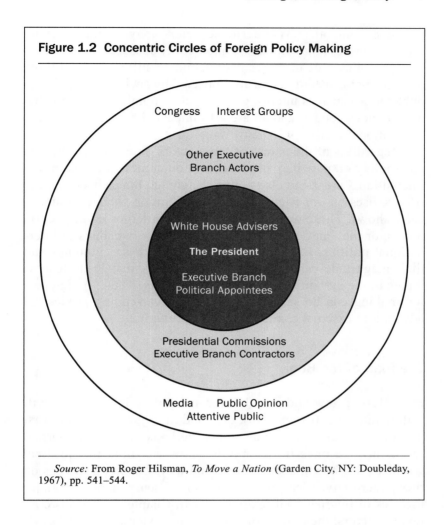

Figure 1.2 Concentric Circles of Foreign Policy Making

Congress   Interest Groups

Other Executive
Branch Actors

White House Advisers

The President

Executive Branch
Political Appointees

Presidential Commissions
Executive Branch Contractors

Media   Public Opinion
Attentive Public

Source: From Roger Hilsman, *To Move a Nation* (Garden City, NY: Doubleday, 1967), pp. 541–544.

ing. Therefore, a more accurate depiction of ongoing interbranch foreign policy interactions is captured by the **shifting constellations model** of power.[3] In a triangular relationship, presidents (along with other White House actors), Congress, and the foreign policy bureaucracies interact to make foreign policy. However, instead of executive branch actors being central to policy making all the time and regardless of the issues involved, each of these three groups has the potential to play a dominant role vis-à-vis the others for some foreign policy issues but not for other ones. The president and other White House actors may dominate some issues, Congress may dominate another set of issues, and various foreign policy bureaucracies may dominate still others. All three of these major sets of actors are impacted by societal forces in the public arena such as interest groups, public opinion, social media, and the news media, and all are also impacted by forces from the international arena.

Regardless of the nature of these actors' interactions, the foreign policy outputs they produce have outcomes—not just in the international arena but also within the United States itself (as tariff increases on imported goods or immigration changes dramatically show). These outcomes may have limited or no impact on others, or they may fundamentally change the dynamics of international politics. Either way, the nature of these outcomes and their magnitude can often produce feedback that leads to new inputs to the system of foreign policy making. Thus, foreign policy making can be seen as a virtually never-ending process of adapting to external challenges and opportunities.

The Plan of the Book

In exploring how and why US foreign policy is made, we will follow the general framework depicted in Figure 1.1. In the first part of the book, we look at inputs. Perhaps the most important inputs are the ones in our minds—how we think the political world works, how it should work, and why. Chapter 2 focuses on these interpretive ideas, which leads to a discussion of four major theories of international relations. Next, Chapter 3 presents contextual factors: the inputs coming from the external political environment of the international arena, the internal political environment within US borders, and the environment of conditioning ideas that shape US behavior.

The next step is to examine various decision-making processes. That's right—processes plural. There are many ways decisions get made, and often the process used depends on who is in the decision-making group. Thus, Chapter 4 goes into greater depth in examining the major governmental actors involved in foreign policy making; Chapter 5 looks at how decisions are made by individuals and small groups; Chapter 6 explores bureaucratic politics and policy making; and Chapter 7 focuses on how Congress participates in foreign policy making. Beyond these governmental actors, other societal groups—interest groups, think tanks, the various elements of the media, and individual opinion leaders—also get involved in foreign policy making. These societal actors, along with other societal factors such as political culture and public opinion, are the focus of Chapter 8. Chapter 9 examines how international actors—individuals, groups, and organizations—also get involved in the making of US foreign policy. Many different actors and their diverging viewpoints combine to shape US foreign policy decisions.

In wrapping up the examination of US foreign policy making, Chapter 10 briefly reviews the types of foreign policy outputs that are the product of this process and the kinds of outcomes that they generate. Chapter 11 presents some concluding thoughts by looking toward the future, including ideas about possible changes in the mix of actors who make US foreign policy, about how the processes of foreign policy making might change, and about how foreign policy outputs may shift in the future.

My goal in this book is to help you understand the people and politics involved in making US foreign policy. To assist in that effort, each chapter begins with learning objectives. Keep them in mind as you read the chapter; they can prove useful in guiding you through the reading. Periodically, boxes are inserted in the chapters. The material in these boxes provides more in-depth, real-life illustrations of the theories, concepts, and relationships discussed. Important terms and concepts appear in **boldface**; these are defined in the chapters and also included in the glossary at the end of the book.

Finally, I hope that by the end of the book you better understand certain things. These include:

- It matters who makes foreign policy.
- What motivates these actors can vary tremendously.
- Policy making is shaped by both international and domestic inputs.
- There are many different ways to reach foreign policy decisions.
- Those resulting decisions have impacts on others.

Once you have a firm grasp of these points, you will know far more about US foreign policy making than most Americans do, and you will be poised to act on that understanding for the rest of your life.

Suggested Reading

Alden, Chris, and Amnon Aran. *Foreign Policy Analysis: New Approaches.* 2nd ed. London: Routledge, 2017.
Hudson, Valerie M. *Foreign Policy Analysis: Classic and Contemporary Theory.* 2nd ed. Lanham, MD: Rowman and Littlefield, 2013.
Neack, Laura. *Studying Foreign Policy Comparatively: Cases and Analysis.* 4th ed. Lanham, MD: Rowman and Littlefield, 2018.
Snyder, Richard C., H. W. Bruck, and Burton Sapin, with new chapters by Valerie M. Hudson, Derek H. Chollet, and James M. Goldgeier. *Foreign Policy Decision-Making (Revisited).* New York: Palgrave Macmillan, 2002.

Notes

1. See Edwin S. Corwin, *The President: Office and Powers* (New York: New York University Press, 1957), 171.
2. Roger Hilsman, *To Move a Nation* (Garden City, NY: Doubleday, 1967), 541–544.
3. See James M. Scott, *Deciding to Intervene: The Reagan Doctrine and American Foreign Policy* (Durham, NC: Duke University Press, 1996).

2

The Impact of Theory

Learning Objectives

- Define a theory.
- Identify the roles played by theories in foreign policy making.
- Differentiate among realism, liberalism, idealism, and constructivism.
- Apply each of these four theories in a case of foreign policy making.

Foreign policy makers typically say they are guided by US national interests, but foreign policies often change—or at least shift—when one administration ends and another begins. US national interests may not have changed, but different policy makers view the world differently. Policy makers may share goals but disagree on the means by which to attain them. Some foreign policy makers don't even agree on the goals of foreign policy. As you will see in Chapter 3, some of these differences are driven by factors arising in the contexts in which these leaders find themselves. However, all policy makers predicate their decisions on the basic and fundamental ideas they have about what is important and how

11

the political world works. Such concerns lie in the realm of theories of foreign policy. The pages that follow discuss the importance of theories, outline four major theories often applied to US foreign policy, and then illustrate those theories with real-life examples.

Theories and International Politics

Theories are sets of interrelated ideas that explain some reality. Often thought of as cognitive maps, theories simplify reality by telling us what matters—and what does not—and what the relationships are regarding the topics that interest us. Like lenses, they bring certain things into focus. You and I use theories every day. We rely on theories of nutrition and how the body works to tell us what to eat and what not to eat, how and when to exercise, what personal habits are associated with long life, and so on. If our car doesn't start, we don't have to be expert auto mechanics to know we should check to see if the battery is dead. We understand some basic relationships about how things are or how they work, and why some things are good and other things are bad. Theories are no more than these bundles of interrelated ideas that help us interpret things. They are tools that aid our understanding.

Further, theories of foreign policy tell us what policy makers care about and why, and theories sometimes prescribe actions to achieve foreign policy goals. Thus, theories help foreign policy makers organize facts and determine appropriate actions in the international arena. Four major theories can be identified that help us understand foreign policy behavior: realism, liberalism, idealism, and constructivism.[1]

Realism

Political realism is the name given to a bundle of ideas that have their roots in the observations of such writers as ancient Greece's Thucydides or the Italian Renaissance's Machiavelli. However, world events in the 1930s and 1940s led writers such as E. H. Carr, Reinhold Niebuhr, and Hans Morgenthau to emphasize how they thought the international system *really was* rather than how we might wish it to be.[2] Their concerns revolved around the **security dilemma**—how states protect their security in a system marked by

anarchy without thereby leading other states to respond by enhancing their own security measures as well. The result could be an unintended arms race that could erupt into violence.

To these thinkers, the most important features of how the international system works, and thus the essence of what they chose to call **realism**, is that (1) humans band together and interact as groups, (2) such groups are motivated primarily by self-interest, and the greatest self-interest is survival, and (3) survival depends on the possession of power.[3] So, for example, a realist explanation of the origins of World War II would stress that Germany and Japan were states on the rise that wanted to ensure their survival and needed to increase their material resources. To do so required them to expand their territory at the expense of others. Thus, Japan attacked China in 1931 and again in 1937, and Germany attacked Poland in 1939 and France the next year. When Japan attacked US forces at Hawaii's Pearl Harbor naval base in 1941 and Germany backed its ally by declaring war on the United States shortly thereafter, the United States was thrust into a global war that grew far beyond its East Asian and European origins.

Of course, reducing the most meaningful aspects of foreign policy to the ideas that societies are greedy and power-seeking means other aspects are minimized, and not all would agree that these points capture the most meaningful aspects of how the international system works. So-called neorealists reject the idea that states are greedy and seek power for its own sake. Instead, neorealists argue that in an international system marked by anarchy and without any coercive authority to which one can turn for protection, it is only prudent to seek, maintain, and increase one's own power resources. In essence, when there is no law enforcement agency to call upon, one has to protect oneself. Thus, **neorealism** sees this inadequacy of the international system itself as the reason states act as they do—not as a result of their inherent bad nature.[4]

Realists also generally share the assumption that states can be considered rational, unitary actors. It doesn't really matter to realists who the country's leaders are at any given point in time, because national interests objectively exist independent of personalities. States face situations in the international system to which they need to respond, and that response is what concerns realists—not who the leaders are. For example, policy makers might think that the most dangerous time for security is when states are undergoing significant power transitions relative to each other. A challenger state may be eager to start a war to demonstrate its growing power, or war could be more likely when the challenger reaches power parity and is dissatisfied with the status quo.[5] Thus, it is not surprising that US policy makers pay careful attention to states such as North Korea and Iran. Both have significant regional military assets, North Korea has tested nuclear weapons and long-range missiles successfully, and Iran was thought to be pursuing nuclear weapons capability prior to the 2015 Joint Comprehensive Plan of Action (better known as the Iran nuclear deal). Thus, US foreign policy makers may often think in such realist terms, and they focus on the power resources of the United States and how they compare with the power resources of others.

However, an oft-heard criticism about realism and its variants is that, by accepting the premise that only military power and national interests really matter, the same old international system is maintained, and wars and other violent conflicts remain the norm. Those who think more positive changes in the international system are possible tend to see the world differently. If they think "what states want is the primary determinant of what they do," then those foreign policy makers wishing for a more peaceful international system can act to create such a system.[6]

Liberalism

Going back to classic political writers such as John Locke, Thomas Hobbes, and Adam Smith, **liberalism** is marked by an emphasis on the rights of the individual person over the rights of the collective state.[7] If individual liberty matters most, then individuals should not only be free from undue state control, they should also have the rights to pursue their own economic opportunities and have a say in their own governance. Consequently, classic liberals stress individual freedom, free-market capitalism, and democracy.[8] Classic liberals also assume that humans are basically cooperative by nature, and such cooperation is possible in international politics as well as in domestic politics. As used here, the term *classic liberalism* is distinguished from the way the term *liberal* is more commonly used in US political discourse. Most Americans who currently use the term *liberal* are generally referring to "welfare liberalism"—a preference for state action on behalf of endangered groups in society—and that's not exactly what is under discussion here.

When applied to foreign policy, classic liberalism produces a pronounced preference for states with some form of democratic or representative government that respects the individual liberties of its citizens and allows capitalism to operate as freely as possible. Not only are such liberal political and economic systems thought to be best for their own citizens, they also produce a **liberal** or **democratic peace**. The historical record shows that well-established liberal democracies do not go to war with other well-established liberal democracies.[9] A variant of this idea is the notion that advanced capitalist systems do not go to war against each other. Such a **capitalist peace** is based on the idea that these advanced capitalist economies are often highly intertwined and wars are thus bad for business.[10]

The idea that liberal regimes foster cooperation and avoid war with each other is not new. Enlightenment writers such as Montesquieu and Immanuel Kant were saying similar things in the eighteenth century.[11] With this line of thinking, then, as the number of liberal democratic regimes increases, an enlarging zone of peace emerges in the international system.[12] Many liberals are thus quite optimistic about the future.

However, the international system is not quite at that stage yet, and the idea of the liberal peace does not mean liberal states do not engage in warfare. They are quite willing to go to war against **illiberal regimes**—those that do not share their values of individual liberty, capitalism, and democracy.[13] Whether such conflicts are motivated by the basic incompatibility of their values or the desire of liberal societies to convert illiberal ones, the results are the same—warfare. Thus, the zone of peace idea only means peace within that group of liberal regimes, not necessarily in the broader international system.

How can wars be discouraged and greater international cooperation advanced? Advocates of neoliberal institutionalism (or simply, **neoliberalism**) think they have the answer. They argue that even under conditions of system anarchy, international cooperation is far more common than confrontation, as states find cooperation advances their national interests.[14] The creation of regional and global international institutions designed to foster cooperation reduces the chances of conflict and war. Whether based on their membership in regional organizations, as with the **Asia-Pacific Economic Cooperation (APEC)** forum or the **European Union (EU)**, or in such global institutions as the **United Nations (UN)** or **International Monetary Fund (IMF)**, as states create more cooperative linkages, they gain more benefits from a peaceful status quo.[15] In short, most states cooperate most of the time. As liberals point out, if realists were right, states would be constantly at war, and they're not.

A number of observers over the years have used the terms *liberalism* and *idealism* interchangeably. However, there's an important distinction to idealism that leads us to consider it separately.

Idealism

Whereas realists stress the likelihood of conflict and the need for self-protection and liberals stress the possibilities of international cooperation to achieve national goals, idealists stress the notion of remaking the world into a better place—often by whatever means necessary. Since the time President Woodrow Wilson brought the United States into World War I in 1917 to "make the world safe for democracy" and stressed the principles of international cooperation in the creation of the League of Nations and its support for national self-determination for all peoples at the end of that war, some foreign policy makers have been motivated to spread what they see as universal values—particularly liberalism's emphasis on democracy, capitalism, and individual freedoms—to new areas of the world. Thus, **idealism** refers to the use of US power and influence to spread a system of liberal, Western values throughout the world and, by doing so, make the world a better place.

It should also be noted that it was Woodrow Wilson's idealism that realists reacted against in the interwar years of the 1920s and 1930s, saying that events in those two decades proved that the United States had neither the will nor the means to act like a world policeman or global parent. Realists counseled instead that the United States should deal with the world as it really was and save scarce US resources (in terms of both blood and treasure) to pursue narrower national interests that could actually be achieved.

Realist thinking dominated the Cold War period beginning in the late 1940s, but toward the end of the Cold War, idealism made a bit of a comeback. In his brief time as president, Gerald Ford tried to make human rights a more important aspect of what the United States was trying to promote internationally. His successor, President Jimmy Carter, agreed with that approach and largely abandoned anticommunism as the guiding force in US foreign policy, instead making the promotion and protection of human rights the guiding force behind how the US government evaluated and reacted to other governments.

The Cold War ended in 1989 during the presidency of George H. W. Bush. President Bill Clinton followed Bush from 1993 to 2000 when George H. W. Bush's son, George W. Bush, was elected. George W. Bush sought to take advantage of the US role as the lone remaining superpower to impose democracy and regime change in the Middle East by force, beginning with Iraq in 2003. The idea was that a democratic Iraq could lead to a more democratic Middle East, free of authoritarian regimes, and this would help solve many international problems arising from this conflict-ridden region.

Realism, liberalism, and idealism have something else in common. Each of these labels denotes what their adherents see as objective beliefs about how the international system works or should work. Another way of understanding international politics is more instrumental in nature. Foreign policy is typically made by groups, and members of groups often agree among themselves about what is important and why, and then they act on the basis of these socially constructed realities. To understand this more subjective social phenomenon, we must consider another theoretical approach.

Constructivism

Unlike the theories discussed to this point, **constructivism** involves a subjective set of ideas about *how* we understand reality, not necessarily about what that objective reality is. Constructivists believe reality is socially constructed.[16] To the extent that members of a group share a set of ideas about how things are and reinforce that set of beliefs in their repeated communications with each other, they typically assume that their ideas are accurate and act on the basis of that socially constructed reality as though it is an objective reality.

For example, during much of the Cold War between the United States and the Soviet Union, most Americans thought communism was an evil menace seeking to destroy them. Given how widespread that societal agreement was, US leaders typically interpreted Soviet actions as threats even when the Soviets did not mean to be threatening. Moving to the present, there is little question that Israel possesses nuclear weapons and in fact has far more nuclear weapons than does North Korea or even Iran, but US leaders worry a lot more about North Korea's nuclear weapons and Iran's nuclear potential than about the actual nuclear weapons possessed by Israel. The difference here is primarily "social." Israel is seen as a friend and de facto ally, and North Korea and Iran are about as far from being seen as friends of the United States as other regimes could be.

The idea that reality is "constructed" is not hard to understand, either. If those with whom we interact regularly keep framing something in positive terms, we typically react to it on that basis. In keeping with the Israel example above, Israel is generally described in the US media and by policy makers as a close friend and a bastion of democracy in a region filled with autocratic regimes. Thus, most Americans tend to give Israelis the benefit of the doubt when the interests of the two countries conflict, which they do occasionally. So, when Israeli forces attacked a US naval vessel (the USS *Liberty*) during the 1967 Six-Day War in the Middle East, US policy makers accepted the Israeli explanation that the attack was a mistake. The United States accepted Israel's apology and negotiated financial compensation for the thirty-four American dead, 170 Americans wounded, and the extensive damage to the ship. One wonders: How would US policy makers have reacted if such an attack had come from Soviet forces during the Cold War instead of Israeli forces? Might the result have risked World War III?

Many constructivists also emphasize the impact of collective identities. For example, the years shortly after the end of World War II witnessed the birth of a number of new international organizations, and the most important of these was the United Nations. The United States was instrumental in helping to create that organization. Thus, as an actor that saw itself as one of the creators of the United Nations, a natural leader in the postwar world, a state that embraced the rule of law, and a state with an overwhelming degree of support from the friendly nations that made up the majority of the UN's membership in its first decade, it is not surprising that US policy makers turned often to the UN as a forum to achieve US national interests. Over time, the majority of the UN's membership came to be composed of states that sought to be nonaligned and saw themselves as victims of Western imperialism or were simply friendlier to the Soviet Union than to the United States. US leaders then began to rely less on the UN as a tool of foreign policy. As far as the American public was concerned, the collective identity of Americans had not changed, but instead the collective identity of the United Nations changed from being pro-United States to anti-United States. Thus, the US orientation toward, and participation in, the United Nations changed, as reflected in the Trump administration's announcement that the United States would withdraw from both the UN Educational, Scientific and Cultural Organization (UNESCO) and the UN Human Rights Council.

Some constructivists also focus on how we use language to construct or mediate social reality. For example, from the mid-1960s until the early 1990s, it seemed that most references to Arabs in US media came when acts of violence were being conducted against Israelis, Western aircraft were being hijacked and their passengers and crews held, airports were being attacked, Israeli Olympic athletes were being killed, and so on. Thus, the word "Arab" was usually followed by the word "terrorist." Soon many Americans seemed to think all Arabs were terrorists, which made dealing diplomatically with Arab regimes difficult and made dealing with Palestinian representatives politically prohibited. After the September 11, 2001, attacks on New York City and the Pentagon, many Americans talked about Muslims as if all Muslims were terrorists, a depiction that Presidents George W. Bush and Barack Obama tried to correct in their public remarks.

Regardless of the approach used, most constructivists would agree on the following: (1) objective or material facts have little meaning until observers assign them a meaning, and (2) those socially constructed meanings are then treated as "facts."[17] These two observations can help us understand differing responses to the problems posed by Saddam Hussein's regime in Iraq. Based on the success of the European Coal and Steel Community evolving eventually into the European Union, Western European leaders typically showed considerable respect for international organizations and multilateral approaches to solving problems. Further, states such as France and Russia had a history of doing business with Saddam

Hussein's Iraqi regime. Thus, when inspectors of the International Atomic Energy Agency (IAEA) failed to find stockpiles of banned chemical weapons in Iraq in the 1990s, a typical European viewpoint was that—given the considerable expertise of those inspectors and the perception that Saddam Hussein's regime no longer represented a military threat—the weapons must no longer exist.

However, the same material fact—that chemical weapons seemed to be missing from Iraq—generated a very different response from top members of the George W. Bush administration. President Bush, Vice President Dick Cheney, Defense Secretary Donald Rumsfeld, and Deputy Defense Secretary Paul Wolfowitz seemed to have somewhat less respect for the United Nations and its associated member organizations, including the IAEA. When such organizations acted contrary to US interests, those organizations were often ignored or circumvented, and such decisions were usually justified by stressing that policy makers were protecting US national sovereignty. Further, Bush, Cheney, Rumsfeld, and Wolfowitz perceived Saddam Hussein as an evil person and his Iraqi regime a threat to both the region and to US national interests. Sharing their distrust of Hussein's regime, these officials could not accept the fact that the weapons were no longer there. In this social construction featuring an evil leader (and possibly less respect for international agencies), top members of the administration constructed a reality that said these chemical weapons must still exist (after all, an evil regime would not just get rid of them), that they must have been hidden away for future use, and this "fact" made the Iraqi regime even more dangerous.[18] For both the Europeans and the Americans, the material facts were the same, but differing social constructions led to very different interpretations of the meaning of those facts.

More recently, free trade has become a contested concept. For most of the post–World War II period, and certainly through the presidencies of George W. Bush and Barack Obama, promoting free trade via participation in such entities as the World Trade Organization (WTO) was socially constructed as a good thing, a way to advance the overall economic interests of the United States. During his campaign and after his election, President Trump railed against the WTO, the North American Free Trade Agreement (NAFTA), and other such free-trade-oriented agreements as being harmful to US interests. After Trump used the words "unfair," "bad," and "a

disaster" to describe the WTO, it is not surprising that his administration raised tariffs on selected imports and threatened trade wars.
White House advisers who disagreed publicly with this policy left
the administration, and thereafter, the socially constructed reality
within the Trump White House was that multilateral trade agreements were bad for America.

Now that the main ideas of these four theoretical approaches
have been outlined, a more detailed illustration can be offered of
how they offer different lenses through which to view, interpret,
and understand foreign policy. Russian interference in the 2016
US presidential election provides a nice example.

The Theories Applied: Russian Intervention in the 2016 US Election

How do these differing theories help us understand who makes
US foreign policy and why such policy is made? The US reactions
to Russian intervention, or "meddling," in the 2016 election provide good examples of these theories in action.

In 2016, the Russian government and its supportive agents
intervened in the US presidential election. The computer networks
of both the Republican National Committee (RNC) and the Democratic National Committee (DNC) were hacked by Russian operatives (led by members of the GRU—Russian military intelligence).
Although no compromising emails or messages from the RNC
were released by the Russians, confidential emails from the DNC
were released to the detriment of the Democratic candidate for
president, Hillary Clinton. Also, Russian entities trolled social-
media networks, targeting swing states with messages designed to
pit Americans against each other, to depict immigrants as criminals and terrorists, and to generally undermine support for the
Clinton campaign by highlighting negative stories about Hillary
Clinton to help the Trump campaign. After the election, the organization of seventeen offices and agencies comprising the US
Intelligence Community (IC) unanimously agreed that Russians
had intervened in the election, and the director of national intelligence tied the computer hacking directly to Russian president
Vladimir Putin.[19] How can the four theories help us understand
the various US reactions to this intervention?

Realism and Russian Intervention

Based on realism, the Obama administration saw the Russian intervention in the election as a way for Russia to advance its national interests by weakening the United States, which made the intervention a threat to US national interests. Obama responded by telling Putin to his face to "knock it off" and by imposing economic sanctions. The sanctions came via executive order and targeted nine named Russian entities and individuals involved in the intervention. Also, Obama closed two Russian diplomatic compounds and expelled forty-two Russian diplomats identified as espionage agents. In July 2017, Congress followed up with additional sanctions against Russia, passing the measure by veto-proof margins in both the House of Representatives and the Senate. In essence, Russia hit the United States and the United States hit back.

Liberalism and Russian Intervention

Liberalism can help illustrate the US reaction to Russian election intervention. States are either naturally cooperative (as per liberalism) or they recognize that cooperation serves their national interests (as per neoliberalism). During and following the Russian intervention in the US election, the US Intelligence Community reached out to allied intelligence agencies to invite their help in identifying the ways the Russians had intervened in the US election and in other countries' elections as well. Particularly important was the coordination by the Five Eyes, which refers to the institutionalized cooperation and sharing of signals intelligence by the intelligence communities of the United States, the United Kingdom (UK), Australia, New Zealand, and Canada. Also, the US Department of Defense's Cyber Command initiated cooperative efforts with Estonia's cyber command. After experiencing a cyberattack from Russia in 2007, Estonia created arguably the most robust anti-cyberattack capability in the Western world. Working with allies, and especially with Estonia, is an essentially neoliberal response to Russia's election intervention. Moreover, liberalism's emphasis on individual rights and democracy was threatened when external actors sought to manipulate voting in the US presidential election. That helps us understand the liberal reaction to the intervention.

Idealism and Russian Intervention

In this case, an idealist interpretation of the US reaction to Russian election intervention starts from the premise that one cannot easily promote democracy, respect for individual rights and freedoms, and a belief in capitalism abroad if those beliefs are under attack at home. The flooding of both conservative news and social media outlets with fabricated stories designed to hurt Clinton and promote Trump weakened the respect for a free press, as many Americans were encouraged to see news they did not like as "fake news." Although many mainstream news organizations tried to offset the idea that they were peddling "fake news," the more they tried, the more some conservative news outlets attacked them. Idealists who want to promote these liberal values saw their defense at home as essential. Moreover, to the extent that the Russian government actively promotes a concept called the Russian World, in which liberal Western values are rejected in favor of more conservative and narrow nationalist values, protecting liberal values here at home became even more crucial to proponents of idealism.

Constructivism and Russian Intervention

As you can see from the above, the US government and societal actors have responded to Russian election intervention in various ways. But the reaction of President Trump and his close circle of advisers still needs to be discussed. A constructivist explanation works very well here. Remember that constructivists believe reality exists only as it is socially constructed. For his part, President Trump rejected the idea that Russians intervened in the election. His White House advisers and media surrogates echoed that idea. The more the president and his closest allies denied and denounced the notion of Russian "meddling," the more the mainstream media challenged that view, and President Trump doubled down on his denials and denunciations. He seemed to take Russian president Putin's word for the fact that Russia hadn't intervened in the election, perhaps because it coincided with his own views. Only after members of his own administration, such as Director of National Intelligence Dan Coats, Central Intelligence Agency (CIA) director Mike Pompeo, and Republican members of the Senate Intelligence Committee agreed that the Russians had interfered in the election did President Trump accept a slightly different narrative. Intervention might have occurred, he said, but it was not clear who was responsible—it could have been someone other than Russia—and he continued to argue that any intervention had not impacted the election's outcome. The president continued to deny the significance of the Russian intervention, and his closest cohort of advisers continued to echo his perception. Thus, the reality socially constructed in the Trump White House was that the intervention either had not happened or if it had, it was insignificant. Other recent illustrations of these theories can be found as well. An evolving illustration involves the United States and international reactions to China's declaration that the South China Sea lies within its control, as discussed in Box 2.1.

Box 2.1 The Chinese Claim to the South China Sea: The View Through Four Lenses

---

Since the 1950s, China has claimed that the South China Sea is, well, Chinese. In the Chinese view, it's called the South China Sea for a reason. Extending far off the Chinese coast, the sea contains hundreds of small, virtually uninhabited islands. According to international law, coastal states can claim up to twelve miles off their coasts as their territorial waters and up to 200 miles off their coast as their exclusive economic zone. Peaceful transit through such exclusive economic zones is allowed, but the coastal state controls access to the sea, the seabed, and their resources. Everything beyond the 200-mile limit is considered the high seas and the common heritage of all humankind, according to the United Nations. The Chinese insist that everything in the South China Sea is theirs, even beyond the 200-mile limit. Other neighboring states have 200-mile zones extending into the South China Sea as well. Thus, states such as Vietnam, the Philippines, Taiwan, Malaysia, and Brunei also claim some of those uninhabited islands and the waters around them.

The United States did not care much about this controversy until China began building artificial islands on some of these reefs in 2014. Some of these artificial islands are now large enough to host Chinese troops and to have airstrips for military aircraft and anti-aircraft and anti-ship missile batteries. China seeks control of these islands and the waters of the South China Sea for several reasons. First, they provide a military bulwark or buffer zone protecting the Chinese mainland. Second, these waters are teeming with commercial fishery resources—and potentially, oil and gas reserves—that the Chinese want for themselves. Third, most international trade involves goods shipped along sea lanes that go through these waters. China's economy is dependent on exported goods and the ability to ship them to markets through these waters. So how do our four theories help us understand this conflict?

The Realist View

For realists, China is simply advancing its national interests at the expense of other states that have not responded in any significant way. However, it is in the US national interest to protect international shipping lanes, and the United States quickly responded to China's provocative island-building. The Obama administration ordered US naval vessels to conduct "freedom of navigation" operations through those waters, sailing close to the Chinese artificial islands. In each case, Chinese warships followed the US warships. The Obama administration also ordered B-52 strategic bombers and then B-1B supersonic strategic bombers to fly over the South China Sea near the Chinese artificial islands. Then, in a largely unprecedented show of force, the Obama administration sent a flight with a B-52 bomber, a B-1B bomber, and a B-2 Stealth strategic bomber through the South China Sea skies. The Trump administration also followed suit by sending naval vessels through these waterways. In 2018, when two navy vessels sailed close to one of the artificial islands, the Chinese navy warned them to leave, but the US ships ignored the warnings. Luckily, by early 2019, no clashes had resulted from these challenges to Chinese sovereignty over these waters.

(continues)

Box 2.1 Continued

The Liberal View

The liberal case to be made here is very straightforward. Liberals emphasize a world system based on peaceful cooperation. The US Navy sent ships through the South China Sea waters and cooperated with US allies that did so as well. Both the British Royal Navy and the Royal Australian Navy sent ships through these waterways. Both the British and the Australians were challenged by the Chinese, but like the Americans, they ignored the warnings. Because of the inherent danger that clashes could occur, one must assume that the US Pacific Command communicated with both the British and the Australian naval commands in the area to coordinate their efforts and share information. Moreover, for liberals, the cooperative responses do not have to be merely military in nature. The Obama administration negotiated the Trans-Pacific Partnership (TPP) as an economic free trade agreement between the United States and eleven other Pacific Rim countries. The treaty noticeably omitted China and was widely seen as an effort to reduce China's ability to use its economic clout to bully its Pacific neighbors, including those with competing claims on the South China Sea. Neoliberals further stress institutionalizing international norms of cooperation, and to them the fact that China is violating the Law of the Sea Treaty, which almost all states respect, reinforces their opposition to China's expansive territorial claims.

The Idealist View

For idealists, the South China Sea issue is about freedom and capitalism. In this case, liberal Western views endorse freedom of navigation on the high seas, and beyond 200 miles, the waters off the Chinese coast are considered part of the high seas. Any country should be free to engage in peaceful transit through or above these waters. The idealist view also sees this in economic terms. Since the Great Depression, liberal Western views have generally endorsed at least freer trade, if not completely free trade, as a means to enhance global wealth and avoid conflicts (remember the capitalist peace idea?). China's actions expressly reject US and Western values and threaten both the global economy and freedom of navigation. Making the world a better place requires protecting both freedom and capitalism, and as a result, the Chinese claims to, and restrictions on use of, the South China Sea must be resisted. China's extraterritorial claims far beyond its coast do not make the world a better place.

The Constructivist View

Constructivists emphasize the danger narrative of allowing China's actions to go unchallenged. The discourse about the Chinese creation of artificial islands and China's attempt to control the entire South China Sea revolves around several common and frightening themes: China's creation and militarization of artificial islands represents a security threat for all who use these Pacific waters; the US ability to exercise its naval and air might in the Pacific could be significantly reduced; the threat could disrupt global trade routes, thereby imperiling the world economy; and America's Pacific and Asian friends are particularly vulnerable to China's actions.

What's your view? Which of these explanations makes the most sense to you? Are China's actions a military threat, an economic threat, or mere posturing on behalf of a government that uses nationalist appeals to build support for its policies? Is the US reaction too little, too much, or just about right?

Conclusion

Foreign policy is made by individuals, either acting alone or more commonly in groups. As individuals, they are guided by fundamental notions of how the political world works and their own ideas of right and wrong; these value premises come from political theories. If policy makers consistently act in terms of US national interests perceived largely as military power, they are relying primarily on realist views. If instead they prefer more often to promote international peace and cooperation by encouraging the protection and expansion of individual liberties, capitalism, and democracy abroad, they are relying primarily on liberalism to guide their actions. If they want to use persuasion or even force to make the rest of the world a better place by making it more like the United States, idealism is motivating their choices. If none of these theoretical lenses seems to capture the thinking of individual policy makers, constructivism may be used to identify how foreign policy makers and those with whom they interact construct the meaning of the facts they perceive and then act accordingly on those meanings at the time. Again, none of us react randomly to events; we react based on what we interpret to be important.

Suggested Reading

Harrison, Ewan, and Sara M. Mitchell. *The Triumph of Democracy and the Eclipse of the West.* New York: Palgrave Macmillan, 2014.

Ikenberry, G. John. *After Victory: Institutions, Strategic Restraint, and the Rebuilding of Order After Major Wars.* New ed. Princeton: Princeton University Press, 2019.

Morgenthau, Hans J., and Kenneth W. Thompson. *Politics Among Nations.* 7th ed. New York: McGraw-Hill Education, 2005.

Perkins, Dexter. *The American Approach to Foreign Policy.* Rev. ed. Cambridge, MA: Harvard University Press, 1962.

Wendt, Alexander. *Social Theory of International Politics.* Cambridge: Cambridge University Press, 1999).

Notes

1. For an introduction to realism, liberalism, and constructivism, see Jennifer Sterling-Folker, ed., *Making Sense of International Relations Theory,* 2nd ed. (Boulder: Lynne Rienner, 2013). For more on realism and idealism, see Sean Kay, *America's Search for Security: The Triumph of Idealism and the Return of Realism* (Lanham, MD: Rowman and Littlefield, 2014).

2. See Thucydides, *The History of the Peloponnesian War,* rev. ed., trans. Rex Warner, ed. M. I. Finley (Baltimore: Penguin Classics, 1954); Niccolo Machiavelli, *The Prince and the Discourses,* introduction by Max Lerner (New York: Random House, 1950); Edward Hallett Carr, *The Twenty Years' Crisis, 1919–1939: An Introduction to the Study of International Relations* (New York: St. Martin's, 1946); Reinhold Niebuhr, *Moral Man and Immoral Society: A Study of Ethics and Politics,* introduction by Landon Gilkey (Louisville, KY: Westminster John Knox Press, 2002); Hans J. Morgenthau and Kenneth W. Thompson,

Politics Among Nations: The Struggle for Power and Peace, 7th ed., rev. (New York: McGraw-Hill, 2005).

3. See William C. Wohlforth, "Realism and Foreign Policy," in *Foreign Policy: Theories, Actors, Cases,* 3rd ed., ed. Steve Smith, Amelia Hadfield, and Tim Dunne (New York: Oxford University Press, 2016), 35–53.

4. See Kenneth Waltz, *Theory of International Politics* (Reading, MA: Addison Wesley, 1979) and Robert O. Keohane, ed., *Neorealism and Its Critics* (New York: Columbia University Press, 1986).

5. For more on the power transition notion, see A. F. K. Organski and Jacek Kugler, *The War Ledger* (Chicago: University of Chicago Press, 1980).

6. Andrew Moravcsik, "Taking Preferences Seriously: A Liberal Theory of International Politics," *International Organization* 51 (4) (1997): 521.

7. John Locke, *Two Treatises of Government* (New York: Everyman Paperbacks/Random House, 1993); Thomas Hobbes, *Leviathan* (Indianapolis: Hackett, 1994); Adam Smith, *The Wealth of Nations* (New York: Bantam Classics, 2003).

8. See Michael W. Doyle, *Ways of War and Peace* (New York: W. W. Norton, 1997).

9. Bruce Russett, *Grasping the Democratic Peace* (Princeton: Princeton University Press, 1994).

10. See Erik Gartzke, "The Capitalist Peace," *American Journal of Political Science* 51 (2007): 166–191.

11. See Baron de La Brede et de Montesquieu, *The Spirit of the Laws,* vol. 36, ed. David W. Carrithers (Berkeley: University of California Press, 1971), and Immanuel Kant, *Perpetual Peace,* ed. Lewis W. Beck (New York: Macmillan, 1957).

12. See Michael W. Doyle, "Liberalism and Foreign Policy," in *Foreign Policy: Theories, Actors, Cases,* 3rd ed., ed. Steve Smith, Amelia Hadfield, and Tim Dunne (New York: Oxford University Press, 2016), 54–78.

13. For more on illiberal regimes, see Fareed Zakaria, "The Rise of Illiberal Democracy," *Foreign Affairs* 76 (6) (1997): 22–43.

14. See Robert Axelrod and Robert O. Keohane, "Achieving Cooperation Under Anarchy: Strategies and Institutions," *World Politics* 38 (1985): 226–254.

15. For more on APEC, see https://www.apec.org/About-Us/About-APEC. For more on the EU, see https://europa.eu/european-union/index_en. For more in the UN, see https://www.un.org/en. For more on the IMF, see http://www.imf.org/external/about.htm.

16. Jeffrey T. Checkel, "Constructivism and Foreign Policy," in *Foreign Policy: Theories, Actors, Cases,* ed. Steve Smith, Amelia Hadfield, and Tim Dunne (New York: Oxford University Press, 2008), 72.

17. See Alexander Wendt, *Social Theory of International Politics* (Cambridge: Cambridge University Press, 1999), 1, and Yale H. Ferguson

and Richard W. Mansbach, *The Elusive Quest Continues: Theory and Global Politics* (Upper Saddle River, NJ: Prentice Hall, 2003), 205.

18. For more on these perceptions, see Kristin Archick, *European Views and Policies Toward the Middle East* (Washington, DC: CRS Report for Congress, Congressional Research Service, March 9, 2005), http://www.globalsecurity.org/military/library/report/crs/44134.pdf. For more on the Bush administration's views on Saddam Hussein, see Bob Woodward, *State of Denial: Bush at War, Part III* (New York: Simon and Schuster, 2006).

19. For a comprehensive timeline of the reporting on Russian meddling, see the CNN fact sheet: "2016 Presidential Campaign Hacking: Fast Facts," https://www.cnn.com/2016/12/26/us/2016-presidential-campaign-hacking-fast-facts/index.html.

3

The Policy-Making Context

Learning Objectives

- Describe the impact of context on foreign policy makers.
- Differentiate among external, internal, and ideational contexts.
- Illustrate the differences between post–Cold War and post–9/11 contexts.
- Assess the current priorities of US foreign policy makers.

Policy makers must envy academics who begin an analysis with the phrase "all other things being equal." In the foreign policy setting, few things are equal and everything seems to affect everything else—especially policy choices. Constraints push policy makers away from some choices, and opportunities lure them toward others. Consequently, policy makers rarely start with the proverbial "blank sheet" when considering a possible policy initiative. They are affected by what is going on in the external political context, the domestic political context, and the ideational context at the time. In this chapter, each of these different contexts comes under discussion, followed by examples showing how such factors can serve as inputs to the process of foreign policy making.

The External Context

The external context can be found in the international political system that lies beyond US borders. This context or setting shapes foreign policy choices in numerous ways, but clearly international norms and power relationships are two of the most important.

International Norms

The international system is like a society, and societies are marked by **norms**—unwritten rules of behavior—and these change over time and impact foreign policy makers. Until the early twentieth century, the international system was dominated by imperial powers governing vast expanses of the globe through a combination of brute force, economic influence, and often the co-optation of local elites. An important norm of this era was that of gunboat diplomacy, of the strong preying on the weak. **Social Darwinism** seemed to justify this approach to international interactions. More powerful societies dominated less powerful ones, and that seemed to be the natural order of things.

   Yet norms changed. As the industrial age made technologies of warfare more lethal and destructive, international society moved to limit the damage. The 1899 and 1907 Hague Conventions began diplomatic processes to promote the peaceful settlement of disputes and establish limitations on the technology of warfare.[1] Although such diplomacy did not prevent the outbreak of wars in the twentieth century, the growing destructiveness of modern warfare—particularly shown in World War II—caused changes in international perceptions. The horrors of the Holocaust and the advent of nuclear weapons increasingly drove states to reject the acceptability of the strong coercing the weak, at least as far as the blatant use of force was concerned.

   The use of force was increasingly seen as a legitimate tool of statecraft to be employed only after other means of influence had failed. Thus, norms involving the peaceful resolution of disputes and a commitment to multilateralism marked the post–World War II period. Given their destructiveness, nuclear weapons became a grave concern, and the norm of nuclear nonproliferation developed in the latter half of the twentieth century.

At the same time, the norm of safeguarding **human rights** became well established in international politics. **First-generation rights** had been around since the 1700s and involve the rights of each individual, for example, civil and political rights such as the freedoms of speech, assembly, and religion. **Second-generation rights** began with the nineteenth-century rise of socialism and Marxism. Such rights include the material rights that should apply to entire societies, such as the rights to education, employment, medical care, and sufficient food. **Third-generation rights** arose after World War II and apply to groups at risk within society, for example, unpopular minorities, women, children, the elderly, and so on.

More recently, the Westphalian norm of state sovereignty based on the inviolability of borders has been seriously eroded. In 2005, the World Summit at the UN General Assembly endorsed the norm that states had a **Responsibility to Protect (R2P)** their population from war crimes, genocide, and other crimes against humanity. In 2006, delegates passed **UN Security Council Resolution 1674**, which reaffirmed the responsibility to protect people from such gross abuses of human rights.[2] Thereafter, the R2P norm evolved in the direction of a more generalized sense that states have a responsibility to protect their population from preventable harm and that if they do not do so, the international community has a right, if not a duty, to intervene on the public's behalf.

Some international norms evolve into more formal international law, but whether they are norms or laws, these ideas matter to policy makers. They become parameters within which options are considered, and consequences arise when US foreign policy fails to conform to these parameters. When policy falls short of these norms, policy makers have to spend considerable time defending the legitimacy of their actions. At the heart of this dynamic is the idea that if most states follow such norms, they expect other states to follow them as well.

The power of such norms was demonstrated when President Trump went to his first NATO meeting in 2017. There he wasted no time in criticizing NATO members for not spending enough on their own defense, pointing out that twenty-three of the twenty-eight member-states were not meeting the agreed target for their defense spending (2 percent of their gross domestic product [GDP]). Trump then shocked his counterparts by refusing to endorse Article 5 of the North Atlantic Treaty, which requires members to consider an attack on one to be an attack on all members and to respond accordingly. The fallout over his apparent rejection of the staunchest American allies, and any commitment to defend them, had multiple members of his administration quickly affirming to the press that "of course the US endorses Article 5." Several times thereafter, President Trump appeared to read prepared scripts in which he said the United States endorsed NATO's Article 5. Given his professed dislike of reading prepared scripts, external pressures may have forced him to endorse international norms contrary to his own views. However, beyond the roles that norms play in setting the context of foreign policy making, power relationships also shape the foreign policy choices of leaders.

Power Relationships

The political realities of power—who has it and how much they have relative to the United States—create both opportunities and constraints to US foreign policy makers and thus provide an array of inputs for the US process of foreign policy making. Consider the current position of the United States in the international system. When the **Cold War** ended in 1989 and the Soviet Union fragmented into fifteen component parts in 1991, the United States was left as the lone remaining superpower. Was that an opportunity for foreign policy makers to expand US national influence, or were there still constraints to be faced?

For many, the answer was simple. The United States had seemingly won the Cold War, its opponent was vanquished, and now US military power eclipsed that of any other state, and if nuclear arms were considered, of arguably all other states combined. According to realists, the United States was poised to pursue any of a number of potential national interests. In the early twenty-first century, the more the top members of the George W. Bush team talked about the possibilities of foreign policy making in this new era, the more they convinced themselves that a new reality was at hand. Inspired by idealist motives, they thought such military power meant the United States could go out and win any objective, right any wrong, and impose its well-intentioned will on the world. For example, backed by American arms, a new democratic Afghanistan could be created, and democracy could be imposed by military force on old nemesis Iraq. Bush administration advocates thought these military moves would remake the Middle East, helping to transform it into a peaceful, democratic region.[3] Supporters and critics alike began talking about a new American empire, linked by a global network of military bases.[4]

Still, the exercise of military power does not come without costs. Even the world's largest single economy was stressed by trying to fight two simultaneous wars on the other side of the world. At least in Afghanistan, some allies came to help. After the Taliban regime in Kabul was deposed, member states of NATO contributed combat or support personnel totaling approximately 50,000 troops to help stabilize the country and consolidate the power of the new regime led by Hamid Karzai.[5] However, the invasion and occupation of Iraq was another story. Few US allies saw any need to overthrow the government of President Saddam Hussein by force, and the UN Security Council refused to authorize military action to oust the regime. So only a few allies agreed to participate in the US-led invasion of Iraq. The failure of other allies to participate left US military resources stretched so thin across both Iraq and Afghanistan that other regimes—such as Iran and North Korea—were emboldened to undertake provocative acts, knowing the unlikelihood of US military response.

External constraints face the United States in nonmilitary arenas as well. Over time, the US economic position relative to others has fallen. Although the US economy is still the largest national economy in the world, others are catching up. As a group, the economies of the **European Union** are larger than the US economy. China is the second-largest national economy in the world and is growing quickly, as is the economy of India. Thus, in either military or economic terms, the United States is still very powerful, but it is not a **hegemon** capable of imposing its will whenever and wherever it desires. Unless a superpower is willing to ask its population to make significant sacrifices in lifestyle to subsidize its foreign initiatives, there are limits to what that regime has the resources to do.

This combination of military, diplomatic, and economic realities provides some interesting challenges for US policy makers. A good illustration came in 2014 when the United States and its allies were unable to stop a Russian-initiated "hybrid war" in Ukraine, which is discussed in Box 3.1.

Box 3.1 Russia's Hybrid War in Ukraine

In 2014, US and European foreign policy makers were shocked when Russia undertook what has been called a "hybrid war" against Ukraine. The result was the annexation of Crimea as a Russian territory and the loss of control by the Ukrainian government of its eastern Donbass region as well. These events began in February, when Ukraine's pro-Russian president, Viktor Yanukovich, was ousted in a revolution. The Russian government quickly proclaimed that native Russian speakers in Ukraine, primarily located in the Crimean peninsula and the eastern Ukrainian provinces known as the Donbass region, were now at risk from Ukrainian fascists. Russian-language television and radio continually broadcast news of the fascist threat to Russian speakers in Ukraine. On February 20, Russian troops in unmarked uniforms began arriving in Crimea, saying they were local militias there to protect the Russian speakers. Agitated by the Russian-language broadcast media, local protesters demonstrated in favor of reunification with Russia, and additional Russian troops seized government buildings in Crimea's capital. On March 16, with these armed "self-defense" units looking on, a referendum was held, and Crimea voted to join the Russian Federation, which agreed to formally annex Crimea on March 18.

Given the speed of events, the crisis in Crimea was over before US and European foreign policy makers were able to fashion meaningful responses to it. The Group of Eight major industrial powers—or G8—suspended Russia from its membership. President Barack Obama imposed economic sanctions on individuals and entities who had assisted the Russian takeover of that territory, and many European states followed suit. Still, Russia possessed Crimea.

However, the process was quickly repeated in the Donbass region of Donetsk and Luhansk in eastern Ukraine. In these Russian-speaking areas, again Russian troops arrived to protect Russian speakers from the threats supposedly posed by the Ukrainian government in Kiev. A separatist conflict broke out, with Russian troops playing a major role (a role denied by the Kremlin at the time). Once more, the hybrid nature of the conflict was apparent, with the early use of Russian communications media to create fear and panic among the people living in the region. Perhaps the culminating event for the international community was the downing of Malaysian Airlines Flight 17 over the region by a Russian-provided anti-aircraft missile, killing all aboard. President Obama responded with economic sanctions on Russian individuals and entities, and the European Union followed suit as well.

Could the United States have done more? Perhaps, but a number of factors made that difficult. First, this hybrid-war technique used a variety of media measures to create real fear among the local population that Russian speakers were going to be persecuted by Ukrainian fascists, to the extent that locals typically welcomed the "polite men in green uniforms" who said they were there to protect the locals. Second, responsibility for these actions was repeatedly denied by the Russian government, causing a few Western allies to wonder if Russia truly was involved. Third, the events moved quickly. Finally, in Washington, the partisan context made getting any kind of congressional authorization difficult. Most Republicans and many war-weary Democrats were very hesitant to get involved in another war, much less one involving another nuclear power operating close to its own borders.

Sources:

"A Look at Key Dates in the Ukraine-Russia Crisis," *France24,* November 29, 2018, https://www.france24.com/en/20181129-ukraine-russia-crisis -putin-kerchstrait-poroshenko-crimea-donbass-eu; Alice Popovici, "Why Russia Wants Crimea: For Centuries It Has Loomed Large for Russian and Soviet Leaders," History.com, July 12, 2018, https://www.history.com /news/crimea-russia-ukraine-annexation; Reuters, "How Russia Took Crimea Without a Fight from Ukraine," *Newsweek,* July 24, 2017, https://www .newsweek.com/russia-crimea-ukraine-how-putin-took-territory-without -fight-640934.

Yet for many liberals, there is reason for cautious optimism in the international system. Mechanisms of cooperation exist and are often used. As noted earlier, NATO accepted an important role in providing military personnel and support for the mission to stabilize Afghanistan. With the help of the **International Monetary Fund,** leaders of both the then Group of Eight (**G8**) major industrial powers and the Group of Twenty (**G20**) largest economies and emerging markets cooperated in trying to adjust their national economic policies to meet the demands of global recovery from the Great Recession of 2008–2010. Even in more contentious situations, cooperation can occur. Despite supporting different sides in the Syrian civil war, US and Russian military commanders coordinated air strikes to avoid any unfortunate accidental clashes between the two. In short, the external context provides a variety of inputs to policy makers—some positive and others less so. But policy makers must also deal with the inputs from the domestic arena.

The Internal Context

Like the external context, the internal context also presents inputs to foreign policy makers in the form of both opportunities and constraints.[6] The values that make up US political culture push policy makers in certain directions and not others. For example, one constant in US political culture is the widely shared idea of **American exceptionalism**. Most Americans believe that the United States is not merely different from other countries or societies, *it is better than others*. US leaders and the public generally believe that the United States is uniquely blessed with a set of liberal values and ideas (e.g., the commitments to individual liberty, representative democracy, and free-market capitalism) that have worked to produce what they see as the most powerful, richest, and best society on the planet.[7]

Such an exceptionalist viewpoint can both pull and push policy makers. On the one hand, if you think you are special, leadership on international issues becomes an easier choice. Being special, you have something valuable to share with others. Pushing other states to embrace democracy or capitalism is a long-standing trait of US foreign policy that flows fairly directly from this sense of exceptionalism. On the other hand, when others see you lead on multiple issues over time, they come to expect it—even when you would prefer *not* to lead. Thus, when US policy makers choose not to lead on high-profile issues—for instance, not intervening to stop genocide in places like Rwanda or Darfur, or not acting to slow global climate change—international criticism ensues. Other international actors that rarely lead on international issues are spared this expectation and potential criticism. When was the last time you heard the Swedes being criticized for a lack of global leadership?

Another important aspect of the domestic context is the nature of the US system of foreign policy making. Compared to that of other states, its fragmented structure makes it very open to inputs from a wide variety of sources. Inputs to foreign policy making can come not only from legislative and executive branch officials but also from domestic opinion makers, public opinion polls, interest groups, think tanks, various types of media, court rulings, foreign officials, and so on. The system is fragmented in the sense that policy-making roles are shared between executive branch actors and members of Congress—and occasionally federal courts. Each can get a piece of the policy-making action. The result of such an open and fragmented system is that with so many trying to get their hands on the helm, the ship of state is difficult to control and steer. Sometimes it goes in directions no specific policy makers sought, directions that instead are the result of compromises or accommodations that became necessary to get anything done at all. Yet beyond the domestic context shaped by values, culture, and the structures of foreign policy making, there is the ideational context—the current state of major ideas about the ends and means of foreign policy and the priorities that thus exist.

The Ideational Context

Overlaying this system of foreign policy making are dominant ideas that provide inputs to policy makers. The open and fragmented system just discussed is populated in part by officials elected as members of political parties, and the ideas that form the basis of partisanship matter in foreign policy, too. Although many will assert that politics *should* stop at the water's edge, it rarely does. There are stereotypical Democratic and Republican agendas of foreign policy, and those policy agendas tend to be different in terms of both ends and means.[8] Regarding ends, in recent years Republican policy makers have generally focused more on global issues involving national security matters or free trade. Although most Democratic foreign policy makers argued they were neither hostile nor indifferent to national security matters, they typically elevated other global issues to a higher priority than their Republican counterparts—for example, environmental protection, human rights, and assuring that basic life necessities were met in developing societies. Democrats also typically favored some restraints on free trade if workers' rights or the environment would be harmed as a result. Regarding means, many Republican policy makers seemed to prefer unilateral approaches that relied primarily on military tools to achieve their goals. Democratic policy makers generally appeared to be more open to multilateral approaches that involved more international actors and a greater use of diplomatic tools to achieve desired ends. Again, these are generalizations. Exceptions to such crude generalizations can always be found (e.g., defense hawks who happen to be Democrats or Republicans committed to protecting the environment), but these generalizations capture something important about what most members of each political party tend to think is important in foreign policy and how such goals should be addressed.

Another aspect of the ideational context is the set of inputs that come from public opinion.[9] Top US foreign policy makers are either elected by the public or appointed by those who are. Thus, public opinion cannot be totally ignored. At times, two broad orientations toward foreign policy held by the public come into play. On the one hand, most Americans believe in **internationalism**. That is, they believe that US national interests are advanced by interacting with other countries and peoples, and regular, ongoing contacts with others may contribute to the greater good of all. Consistently in public opinion polls since the end of the Vietnam War, at least two-thirds of the American public has favored regular engagement with the world beyond US borders. Such internationalists may feel either that it is simply good to know more about other societies and peoples or that there are distinct advantages to be gained through interaction—such as military allies or expanded opportunities for US trade.

On the other hand, some Americans are isolationists. **Isolationism** refers to the belief that the dangers of regular and ongoing engagement with the world beyond US borders outweigh the advantages. Isolationists may stress that such engagement draws the United States into other people's wars or that contact with other cultures undermines traditional American values. Isolationism was stronger in the 1930s than now, but since the end of the Vietnam War, between 10 and 20 percent of Americans typically express isolationist themes in public opinion polls.[10] Recently, isolationists have gotten somewhat of a boost by the election of Donald Trump. His foreign policy agenda suggests a general withdrawal from ready US participation in the kinds of multilateral institutions that the United States helped to create after World War II. President Trump prefers bilateral agreements with other countries rather than support for broader multinational institutions such as the World Trade Organization, for example. However, the intense support shown by his supporters should not obscure the fact that such withdrawal from the international architecture the United States helped to create has only appealed to a minority of Americans over the last seventy years.

More generally, public opinion about specific issues may push policy makers in certain directions—toward some possible options but not others. Depending on the congruence between what the public and key policy makers seem to want, public opinion can either constrain or empower those policy makers. In some instances, the public may not care about an international issue. In those circumstances, policy makers may be relatively free to do whatever they think is best. In other instances, public opinion may be strong enough to force policy makers to address an issue and to do so in a particular way, such as imposing economic sanctions on South Africa over its **apartheid** policy in the 1980s. Thus, public opinion often sets parameters within which US foreign policy makers can operate with less fear of domestic backlash.

Foreign policy goals are part of this ideational context as well. It would be easy to say that US foreign policy makers confront three overarching foreign policy goals: enhancing US security, power, and interests.[11] But what such overarching goals involve varies in the eye of the beholder. Like policy makers in other countries, US foreign policy makers share the minimalist goal of guarding the physical safety of their population and protecting territorial possessions from attack. More ambitious goals include actively safeguarding the economic security of their population as well. However, the combined effects of American exceptionalism and a commitment to liberal values often mean that US policy makers publicly embrace maximalist goals such as making the world safe for democracy, expanding the number of democratic states, acting as a global policeman to protect the weak from bullies abroad, or, more broadly, just going out to "do good" in the world.

How and when foreign policy makers choose to act on these goals reflects their policy priorities at that moment in time, and those priorities are shaped by the external, internal, and ideational contexts in which policy making occurs. In addition to the points covered earlier, that setting is shaped significantly by what happened in the past, particularly in the recent past. The impact of history is part of the context of ideas that shape US foreign policy, but because history is so important, a brief historical review follows to show how the United States came to be in its present situation.

Recent US Foreign Policy History

From roughly the end of World War II until the Berlin Wall was torn down in 1989, the Cold War dominated US foreign policy. Rivalry with the Soviet Union—political, economic, and military—produced an era in which small wars between the client states of each superpower could erupt at any time. Yet the overwhelming concern was preventing the two superpowers from going to war directly with each other, as that seemed likely to lead to nuclear war and **mutual assured destruction (MAD)**.

When economic weaknesses caused the Soviet Union's collapse and the Cold War ended, many assumed a new, more peaceful era had arrived.[12] Events proved otherwise. The administration of George H. W. Bush took a cautious approach to the newly independent Russian Federation, the largest part of the old Soviet Union. Despite Russia's economic collapse and its vital need for economic assistance, most of the economic assistance it received came from Europe—primarily from Germany. US economic aid went more quickly to the former Soviet states in Eastern Europe, and what aid went to Russia only came later and was viewed in Russia as "too little, too late." Thus, a gradual deterioration in US-Russian relations began in the post–Cold War period.

A highlight of Bush's foreign policy was the international response to Iraq's invasion of Kuwait in 1990. The United States engineered a multinational coalition of over fifty countries to return control of Kuwait to its rightful government, receiving a UN Security Council resolution endorsing such action, and the resulting 1991 Persian Gulf War succeeded in ousting Iraqi forces from Kuwait. However, as the Bush administration was nearing its end, it supported a United Nations call to send peacekeepers to help safeguard refugee aid sent to Somalia, and US troops were deployed there.

The new administration of President Bill Clinton inherited that Somali intervention, and it went badly. Initially thought to be peacekeepers, US troops quickly found themselves to be participants in a Somali civil war. The low point came in 1993 during a dramatic firefight in the Somali capital—immortalized in the movie *Black Hawk Down*—in which two US helicopters were shot down, eighteen US troops were killed, and their bodies were dragged through the streets. Not long after, Clinton ordered the US troops out of Somalia. Perhaps because of this searing experience, in 1994 Clinton was reluctant to send any troops to stop the genocide in Rwanda or to intervene to stop the genocide ongoing in the Bosnian civil war.

A new threat arose during the Clinton years. Angered by the continuing US presence in Saudi Arabia and US support for Israel, a Saudi named Osama bin Laden pointed his militant group **al-Qaeda** at the United States. The group was linked to the 1993 bombing of a parking garage beneath New York City's World Trade Center. That attack killed six and injured about 1,000 (but failed to bring down the building). After several other attacks against Americans in the Middle East, in 1996 bin Laden issued a religious directive (called a fatwa) urging all devout Muslims to take up arms against Americans in the Middle East. Shortly thereafter, an apartment building housing US military personnel in Khobar, Saudi Arabia, was bombed, killing nineteen US service members. In 1998, bin Laden issued a second fatwa calling on Muslims to kill Americans and Jews wherever the opportunity presented itself (this time specifically including women and children to be killed), and truck bombs went off at the US embassies in both Kenya and Tanzania. Over 200 people, mostly Kenyan passersby, were killed, and Clinton responded by ordering cruise missile attacks on al-Qaeda training bases in Afghanistan and on a Sudanese pharmaceutical plant that had been linked (apparently erroneously) to chemical weapons and bin Laden. In 2000, two suicide bombers attacked the USS *Cole* as it arrived in the port of Aden, Yemen, killing seventeen members of its crew.

When President George W. Bush took office in January 2001, he hoped to stress such domestic initiatives as education reform and tax cuts over foreign policy matters. However, on September 11, 2001, four civilian airliners were hijacked by nineteen members of al-Qaeda. Two of the aircraft were flown into the twin towers of New York City's World Trade Center, killing more than 2,600 people. Another airplane flew into the US Department of Defense headquarters building—better known as the Pentagon. The death toll from that attack was 125. The fourth airplane crashed in a Pennsylvania field. The passengers on board that aircraft apparently learned of the other incidents and forced the airplane down short of its target—thought to be either the Capitol building or the White House in Washington, DC. The death toll of the individuals on the four combined aircraft was 256, making a total of nearly 3,000 dead in this coordinated attack. The tally thus exceeded the death toll of the 1941 Japanese attack on Pearl Harbor.[13] Right after the 9/11 attacks, President Bush declared the US War on Terror, targeting terrorists wherever they were located as well as targeting those who supported terrorists. In late 2001, the United States went to war against the Taliban regime in Afghanistan that had sheltered bin Laden. Despite an aggressive bombing campaign and a ground assault by indigenous anti-Taliban Afghan forces known as the Northern Alliance, bin Laden escaped capture by slipping into Pakistan.

In 2003, the George W. Bush administration's focus turned to Iraq. Saddam Hussein's regime had used chemical weapons in the past, and intelligence reports suggested the regime was pursuing biological and nuclear weapons as well. Given these factors, administration officials claimed that the Iraqis might make weapons of mass destruction available to international terrorists, and some officials (prominently led by Vice President Dick Cheney) said they would not be surprised to learn that Iraq was somehow involved in the 9/11 attacks. When the UN Security Council refused to authorize a collective attack on Iraq, a force composed primarily of US and British troops (along with some from other allies) invaded Iraq, overthrew the Hussein regime, and ultimately created a new Iraqi government led by Prime Minister Nouri al-Maliki.[14]

Although the invasion of Iraq was an immediate success, the occupation of Iraq proved difficult. Sectarian tensions between

Iraqis quickly arose, and armed resistance to the US military occupation followed rapidly. Although Iraq was not a stronghold of al-Qaeda prior to 2003, after the US-led intervention, foreign **jihadists** flocked there, and the group known as "al-Qaeda in Iraq" was formed, which later evolved into **ISIS**—the Islamic State in Iraq and Syria. In 2007, the momentum of the Iraqi occupation began to change. Prompted by the indiscriminate killing of Iraqis by al-Qaeda in Iraq, many **Sunni** insurgents stopped fighting the US occupation troops, began working with US troops to fight the largely foreign al-Qaeda forces, and were later put on the US payroll for their support. US efforts to identify, track, and assassinate the leaders of al-Qaeda in Iraq helped neutralize the group's effectiveness. Also effective was the military surge in 2007, an increase of approximately 30,000 more US troops deployed to Iraq, bringing the total number there to approximately 130,000.[15] Thereafter, US troop totals in Iraq gradually declined, and by 2018, the number of US troops there was down to about 5,000.

The War on Terror resulted in thousands of terrorist suspects rounded up in Afghanistan, Iraq, and other locations and detained indefinitely. Hundreds were housed at the US military base at Guantanamo Bay, Cuba, where they were held without charges or legal representation. Ultimately, the US Supreme Court ruled that such detainees could not be held indefinitely without recourse to the legal system.[16] The fact that the tactics used in the War on Terror seemed to put traditional US values at risk created disillusionment both at home and abroad. Such disillusionment increased when it was learned that some detainees had been subjected to "enhanced interrogation techniques," tactics many others called torture. Also, detainees at the **Abu Ghraib** prison in Iraq were abused and humiliated by US military personnel, and the National Security Agency illegally engaged in warrantless electronic eavesdropping on US citizens.[17] Actions such as these made US statements that it was a nation that followed the rule of law seem hypocritical, and the international image of the United States was tarnished.

Beyond the War on Terror, a second theme of the Bush administration was to avoid constraints on how the United States chose to act in the international arena. However, unilateralism was nothing new. During the Clinton administration, the United States chose not to go along with multilateral approaches to address a number of global problems that had been endorsed by US friends and allies. Among other examples, these multilateral efforts to deal with global problems included the **Kyoto Protocol** to limit global climate change and the creation and operation of the **International Criminal Court (ICC)**. Unlike his father's administration, the George W. Bush administration preferred unilateral initiatives that preserved US sovereignty or US freedom of action over multilateral efforts based on cooperation. Regarding the Kyoto Protocol, President Bush opposed mandatory restrictions on fossil fuel emissions because imposing them would hurt the US economy. Bush not only opposed the creation of the ICC, which in the future might bring US military personnel to trial, he rescinded the US signature on the treaty creating the court and instead signed the **American Service-Members' Protection Act** in 2002, which made it illegal to cooperate with the ICC. That act also threatened non-NATO countries with the loss of US military aid if they did not sign Status of Forces Agreements exempting US forces from being turned over to the ICC.

Perhaps the most potent illustration of US unilateralism came with the **US National Security Strategy** announced in 2002. This statement stressed that the nature of the threats facing the country had changed. With weapons of mass destruction becoming increasingly commonplace and with nonstate actors as enemies, the strategy said some of the old rules of conflict no longer applied. International law's traditional justification of the use of force only in self-defense meant one had to let an aggressor attack first before retaliating. As President Bush noted, letting the opponent strike first might condemn an entire US city to destruction. Similarly, past deterrence strategies worked against state actors whose cities provided immovable retaliatory targets, but nonstate actors (whose members could easily move about) could not be so readily deterred by threats of retaliation. Thus, this new **Bush Doctrine** stated that the United States would not wait for the first blow; it would strike preemptively against potential aggressors. To critics, this "strike first" approach meant those who earned the ire of the administration could be labeled as either terrorists or supporters of terrorism and then attacked. In their eyes, the invasion of Iraq in 2003 aptly demonstrated their fears of a hegemonic power using force as a first resort simply because it could. Thus, the propensity of foreign audiences to view the United States as a threat grew as a result.[18]

A third major theme for the George W. Bush administration was another carryover from the Clinton administration. It involved largely ignoring Russia's concerns when pursuing US national interests. During both the Clinton and Bush administrations, US officials seemed to expect the Russians to respect US views without any need for the United States to respect Russian perspectives in return. This dynamic was well illustrated in debates about NATO expansion. The Russians were alarmed at the acceptance of Hungary, Poland, and the Czech Republic into NATO in 1999, which from the Russian perspective meant that NATO had crept into the former Soviet sphere of influence. In 2004, Russians were further alarmed when four more former Soviet-sphere states were added (Slovenia, Slovakia, Bulgaria, and Romania) along with three countries that had actually been part of the Soviet Union itself (Estonia, Latvia, and Lithuania). Now NATO members actually abutted Russian borders, and Russian president Vladimir Putin warned NATO against stationing any troops in these forward areas. Despite Russia's repeated objections, Albania and Croatia were invited to begin the process of joining NATO in April 2008. At that time, President Bush supported an invitation to Ukraine and Georgia to join as well, but other NATO members did not agree. The August 2008 Russian invasion of Georgia could be seen as Russia's attempt to forcibly prevent Georgia's entry into NATO and as its delayed response to NATO's war on Russian ally Serbia in 1999. In 2009, Albania and Croatia formally joined NATO, and Montenegro was added in 2017.

Another illustration of the United States pursuing its interests at the expense of Russian interests involved the creation of a new missile defense system. In 2008, the Bush administration signed agreements that would create a theater missile defense system in Europe by placing a radar installation in the Czech Republic and interceptor missiles in Poland. According to US officials, the system was to defend Europe and North America against missile launches from Iran or other "rogue" regimes in the Middle East. However, for years top Russian officials had said that the real target of such a defense system was Russia, because Russia had nuclear missiles and Middle East states did not. Russian leaders warned that they would be forced to target Russian missiles at such a European antimissile system in the future. In each of these instances—NATO expansion and European missile defense—US leaders paid little or no heed to Russia's perceptions of its national interests, and Russian hostility grew.

The new Obama administration sought to reverse many of these Bush-era initiatives by reengaging with traditional allies, listening to others more, and seeking multinational responses to global problems, for example, the 2008–2010 Great Recession, which began in the United States but quickly went global. By simply changing the tone of US foreign policy, President Obama was awarded the 2009 Nobel Peace Prize. Despite a call for global nuclear disarmament and the negotiation of the **New START** treaty with Russia (which reduced the number of US and Russian deployed nuclear warheads to 1,550 per side and limited each side to no more than 700 deployed heavy bombers and missiles), the relationship with Russia continued to deteriorate. One source of persistent tension was the continued expansion of NATO eastward into what Russians saw as their traditional sphere of influence. Another was the fact that Obama continued the Bush-era plans for a missile defense system for Europe, a system the Russians saw as a hostile act aimed at reducing the value of their nuclear arsenal.

In the administration's view, the good news in 2011 was that the raid on Osama bin Laden's compound in Pakistan resulted in bin Laden's death and the capture of considerable intelligence information. However, 2011 also brought the surprise of the Arab Spring, when popular opposition to Middle East tyrants mushroomed in major cities across the Arab world. American policy makers were caught in a dilemma: Should the United States support democratic protesters or protect long-standing but autocratic allies such as Egypt and Saudi Arabia? The Obama administration chose to support the pro-democracy demonstrators, but only in Tunisia did a real democracy result. In most other affected countries, authoritarian regimes managed to retain control. Both Libya and Syria descended into vicious civil wars. In each case, the Obama administration tried to intervene, but opposition back home—by many in the Democratic Party who wanted no more US involvement in Middle East wars—kept the US role from being determinative in either conflict. More significant, Obama said that any use of chemical weapons by the Bashar al-Assad regime in Syria against its own people would result in crossing a "red line," normally a euphemism for saying the action would elicit a military response. Yet when the Assad regime used chemical weapons against Syrians, Obama sought congressional authorization to respond and failed to get it. Thus, the "red-line" warning produced no penalty. The final highlights of the administration came in 2015 with the Paris Agreement on climate change to take voluntary steps to hold the average increase in the earth's temperature to no more than 2 degrees Celsius and the negotiation of the **Joint Comprehensive Plan of Action**, better known as the **Iran nuclear deal**. Negotiated by the five permanent members of the UN Security Council (the United States, United Kingdom, France, Russia, and China) plus Germany, the deal significantly slowed the Iranian development of nuclear weapons by closing one nuclear plant, changing the form of another so it could no longer produce weapons-grade nuclear fuel, putting into storage about 3,000 of Iran's modern centrifuges used to enrich uranium fuel, moving 98 percent of Iran's enriched uranium out of the country, and verifying all of this through international inspections. In return, Iran got access to approximately $100 billion in Iranian bank accounts that had been frozen in Western banks since 1979.

Beginning in 2017, the new Trump administration sought to change the course of US foreign policy dramatically. Three broad themes connected many of Trump's policies. The first was an almost isolationist reduction in foreign contacts. After one week in office, President Trump banned the entry of immigrants from seven predominantly Muslim countries. As noted in Chapter 1, this action produced chaos at airports, and given Trump's campaign promise to ban Muslims from entering the United States, multiple federal courts overturned the ban as an impermissible religious test. Only when Iraq was dropped from the list and two non-Muslim states (North Korea and Venezuela) were added did the Supreme Court endorse the ban. As noted earlier, Trump challenged NATO allies to spend more on defense and implied that the United States might not come to their aid if they did not do so. Tariffs on imported steel and aluminum, which came primarily from long-standing US allies, were imposed, and trade wars with China and Europe were threatened or pursued. Throughout the first years of his administration, Trump unsuccessfully sought significant funding for a wall along the US-Mexican border.

A second theme was to reverse as many Obama-era policies as possible, both at home and abroad. In foreign policy, Trump decertified the Iran nuclear deal and sought new sanctions on Iran. He also rejected the Trans-Pacific Partnership (TPP), negotiated by the Obama administration to improve US economic ties with eleven Asian and Pacific states at the expense of China. The Paris Agreement was abandoned, and many regulations at home to protect the environment were weakened or eliminated. Trump also embraced conservative Saudi, Egyptian, and Israeli leaders, after the Obama administration had distanced itself from those regimes. Trump held the first-ever US summit conference with a North Korean leader—Kim Jong-un, a leader representing a rogue regime known for its human rights abuses and its provocative nuclear weapons and missile programs. Trump agreed to stop the regular military exercises between the United States and South Korea and declared after the summit that the North Korean nuclear threat had been eliminated. Unfortunately, the administration later learned that North Korea refused to make significant cuts in its nuclear arsenal and continued to expand its weapons and missile programs. It appeared the Trump administration had been "played" by the North Koreans.

However, the third theme of the new administration was arguably the most controversial. Trump doggedly sought to improve relations with Russia, to such an extent that his critics suggested that he sought to achieve Russian national interests at the expense of American national interests. President Trump initially took President Vladimir Putin's word that Russia had not intervened in the 2016 election, despite the unanimous conclusion by the US Intelligence Community that Russia had done so with the intent to help Trump and hurt his opponent, Hillary Clinton. When pressed to do so by his own advisers, Trump conceded that an intervention in the election had occurred, but he said it could have been by Russia or by someone else. As Trump sought to improve his relationship with Putin, most notably in a summit with Putin in Helsinki, Finland, Congress imposed additional sanctions on the Russian regime and Russian officials for their intervention in the 2016 election. For more on this issue, see Box 3.2.

As this historical account shows, the international environment facing US foreign policy makers in 2019 is complex. On the one hand, the United States is unquestionably the leading military power of the early twenty-first century. Its defense spending leads the world. However, this does not mean the United States is

Box 3.2 Have Republicans Embraced Russia?

For anyone who grew up during the Cold War years, the idea that Republican Party members would cozy up to a Russian Federation led by a former KGB agent seems pretty far-fetched. After all, it was the Republicans who led the House Un-American Activities Committee investigations into Soviet subversion in the United States in the 1940s, and it was Republican senator Joseph McCarthy who alleged widespread Communist subversion in the United States in the 1950s. However, facts are facts, and the closer relations between some Republicans and Russian officials goes far beyond President Donald Trump's apparent willingness to court President Vladimir Putin at every opportunity. A number of events give a glimpse into this changing relationship between the Republican Party and Russia. First, at the events surrounding the 2016 Republican Presidential Nominating Convention in Cleveland, Russian ambassador to the United States Sergey Kislyak made the rounds, speaking with or attending meetings with Jeff Sessions (later attorney general), Carter Page (then a national security adviser to the Trump campaign), and K. T. McFarland (later Trump's deputy national security adviser). After speaking with Kislyak at the convention, Trump campaign officials got the party's platform statement on Russia's intervention into Ukraine weakened. Following the election, National Security Adviser–designate Michael Flynn also met with Kislyak to discuss the termination of US sanctions against Russia. Lying about what they discussed ultimately cost Flynn his job, and he later pleaded guilty to lying to the Federal Bureau of Investigation (FBI) about these matters.

Second, some Republicans in the House of Representatives appeared in Russia-related news. In February 2018, Devin Nunes, the chairman of the House Intelligence Committee, drafted a memo saying that his committee's investigation revealed no evidence of Russian interference in the 2016 election. The other Republicans on the committee voted to release the memo to the public, but all the committee's Democrats voted against its release, saying its analysis was

(continues)

52

Box 3.2 Continued

---

fundamentally flawed. For their part, the Senate Intelligence Committee's investigation (also led by Republicans) determined that the Russians had interfered in the election. Also, in the House, Republican Dana Rohrabacher was warned in 2012 that Russian agents were trying to recruit him. Despite this warning from the FBI, Rohrabacher remained one of Russia's most consistent champions in Congress until he was defeated for reelection in 2018.

Third, there's the Russian attempt to gain inroads into the National Rifle Association, which is closely tied to the Republican Party. The NRA donated $30 million to the Trump campaign, three times more than it contributed to support Republican Mitt Romney in 2012. Did some of that money illegally come from Russian sources? It's possible. Alexander Torshin has been described as a Russian legislator, the deputy governor of Russia's Central Bank, a Putin confidant, and a Russian mafia don, and Torshin long sought close ties with the NRA. He attended multiple NRA meetings over the years, began a Right to Bear Arms group in Russia, and funded Russian Maria Butina's efforts to gain inroads into the NRA's top leadership. In December 2018, Butina pleaded guilty to the charge of acting as an unregistered foreign agent and said her role was part of an organized attempt to go through the NRA to influence conservatives and Republicans on behalf of Russia. Some of these Russian funds may have gone to other Republican legislators as well.

To be fair, there are many Republicans in Congress who believe the Russians are an adversary and did interfere in the 2016 election. In 2018, a delegation of Republican legislators journeyed to Moscow. On July 4, Senators Richard Shelby (AL), Steve Daines (MT), John Thune (SD), John Kennedy (LA), Jerry Moran (KS) and John Hoeven (ND), and Representative Kay Granger (TX) met with Russian officials. They asked about Russian meddling in the 2016 election, receiving denials of any such meddling from all the officials with whom they spoke, but they warned Russia not to interfere in the 2018 midterm elections. Ironically, their meeting was on the same day that the Republican-led Senate Intelligence Committee released its report saying the Russians had interfered in the 2016 election in an attempt to help Donald Trump. None of this, however, changes the fact that the president and at least some other Republicans reached out to Russia, which is quite surprising, given the party's historical anti-Russian stance.

Sources:

Matt Apuzzo, Adam Goldman, and Mark Mazzetti, "F.B.I. Once Warned G.O.P. Congressman That Russian Spies Were Recruiting Him," *New York Times,* May 19, 2017, https://www.nytimes.com/2017/05/19/us /politics/dana-rohrabacher-russia-spies.html; Emily Birnbaum, "GOP Senators Visited Moscow on July 4, Warned Russia Against Meddling in 2018 Election: Report," *Hill,* July 5, 2018, http://thehill.com/homenews /senate/395719-gop-senators-visited-moscow-on-july-4; Tom Jackman and Rosalind S. Helderman, "Alleged Russian Agent Maria Butina Ordered to Remain in Custody After Prosecutors Argue She Has Ties to Russian Intelligence," *Washington Post,* July 18, 2018, https://www .washingtonpost.com/local/public-safety/alleged-russian-agent-maria -butina-had-ties-to-russian-intelligence-agency-prosecutors-say/2018 /07/18/a1a4042c-8a01-11e8-a345-a1bf7847b375_story.html?noredirect =on&utm_term=.e47deb920236; Andrew C. McCarthy, "Collusion 3.0: Russia and the NRA," *National Review,* January 20, 2018, https://www .nationalreview.com/2018/01/russia-national-rifle-association-trump -campaign-alexander-torshin-maria-butina-organized-crime/; Brian Naylor, "How the Trump Campaign Weakened the Republican Platform on Aid to Ukraine," *National Public Radio,* August 6, 2016, https://www .npr.org/2016/08/06/488876597/how-the-trump-campaign-weakened-the -republican-platform-on-aid-to-ukraine; Steve Reilly, "Exclusive: Two Other Trump Advisors Also Spoke with Russian Envoy During GOP Convention," *USA Today,* March 2, 2017, https://www.usatoday.com /story/news/2017/03/02/exclusive-two-other-trump-advisers-also-spoke -russian-envoy-during-gop-convention/98648190/.

omnipotent. Conflicts in both Iraq and Afghanistan have stressed US military resources to the point that major new military initiatives could not readily be undertaken, and others know this. When the George W. Bush administration pressed Iran over its nuclear program, Supreme Leader Ali Khamenei pointedly asked what the

United States could do about it, given that US forces were over-stretched in both Iraq and Afghanistan at that time.

Further, other major regional powers insist on being taken seri-ously today. China has been a rising military power in recent years, and India's deployment of its first self-built nuclear-powered sub-marine completes its efforts to join the United States, Russia, France, the United Kingdom, and China in being able to launch nuclear weapons from land-based missiles, sea-based missiles, or bomber aircraft.[19] Russia remains a major military power in the Eurasian region—as shown by its war with Georgia in 2008 and its 2014 annexation of Crimea and seizure of Ukraine's eastern Don-bass region—and Russia demands that its interests be considered in Asia, Eastern Europe, the Balkans, and the Caucasus. European leaders have sought to make NATO a military alliance that has the ability to act without requiring US participation, and the EU pos-sesses a larger economy than that of the United States.

Economically and socially as well, the United States faces sig-nificant rivals and challenges. As noted earlier, the US economy is the largest single economy in the world, but in recent years the story of the international economy has been "the rise of the rest."[20] Unless growth rates change, the length of time it takes for the **gross domestic product (GDP)** of China to overtake that of the United States will be measured in a few years, not decades or cen-turies. China's economy has consistently grown faster than that of the United States. When wealth is measured in terms of nominal GDP per capita, the United States typically ranks behind such countries as Luxembourg, Norway, Denmark, and even Qatar. In terms of the human development index—a figure created by the United Nations that combines life expectancy, literacy, education, and standard of living—the United States typically ranks behind countries such as Norway, Australia, Switzerland, Germany, Den-mark, Singapore, the Netherlands, and Ireland.

In summary, the current historical context provides a mix of both positive and negative inputs to policy making. The United States is the primary power, if not a superpower, and others in the international system expect US leadership on important issues. Yet there are limits on its freedom of action; the United States is not a hegemon and thus cannot readily impose its will on others. Similarly, American exceptionalism at home pushes the United States to lead on international issues, but the effects of the global recession have made some wary of the financial costs of such leadership, and growing isolationist tendencies at home have made more Americans leery of globalization and foreign contacts. Partisan gridlock in the nation's capital complicates efforts, as Democrats and Republicans typically disagree on both the ends and the means of foreign policy. Thus, policy makers have to contend with a global foreign policy agenda that receives mixed signals from both home and abroad.

Conclusion

A number of contextual trends, long in the making, came together with the election of Donald Trump as president. His campaign slogan—"Make America Great Again"—was obviously popular and meaningful to many voters. But what does that slogan suggest? Is the United States a rising or declining power? Certainly, other countries are catching up to the United States on various dimensions, so in a relative sense, the country is in decline because its lead over other states has shrunk. But what are the means to make it great again? Most recent presidents tried to lead within the context of the global institutions that the United States helped to create after World War II. Trump wants to replace American participation in such global norm-setting institutions with individual bilateral transactions in which the United States repeatedly comes out on top. Is that possible? Is it even desirable? Reasonable people can disagree on these matters.

Then there's the cost of global leadership. The national debt grew by $2 trillion in Trump's first two years in office. Given the cost of paying the interest on that debt each year, much less potentially paying the debt off at some point, which foreign policy priorities will get more funding and which will get less? Many Americans have long chafed at the money spent abroad, but what are the costs of letting someone else lead? Is letting others lead a better deal, or a worse one?

In the current environment, what issues will rise enough in importance to demand funding? President Trump's rhetoric and policies suggest that unchecked immigration, lax border security, Latin American gang presence, and economic competition are among the highest threats facing the country. On the other hand, his national security team produced a 2018 defense strategy statement that listed China and Russia as the greatest threats to the United States, followed by North Korea and Iran. Trump's rhetoric has been very pro-Russian, but US policies—often forced on him by Congress—have been harsher on Moscow. What are the primary threats facing the United States? Again, people disagree. The changing nature of the domestic, external, and ideational contexts provides many mixed signals to US foreign policy makers in the early twenty-first century. Moreover, there are many such policy makers in the US government, and they are the next subject.

Suggested Reading

Haass, Richard. *A World in Disarray: American Foreign Policy and the Crisis of the Old Order.* New York: Penguin Books, 2017.
Hunt, Michael H. *Ideology and U.S. Foreign Policy.* New Haven: Yale University Press, 1987, 2009.
Kaufman, Joyce P. *A Concise History of U.S. Foreign Policy.* 4th ed. Lanham, MD: Rowman and Littlefield, 2017.
Trubowitz, Peter. *Defining the National Interest: Conflict and Change in American Foreign Policy.* Chicago: University of Chicago Press, 1998.

Notes

1. For more on the laws of war, see "The Laws of War," part of the Avalon Project, Yale Law School, http://avalon.law.yale.edu/subject_menus/lawwar.asp.
2. See "Key Developments on the Responsibility to Protect at the United Nations, 2005–2010," International Coalition for the Responsibility to Protect, http://responsibilitytoprotect.org/ICRtoP%20Latest%20Developments%20at%20the%20UN%20Aug%202010(2).pdf.
3. See Thomas E. Ricks, *Fiasco: The American Military Adventure in Iraq* (New York: Penguin, 2006), or Bob Woodward, *State of Denial: Bush at War, Part III* (New York: Simon and Schuster, 2006).
4. For an approving viewpoint on American empire, see Robert Kagan, "The Benevolent Empire," *Foreign Policy* 111 (Summer 1998): 24–35, or Sebastian Mallaby, "The Reluctant Imperialist: Terrorism, Failed States, and the Case for American Empire," *Foreign Affairs,* 81 (March–April 2002): 2–7. For a disapproving viewpoint, see Andrew J. Bacevich, *American Empire: The Realities and Consequences of U.S.*

Diplomacy (Cambridge, MA: Harvard University Press, 2004), or Chalmers Johnson, *The Sorrows of Empire: Militarism, Secrecy, and the End of the Republic* (New York: Holt Paperbacks, 2004).

5. See "NATO's Role in Afghanistan," http://www.nato.int/cps/en /natolive/topics_8189.htm.

6. For a classic view on the interaction of these contexts and modern interpretations thereof, see Richard C. Snyder, H. W. Bruck, Burton Sapin, Valerie M. Hudson, Derek H. Chollet, and James H. Goldgeier, *Foreign Policy Decision Making (Revisited)* (New York: Palgrave Macmillan, 2002). For a more recent treatment of the importance of political context, see Barbara Farnham, "Impact of the Political Context on Foreign Policy Decision Making," *Political Psychology* 25 (3) (2004): 441–463.

7. For more on American exceptionalism, see Seymour Martin Lipset, *American Exceptionalism: A Double-Edged Sword* (New York: W. W. Norton, 1996).

8. Identifying differences in foreign policy ends and means based on one's partisanship goes back a long way. See, for example, George Belknap and Angus Campbell, "Political Party Identification and Attitudes Toward Foreign Policy," *Public Opinion Quarterly* 15 (Winter 1951– 1952): 601–623.

9. See, for example, Ole R. Holsti, "Public Opinion and Foreign Policy: Challenges to the Almond-Lippmann Consensus," *International Studies Quarterly,* 36 (1992): 439–466.

10. See the surveys conducted periodically by the Chicago Council on Global Affairs, www.thechicagocouncil.org.

11. For the classic version of these ideas, see Hans J. Morgenthau, *Politics Among Nations: The Struggle for Power and Peace,* 3rd ed. (Chicago: University of Chicago Press, 1954). For a more contemporary discussion, see Daniel Deudney and Jeffrey Meiser, "American Exceptionalism," in *US Foreign Policy,* ed. Michael Cox and Doug Stokes (Oxford: Oxford University Press, 2008).

12. See Francis Fukuyama, *The End of History and the Last Man* (New York: Free Press, 2006).

13. See *The 9/11 Commission Report: Final Report of the National Commission on Terrorist Attacks on the United States,* https://www. 9-11commission.gov/report/911Report.pdf. The number of dead attributed to this attack can be expected to rise over time, as first responders and others affected there at the time succumb to long-term illnesses caused by their exposure to the toxic chemicals produced by the fires and collapse of buildings.

14. At its height, the "coalition of the willing" in Iraq produced a force of about 300,000 troops. About 250,000 of those were US troops and 40,000 were British. The remaining contributions to the coalition varied, from 2,000 Australians to seventy Albanians. So while the coalition was officially composed of thirty-eight states, the Iraqi invasion and occupation was fundamentally a US-British military operation. See Chelsea

J. Carter, "Last Two Partner Nations of U.S. Pull Forces Out of Iraq," Associated Press, *Fort Worth Star-Telegram,* August 2, 2009.

15. For more on how and why the Iraqi response to the occupation changed, see Bob Woodward, *The War Within: A Secret White House History, 2006–2008* (New York: Simon and Schuster, 2008).

16. For a good discussion of the rights of detainees, see Linda Cornett and Mark Gibney, "The Rights of Detainees: Determining the Limits of Law," in *Contemporary Cases in U.S. Foreign Policy: From Terrorism to Trade,* 5th ed., ed. Ralph G. Carter (Washington, DC: CQ Press, 2014), 409–434.

17. For more on the warrantless eavesdropping, see Louis Fisher, "NSA Eavesdropping: Unchecked or Limited Presidential Power?" in Carter, ed., *Contemporary Cases in U.S. Foreign Policy.*

18. To track such global public opinion, see the Pew Global Attitudes Project, http://pewglobal.org.

19. Ashok Sharma, "Nuclear-Powered Sub Built in India Makes Its Debut," Associated Press, found in the *Fort Worth Star-Telegram,* July 27, 2009.

20. Fareed Zakaria, *The Post-American World* (New York: W. W. Norton, 2008), 2.

4

Actors in the Policy-Making Process

Learning Objectives

- Identify the major governmental actors making US foreign policy.
- Explain the roles typically played by executive branch, congressional, and judicial foreign policy actors.
- Analyze the circumstances that favor executive branch, congressional, or judicial foreign policy actors.
- Evaluate the degree to which separate governmental institutions share power in making foreign policy.

So far we have looked at the nature of foreign policy making, the theoretical ideas that help us (and foreign policy makers) interpret and understand international phenomena, and the inputs that can come from the external, internal, and ideational contexts in which foreign policy is made. Let's now turn our attention to the major actors who participate in making US foreign policy and the processes by which they do so. This entails examining how policy inputs are transformed into policy outputs and by whom. This chapter also covers the major governmental actors and their roles in foreign policy making. The chapters that follow then take up typical decision-making processes.

To begin, who actually makes US foreign policy? Such a simple question defies easy answers. As illustrated in Chapter 1, the "concentric circles" model of policy making puts the president (assisted by advisers) at the center of the process, and with good reason. Presidents are usually the most influential foreign policy makers for many foreign policy issues. However, they are not the only foreign policy makers, and according to the shifting constellations model of policy making indicated in Chapter 1, they are sometimes not the most important ones. Other governmental actors are significantly involved in foreign policy making as well. The sections below examine these actors, taking executive branch actors first, congressional actors next, and judicial actors last.

Executive Branch Actors

There are many different officials and agencies in the executive branch that help shape US foreign policy. The president is the single most important, so a review of the presidency should begin this exploration.

The President

Presidents shape US foreign policy through their words and deeds. As noted in Chapter 1, the Constitution makes the president the commander in chief of the military, the chief executive, and effectively the country's chief diplomat. These roles put presidents in a position to control the general direction of US foreign policy through their control of the governmental agenda. Such powers implicitly put presidents in the position to be, as the US Supreme Court noted in 1936, the "sole organ" representing the nation in foreign affairs.[1] Thus, presidents can use their access to the media to assert what the foreign policies of the United States are, ask Congress to authorize and/or fund such policies as required, order executive branch officials and personnel to carry out such policies, and negotiate and sign treaties or other executive agreements affirming such policies as necessary.

When it comes to foreign policy, presidents are clearly *more* than just the "first among equals," but they are not dominant across the board, as their power lies primarily in the power of persuasion.[2] Presidential influence over foreign policy is often like a driver's control of a vehicle traveling on an ice-glazed street. Presidents can point the government in a preferred policy direction, but rarely do they have precise control over what happens next, for at that point other actors (both at home and abroad) often get involved and events take their own course. Still if you want to influence US foreign policy, it's hard to beat being president.

Presidential Advisers

The good news for presidents is that they receive lots of help in shaping US foreign policy. A number of advisers are available to assist presidents. Some occupy formal roles, and others are selected on an as-needed or as-desired basis.

Three official forums for such advisers are the National Security Council, the Homeland Security Council, and the National Economic Council. The **National Security Council (NSC)** dates back to the **National Security Act of 1947**. Its purpose is to advise the president on national security matters and coordinate US national security policy across the various governmental actors and agencies involved. Its statutory members are the president, the vice president, and secretaries of the Departments of State and Defense. By statute, the director of the Central Intelligence Agency advises the NSC on intelligence matters, and the chairman of the Joint Chiefs of Staff (JCS) advises it on military matters. Other officials are routinely invited to its meetings, as dictated by the issues involved and the president's preferences.

However, the NSC as a whole typically does not meet often. Instead, it subdivides its work through a series of interagency committees. The Principals Committee is composed of secretaries of relevant cabinet departments; the Deputies Committee is composed of deputy secretaries from those departments; and a third grouping is composed of Interagency Working Groups (also known as Interagency Policy Committees), typically organized around recurring issues (e.g., nonproliferation or international narcotrafficking) or specific geographic regions. The work of the Principals Committee and the Deputies Committee is guided by the national security adviser and that person's deputy. The Interagency Working Groups are typically chaired by an assistant secretary from the most relevant cabinet department concerned, and their members come from experts drawn from across the administration's various units. All these NSC committees are assisted by members of the NSC staff, who also do their own research and draft position papers on anything falling within the realm of national and international security.

The **Homeland Security Council (HSC)** was created by an executive order in 2001 by George W. Bush following the 9/11 attacks on New York City and the Pentagon. Like the NSC, its purpose is to coordinate planning and policy for the many different areas that fall under the heading of protecting US citizens at home. Although some of these threats have natural sources (e.g., hurricane damage), others may be intentional (e.g., terrorism, threats of weapons of mass destruction, or even biological warfare concerns). The council's structure is similar to that of the NSC. Originally, it had its own staff, and the president's homeland security adviser coordinated its operations. However, under President Barack Obama the staffs of the NSC and the HSC were merged into a new entity, the **National Security Staff (NSS)**.

The **National Economic Council (NEC)** is the NSC's counterpart for advising the president on domestic and international economic issues and coordinating economic policy across the various governmental actors and agencies involved. The NEC was created by an executive order in 1993 by President Bill Clinton, and the assistant to the president for economic policy serves as its director. Those who attend its meetings typically include the vice president and secretaries of the Departments of Agriculture, Commerce, Energy, Health and Human Services, Housing and Urban Development, Labor, State, Transportation, and Treasury. Although international economic policy is always important, the global scope of the Great Recession of 2008–2010 reminded all of how quickly economic matters can become high-visibility foreign policy issues.

Among other presidential advisers, the best known is the **national security adviser** (also known as the assistant to the president for national security affairs). Part of the Executive Office of the President, the national security adviser's importance is based on legal statute and frequent contact with the president. The role originated in the National Security Act of 1947, which reorganized parts of the executive branch to handle the looming challenges of the Cold War. National security advisers have considerable contact with the presidents they serve. They typically brief the president each day about relevant happenings that could affect US foreign and security interests, and their offices are located in the West Wing of the White House, along with the president's Oval Office and private study. They normally travel with the president as well. In practice, national security advisers have evolved from directors of the NSC staff to influential actors in their own right who help shape the content of foreign policy. A few have been particularly associated with certain initiatives— Henry Kissinger with the opening of relations with the People's Republic of China and negotiating the withdrawal of US forces from Vietnam, Robert McFarlane and John Poindexter with arming the rebel Contra forces in Nicaragua, and so on.

Presidents listen to others in the West Wing of the White House as well. As a result of proximity and contact, the president's chief of staff is always in a position of potential policy influence, as when Trump's then chief of staff John Kelly argued that separating families of undocumented immigrants would serve to deter others from entering the country illegally. Other advisers include those with titles such as counselors to the president, senior advisers to the president, press secretaries, and speechwriters. Presidents also often rely on other, more informal advisers. These advisers may be their spouses, other family members, childhood friends, old college buddies, or other acquaintances whose judgment or expertise they trust. For example, two iconic moments in President John Kennedy's administration were traceable to one person. Kennedy got the ideas for both the Peace Corps and his famous "I Am a Berliner" speech (made following the 1961 Berlin Crisis) from Representative Henry Reuss, a Democrat and German American from Milwaukee who had helped Kennedy reach out to German American voters during the 1960 presidential campaign.[3]

Another increasingly important presidential adviser is the vice president. For years, the vice presidency was not considered an influential position. As vice president to President Franklin Roosevelt, John Nance Garner is alleged to have said, the job "was not worth a bucket of warm [spit]."[4] The constitutional mandate for the vice president is to preside over the Senate. However, in a chamber with relatively unlimited debate, the importance of that role is so reduced that most of the time it is filled instead by the most junior senator available. Vice presidents tend to preside only when a close vote is anticipated on legislation deemed important by the administration, just in case a tie-breaking vote is needed. Beyond that, the vice president's importance used to be solely to help get the president elected and to fulfill the duties of office should the president die or become incapacitated.

Yet in recent administrations, the role of the vice president has dramatically changed. Under Bill Clinton, Vice President Al Gore was delegated primary responsibility for two important bundles of issues—environmental issues and US-Russian relations. George W. Bush also gave a prominent role to his vice president. Particularly during his first term, Bush listened closely to Vice President Dick Cheney on a wide array of issues involving national security, the administration's War on Terror, policies regarding detainees from that conflict, the invasion of Iraq, and energy policy. Cheney consistently encouraged the president to pursue policies and actions that emphasized a presidency that was greatly empowered at the expense of Congress.[5] Following this trend, Barack Obama picked Joe Biden as his running mate, in part because of Biden's long history of foreign policy expertise as chair of the Senate Foreign Relations Committee. Once in office, Biden served as a key adviser regarding the war in Afghanistan and the response to the Great Recession and often played the important role of devil's advocate in decision-making sessions to ensure that multiple points of view were considered.

Cabinet Officials and Departments

There is always the possibility that cabinet officials will be asked for their views on foreign policy topics. When those requests come, cabinet officials must decide whether to present the views of the organization they lead or their own personal views. At times these views coincide, but not always. The chances for meaningful foreign policy input will be greatest for the secretaries of state and defense, so let's take a closer look at their roles.

The secretary of state has three different roles: serving as the nation's top diplomat and spokesperson, as the manager of the State Department, and as a presidential adviser. All these roles take considerable effort. Whether the secretary of state also serves as an influential shaper of foreign policy depends on the person filling the role and the president's willingness to listen. For example, Presidents Harry Truman and Dwight Eisenhower listened to their secretaries—Dean Acheson and John Foster Dulles, respectively. Both were reputed to have considerable foreign policy influence.[6] Colin Powell wanted to play such a role for George W. Bush, but the president did not seem predisposed to listen.[7] Hillary Rodham Clinton developed a reputation as a sound manager of the State Department, a very well-traveled diplomat, and a serious voice in the White House regarding diplomatic and national security affairs. More recently, President Trump appeared to listen more to Mike Pompeo in this role than he did when the role was held by Rex Tillerson.

Beginning in the 1960s, secretaries of defense began to loom larger as foreign policy advisers to presidents, sometimes pushing secretaries of state into subordinate positions of influence. Part of this shift was due to the personalities and styles of some less assertive secretaries of state (e.g., Dean Rusk under Presidents Kennedy and Johnson and Warren Christopher under President Clinton), part was due to some strong-willed secretaries of defense (e.g., Robert McNamara under President Kennedy and Donald Rumsfeld under President George W. Bush), and part was due to the frequent use of military force as an instrument of foreign policy that would propel the secretary of defense into policy discussions more frequently.[8] Robert Gates developed quite a reputation as a very influential secretary of defense, serving as a key adviser to both George W. Bush and Barack Obama. Secretary of Defense James Mattis often pushed policy stances at odds with President Trump's rhetoric, and many of those contrary policy stances were implemented (such as naming China and Russia as the greatest threats in the National Security Strategy Statement of 2018 or defending the right of transgendered troops to serve in the military). Ultimately, however, these disagreements led Mattis in late 2018 to resign in protest, citing the president's lack of respect for allies and his courting of traditional adversaries. In turn, President Trump then fired Mattis.

The functions and size of each of these two departments also impact their foreign policy roles. The primary functions of the State Department are to staff a network of embassies and consulates abroad, conduct diplomatic communications and negotiations, and administer programs such as foreign assistance. Since the early 1960s, the State Department's budget has diminished steadily when adjusted for inflation.[9] Although the State Department has always served as the channel for official US communications to other international actors, its role in diplomatic negotiations varies. State Department personnel are more likely to be engaged early in the negotiations process and when the issues involved are considered highly technical or complex. After 1962, the funding for foreign assistance generally trended down in constant dollar terms until the George W. Bush administration, when its budgeting for programs in Africa and the reconstruction of Iraq pushed the totals back up.[10] On the other hand, President Trump came into office advocating a cut of 37 percent in the State Department budget, and then Secretary of State Rex Tillerson said he thought more than that could safely be cut.

By contrast, the Defense Department always looms large in US foreign policy making and policy implementation. Entrusted with the maintenance and operation of the air force, army, marines, and navy, the military's budget has steadily trended upward since 1950 when measured in constant dollars, with the only exception being the years of the Obama administration.[11] With over 1 million uniformed personnel, the largest naval and air forces in the world, and more "smart weapons" than any other country, the Defense Department gives the United States the ability to project force globally. Based on these considerations, the chairman of the JCS, the other members of the JCS, and the overall combatant commanders of important unified regional military commands can also be significant foreign policy makers. Elected political leaders often defer to uniformed generals and admirals in terms of how the military should be used, and some of these generals and admirals shrewdly exploit this influence. For example, General Colin Powell, the chairman of the JSC, and General Creighton Abrams, the army chief of staff, both recommended policy and procedural changes designed to make it harder for civilian leaders to risk the lives of military personnel in combat unless it was absolutely necessary.[12] More recently, President Trump allowed combat commanders to have more freedom of action to do what they thought best without having to seek clearance from the administration.

The Defense Department's foreign policy uses are many: to deploy forces for combat, to use the threat of force to send a signal to a potential opponent, to affirm commitments to allies, to suggest

US resolve, to act as de facto diplomats, to rebuild war-torn or failed states, and so on. The military also possesses significant intelligence resources (see the next section). The human and financial resources devoted to the Defense Department dwarf those of any other foreign policy–related actor. Consequently, it is not surprising that when US foreign policy makers reach into their statecraft toolbox, they often pull out a military tool. Interestingly, a call for redressing the glaring imbalance of funding between the State and Defense Departments was made by none other than Defense Secretary Robert Gates. In November 2007, he noted that the State Department's budget was only $36 billion, and the total number of US diplomats (6,600) was equivalent to the number of personnel for one US naval aircraft carrier strike group. As a consequence, he urged more spending on the State Department and Central Intelligence Agency, arguing that if more were spent on diplomacy and intelligence, less might be needed for defense.[13]

Beyond the Departments of State and Defense and their leaders, other cabinet departments play foreign policy roles. The secretaries of the Departments of Homeland Security, Treasury, Commerce, Energy, and Agriculture can all play important foreign policy roles at times. Depending on the issues involved, attorneys general may also get involved in foreign policy discussions. However, the remaining part of the executive branch that typically gets the most attention is the Intelligence Community.

The Intelligence Community

When most people think of intelligence or counterintelligence, they typically think first of the **Central Intelligence Agency (CIA)**. However, the CIA represents only one of seventeen entities that comprise the **Intelligence Community (IC)**, which is nominally led by the **director of national intelligence (DNI)**. The position of DNI was created in 2004, after post-9/11 investigations found that different parts of the IC had different pieces of information suggesting that some sort of terrorist incident might be imminent. However, such information was not shared, and no one was in a position to put all the pieces of information together.[14] Unfortunately, the ability of the DNI to effectively pull the various parts of the IC together seems unlikely. The largest parts of the intelligence budget are found in the Defense Department and are thus out of the DNI's control, and bureaucratic loyalties and careerism generally inhibit the sharing of information. Although there are numerous components of the IC, two of the most prominent ones are the CIA and the National Security Agency, both of which are discussed below.

The CIA is the nation's primary civilian intelligence agency. Like intelligence agencies the world over, the CIA engages in intelligence gathering (the collecting of information thought to be useful in policy making), analysis of what that intelligence means, and counterintelligence (preventing others from obtaining information the United States would prefer not to share publicly). Where the CIA differs from other intelligence agencies is in the degree to which it conducts its own covert or paramilitary operations—direct actions abroad designed to bring about a desired result without that action being traced back to the US government. Although specific finance figures are classified, it is thought the CIA's budget is somewhere around $13–14 billion per year.[15] Reports suggest that approximately 20,000 employees may work at the CIA headquarters in Langley, Virginia, but no data are available for the number of CIA personnel who work in other locations or abroad, or how many private contractors are employed by the CIA.[16]

Far larger in personnel terms is the **National Security Agency (NSA)**. The job of the NSA is conducting information assurance by preventing vital information from falling into the hands of other powers (often through the use of cryptography), collecting signals intelligence (by eavesdropping on the communications of others), and conducting the research necessary for both information assurance and signals intelligence.[17] According to a 1990s estimate, the NSA employed nearly 40,000 people and had a budget of nearly $4 billion per year.[18] By the turn of the twenty-first century, NSA staff levels had dropped to approximately 32,000—a number that does not include the 25,000 people employed by the Central Security Service to staff listening posts for NSA—and the budget dropped to something in excess of $3 billion per year.[19] After the terrorist attacks on 9/11, spending on electronic surveillance surged, and in 2012, the NSA's budget was the second largest in the IC, at $10.8 billion. By 2000, the NSA was reported to be the source for almost 80 percent of the intelligence information relayed to the rest of the US government, and that percentage may be higher now.[20]

The largest components of the IC in terms of budgets and personnel are the individual military branch intelligence agencies and the **Defense Intelligence Agency (DIA)**, which has both civilian employees and personnel from all the military service branches as well. Numerous other government entities have IC components, as shown in Table 4.1.

Table 4.1 Member Agencies of the Intelligence Community

Air Force Intelligence	Federal Bureau of Investigation
Army Intelligence	Marine Corps Intelligence
Central Intelligence Agency	National Geospatial-Intelligence
Coast Guard Intelligence	Agency
Defense Intelligence Agency	National Reconnaissance Office
Department of Energy	National Security Agency
Department of Homeland Security	Navy Intelligence
Department of State	Office of the Director of National
Department of Treasury	Intelligence
Drug Enforcement Administration	

Source: "About the Intelligence Community," Intelligence Community website, https://www.intelligence.gov/how-the-ic-works.

All told, the IC represents much of the federal government's eyes and ears. Beyond their own monitoring of open news sources, foreign policy makers rely on the IC to tell them what is happening in the world, how that information may affect US national interests, and what may be done to further US national interests as a result. As noted earlier, members of the IC may be relied upon to undertake direct actions to further US national interests as well.

Of course, all presidents would like the support of all the various agencies and officials who work in their administration, but that doesn't always happen. Sometimes different parts of an administration take opposing views on a foreign policy matter, as illustrated in Box 4.1. If they haven't been involved up to that point, members of Congress often get more involved then, as explained in the next section.

Congressional Actors

Congress as a whole, a variety of its components, and its individual members play a number of significant foreign policy roles. Each of these perspectives on Congress deserves attention.

Box 4.1 Who Decides When Foreign Investment in the
United States Is Bad?

Normally, it would be considered a good thing if people wanted to invest in the United States, the underlying idea being that a strong American economy lures investment dollars and additional financial capital can fund research and development or create jobs. But is there a downside if the investors come from other countries? Perhaps.

What if individuals or corporations from other countries wanted to invest in US defense contractors or in corporations that are part of sensitive infrastructure such as the electric grid? Might such foreign investment create national security risks? To make sure that such risks did not occur, in the mid-1970s President Gerald Ford created the **Committee on Foreign Investment in the United States (CFIUS)**. Composed of representatives of the State, Defense, Justice, Commerce, Energy and Homeland Security Departments and the Offices of the U.S. Trade Representative and Science and Technology Policy (as well as representatives of any other federal agency the president wishes represented in a specific case), CFIUS is led by the treasury secretary. Its purpose is to review any foreign investment that could jeopardize US national security. Congress passed the Exon-Florio Amendment in 1988, making it clear that the president had the authority to veto any foreign investment that threatened national security.

Normally, CFIUS reviews do not generate much controversy, but in 2006 the committee approved the transfer of the operation of six major US ports from a British-owned company to an Arab-owned company. In a deal that looked as if it could pose a potential terrorist risk to major American ports, President George W. Bush admitted that he learned of the approval only when he read about it in the newspapers, raising questions about who was making sensitive US policy. Members of Congress threatened retaliation, and the Arab-owned company (Dubai Ports World) withdrew its takeover bid. Since then, the Obama administration used CFIUS to deny a Chinese company the right to buy a wind farm located near a Department of Defense facility, and it prevented a Chinese investment company from buying a German-owned investment company conducting business in the United States. In 2017, the Trump administration used CFIUS to block a Chinese firm from buying a US semiconductor manufacturer, and in 2018, it blocked the acquisition of Qualcomm by a Singaporean telecommunications company. In late 2017, legislation was introduced in Congress to add thousands of US corporations to the list of those subject to CFIUS review. IBM opposed the legislation, saying it would hurt US businesses.

So, should foreign investment in the United States be regulated? If so, by whom? The potential regulators often are motivated by very different goals and threat assessments.

Sources:

CFIUS website, https://www.treasury.gov/resource-center/international/foreign-investment/Pages/cfius-members.aspx; Congressional Research Report on CFIUS, https://news.usni.org/2018/06/15/report-congress-committee-foreign-investment-united-states-2; Kevin Granville, "CFIUS, Powerful and Unseen, Is a Gatekeeper on Major Deals," *New York Times,* March 5, 2018, https://www.nytimes.com/2018/03/05/business/what-is-cfius.html.

Congress as a Whole

As indicated in Chapter 1, Congress actually has a wider array of foreign policy–making powers than does the president.[21] These include declaring war, approving treaties and appointments, regulating foreign trade, and so on. However, Congress's most significant powers are the ability to pass legislation authorizing some action or policy statement and the ability to provide the funds the federal government needs to work. Thus, except for the granting of diplomatic recognition to other regimes, Congress can basically set almost any aspect of US foreign policy by what it chooses to authorize, fund, or require the administration to do. In short, Congress has tremendous foreign policy powers if and when its members choose to use them.

The degree to which Congress uses these powers varies according to the situation. For example, Congress has historically been quite willing to tell the administration what it can or cannot do based on what Congress is willing to fund. Immigration policy is another arena that Congress has generally reserved for itself. Nor does Congress hesitate to send signals to an administration. For example, when the Clinton administration was considering the 1997 Kyoto Protocol on global climate change (which would require Senate approval to be binding on the United States), the Senate voted 95–0 for a nonbinding "sense of the Senate" resolution that essentially said: "Don't send us that treaty."

Another way to use the power of money is through the imposition of economic sanctions. Putting economic sanctions on an offending regime, its leaders or officials, or its banks and corporations has become a recurring instrument of US foreign policy in recent years. Congress seemingly loves this tactic, as it sends a signal to the offending regime and might impose some real hardships on the offender, but it doesn't result in any US personnel dying and satisfies the political imperative to "do something!" For example, after Russia's nerve agent attack in 2018 on a former spy and his daughter living in the United Kingdom, economic sanctions were imposed on Russia.

One situation in which Congress has an uneven record involves use-of-force decisions. On the one hand, Congress has not declared war on another state since World War II, and since then there have been numerous presidential use-of-force decisions. For this reason, Congress is often depicted as not wanting the responsibility for use-of-force decisions, as being reluctant to challenge presidential war-making unless things go very badly and reluctant to be put in a position that could be described as not supporting the troops. However, there is another way to look at this. Presidential uses-of-force require money, and Congress has the power to cut off funding for such ventures, as it did when it stopped funding for the Vietnam War. That cutoff forced President Nixon to end the war. Also, the **War Powers Resolution** of 1973 requires presidents to inform Congress when troops are sent into areas of current or imminent hostilities, and it gives Congress the opportunity to authorize or not authorize such uses of force.

Overall, then, what is the impact of these considerations? According to a comprehensive study of presidential uses-of-force, presidents who face at least one chamber of Congress controlled by the opposition party are less likely to use force and wait longer before choosing to use force. Moreover, presidents are wary of Congress's ability to swing public opinion against a decision to use force or to suggest to foreign audiences that the president lacks important political support back home for the use of force.[22] In short, congressional influence over use-of-force decisions can be blunt and direct or subtle and indirect. In the examples just discussed, Congress acts collectively; but there are also parts of Congress that can play independent roles.

Congressional Components

Congress contains various structural components, and some of them have clear foreign policy roles. Congress is organized to process legislation and engage in policy oversight via its structure of committees and their various subcommittees. Both the House of Representatives and the Senate have standing committees dealing with armed services, foreign relations/foreign affairs, and homeland security. Both have special or select committees dedicated to intelligence matters. Many other standing committees have jurisdictions that touch on foreign policy concerns as well. For example, the energy committees focus on national energy policy; the commerce committees regulate foreign trade; the finance committees deal with the taxation of foreign trade; the judiciary committees' jurisdiction involves a variety of issues such as imprisonment of detainees, the protection of intellectual property (e.g., patents, copyrights, and trademarks), immigration, and international criminal matters; and the natural resources committees deal with maritime and fishery resources as well as some petroleum-related matters.

Significant policy actions take place in these committees. Once legislation is introduced, the closest scrutiny typically comes at the subcommittee and committee level. The actual wording and substance of bills are often determined by these committees. Although the wording of legislation can be changed on the chamber floor, most of the time it is not, and it reflects the will of those subcommittee and committee members. Unless approved by these committees, legislation typically dies and would have to be reintroduced to be reconsidered. These committees also influence policy by holding hearings, conducting investigations of foreign policy–related matters, and overseeing the activities of the administration.

Members of Congress also form caucuses (ad hoc organizations of congressional members interested in particular sets of issues) to coordinate action on those issues of mutual concern.[23] There are about twenty-five caucuses in the Senate but over 200 in the House of Representatives.[24] For example, there are caucuses focused on specific foreign countries (among them Armenia, Brazil, Croatia, Greece, the Netherlands, North Korea, Sudan), regions (e.g., Central America), global issues (e.g., climate change, human rights, HIV/AIDS, narcotics control, workers' rights), and national security (e.g., energy security, port security, the uniformed military services, the Out of Iraq Caucus).[25] Although caucuses have no official role in policy making, informally they can be very important. They provide a forum for concerned members to coordinate their policy-making efforts, garner public attention for the issues that motivate them, and define the problem agenda in a favorable way.

Finally, other component parts of Congress that can play foreign policy roles are nonpartisan research organizations such as the **Congressional Research Service (CRS)** and the **Government Accountability Office (GAO)**. Members of Congress can request CRS reports on policy issues, and those reports can help set the agenda and context of foreign policy making. For example, in a period of rapidly rising global food costs, a CRS report might show Congress what the administration is proposing in the way of food aid in the short-term future and how such aid should be used.[26] The GAO performs similar research and analysis on financial questions. For example, the GAO can evaluate ways to enhance the delivery of civilian foreign assistance to a recipient country and make specific recommendations to Congress regarding how to proceed.[27]

However, perhaps the most overlooked and underestimated way Congress can influence foreign policy is through the individual actions of its members.

Individual Members of Congress

In the final analysis, Congress is composed of 535 individuals, some of whom care about foreign policy issues and will act in the name of Congress.[28] Members of Congress can employ means that are direct (seeking to address a particular issue) or indirect (seeking to shape the broader context or policy making setting) and legislative (specific to a piece of legislation) or nonlegislative (not tied to a targeted piece of legislation). Thus, members of Congress can choose direct-legislative means, indirect-legislative means, direct-nonlegislative means, and indirect-nonlegislative means. These dichotomies produce four avenues they can use to shape foreign policy, and examples of them can be found in Table 4.2.[29]

Some members of Congress choose to act on their own foreign policy agendas without waiting for the administration to do so; these are considered **congressional foreign policy entrepreneurs**. In the past, they came more often from the Senate than the House, although over time this difference has narrowed to the point that foreign policy entrepreneurship is now almost as likely in the House as in the Senate. These members of Congress also tend to be from the majority party controlling their chamber and tend not to be members of the president's political party. They gravitate toward all four of the avenues of influence mentioned earlier. For example, they can introduce legislation to keep otherwise out-of-work Russian nuclear weapons engineers employed in peaceful tasks or reject the Comprehensive Test Ban Treaty (direct-legislative avenues); introduce procedural legislation to oversee the IC more carefully or prohibit political contributions by foreign agents (indirect-legislative); provide the administration with the idea for how to bail out the Mexican peso during a currency crisis or

Table 4.2 Congressional Avenues of Influence

	Direct	Indirect
Legislative	Legislation Appropriations Treaties (Senate)	Nonbinding legislation Procedural legislation Appointments (Senate)
Nonlegislative	Letters, phone calls Consultations, advising Hearings Oversight activities Litigation	Agenda setting Framing debate Foreign contacts

Source: Adapted from James M. Scott, "In the Loop: Congressional Influence in American Foreign Policy," *Journal of Political and Military Sociology* 25 (1997): 47–76.

encourage US citizens to stop funding the activities of the Irish Republican Army (direct-nonlegislative); or promote peace negotiations in Central America or hold hearings questioning the wisdom of US participation in the Vietnam War (indirect-nonlegislative).[30] By the way, all these examples really happened.

The policy impacts of these entrepreneurs are often significant. Such entrepreneurs stopped US involvement in foreign conflicts (e.g., the Vietnam War and Somalia interventions) and made it harder for presidents to commit troops abroad thereafter.[31] They shifted US policy regarding particular regimes, making relations with some more positive (Spain in the 1950s, Mexico and Russia in the 1990s) and some more negative (South Africa in the 1980s, Cuba and Iran in the 1990s and 2000s). They encouraged closer US relationships with international organizations (in the 1940s and 1950s) and discouraged closer ties with international organizations that might infringe on US sovereignty (in the 1990s). They pushed administrations to work to topple some foreign governments (e.g., Iraq and Iran) and prevented administrations from toppling others (e.g., Nicaragua). They pressed for greater US participation in efforts to solve some global problems (e.g., AIDS in Africa or the trade in conflict diamonds) and for less US participation in solving others (e.g., global climate change).

Some of their policy impacts were significant but ultimately counterproductive. The efforts of Representative Charles Wilson (D-TX) and others to arm the Afghan mujahedin in the 1980s led to expulsion of the Soviet Red Army from Afghanistan and hastened the end of the Cold War. However, that effort also helped give birth to Osama bin Laden's al-Qaeda and provided it with arms to later attack US military and civilian personnel.[32]

In many ways, the presence of congressional foreign policy entrepreneurs is a stealth phenomenon, because such policy entrepreneurs are usually more interested in getting the desired change in policy than in getting individual credit for doing so. As a result, presidents often take credit for ideas that come from these members of Congress, and in other instances, administration officials anticipate the reactions of these members of Congress and build many of their policy preferences into administration proposals.

Although it is true that most members of Congress do not choose to become heavily involved in foreign policy innovation, a number have always done so. The numbers of congressional foreign policy entrepreneurs have been significant and growing in the post–World War II era.[33] Major public policy changes rarely occur in the United States without individual members of Congress taking public stances on them, and almost one-fourth of all such public stances taken by members of Congress since 1789 have involved foreign policy.[34]

In many ways, most US foreign policy is directly made by presidents, other executive branch officials, and members of Congress. However, in rare instances courts get involved as well.

Judicial Actors

The federal courts rarely get involved in foreign policy making, because judges tend to see most foreign policy matters as "political questions"—issues most appropriately resolved by elected officials rather than courts of law. However, as the final arbiters of what the federal government can legally do (and sometimes how it can be done), there are circumstances when judicial input is required. The federal courts cannot act unless someone files a lawsuit, and those suits can involve corporations, individuals, or other government officials.

Several highly significant legal rulings came from cases involving corporations. The 1936 *United States v. Curtiss-Wright Export Corporation* case involved a US aircraft manufacturer that wanted to sell bomber aircraft to Bolivia despite a presidential order banning such exports. The US Supreme Court ruled that since Congress had previously authorized the president to embargo the sale of arms in South America, the president had the power to do so and that, moreover, the president should serve as the country's primary spokesperson in foreign policy.[35] However, the Court also ruled later on that such presidential power was not unlimited. During the Korean War, President Truman seized control of a steel factory idled due to a strike. In the *Youngstown Sheet and Tube Co. v. Sawyer* case, the US Supreme Court ruled that the administration did not have the power to take such an action, specifically because strike-related remedies open to the administration were included in the recently passed Taft-Hartley

Act of 1947.[36] Overall, as long as Congress carefully spells out what administrations are authorized to do in prior legislation, administrations are bound by those specific congressional authorizations. If, on the other hand, those congressional authorizations are vaguely worded or don't exist, courts generally allow presidents considerable leeway in foreign policy actions.[37]

In some instances, other government officials will file suits over US foreign policy matters. For instance, Senator Barry Goldwater (R-AZ) objected to the fact that President Jimmy Carter extended official diplomatic relations to the People's Republic of China, thereby decertifying the Republic of China (now better known as Taiwan) as *the only* China in US eyes. Goldwater argued that the US Senate had previously approved a mutual security treaty with Taiwan and the president's action put that treaty into doubt, and furthermore, the president could not break that treaty without the Senate's input. The Supreme Court ruled against the senator, saying that the Constitution was clear; the Constitution gave the president the sole power to determine official diplomatic relations. Other treaties did not rise above this constitutional prerogative.[38] In 2011, a bipartisan group of ten US representatives, led by Dennis Kucinich (D-OH), filed a federal lawsuit challenging the Obama administration's right to use force in Libya. Although subsequent events rendered it moot, the lawsuit called upon the courts to prevent presidents from going to war, participating in NATO military missions, or participating in UN-authorized military missions without the express approval of Congress.[39] Sometimes lawsuits come from private citizens, such as Larry Klayman's lawsuit challenging the legality of the NSA's metadata program that kept dialing records of all phones in the United States. A federal district court ruled the metadata program to be unconstitutional in 2013, but the case was reversed on appeal and later dismissed.

In recent years, difficult legal issues have arisen regarding the status of detainees captured in the War on Terror. These are discussed in more detail in Box 4.2. These issues are troubling, because reasonable people differ greatly in finding a line that separates the benefits of following the rule of law from the benefits of protecting US lives from terrorist attack. After reading this box, you'll be more able to add your view to the mix.

**Box 4.2 The Courts and Detainee Rights: Determining the
Limits of the Constitution**

When the post-9/11 War on Terror began in earnest, the result
was the capture of thousands of people in Afghanistan who were
initially labeled as "enemy combatants." The question quickly
arose as to what to do with them. Although many were imprisoned in Afghanistan and later Iraq, some were transported to the
US naval base at Guantanamo Bay, Cuba. White House and Justice Department lawyers wrote memorandums for President
George W. Bush, arguing that such detainees were neither criminals (and thus not deserving of due process rights under the US
Constitution) nor prisoners of war, as they did not represent
nation-states or wear military uniforms (and thus were not
deserving of rights under the Geneva Conventions).

Therefore, these individuals existed in a kind of legal limbo.
The administration claimed that the president's authority as commander in chief *in time of war* allowed him to keep the detainees
locked up indefinitely as many were considered too dangerous to
release, because they had taken up arms against the United States
or were motivated to do so now after their imprisonment. Further,
these detainees might know things that would help prevent future
terrorist attacks. So, administration lawyers wrote memorandums
justifying the use of aggressive interrogation techniques—which
others would later call torture—in an attempt to gain useful intelligence information from them.

Critics of the administration's actions (including numerous
State Department lawyers) were aghast; to them, it was illegal
and un-American to simply lock people up and throw away the
key, thereby denying prisoners any chance to protest their inno-
cence or challenge their detention. Others also could not abide the
idea of aggressive interrogation techniques that included at times
the simulated drowning of prisoners (i.e., waterboarding). Even
more troubling, a few of those incarcerated were US citizens,
and the Bush administration's position was that they had for-
feited their constitutional rights by fighting for the enemy. Not
surprisingly, a number of lawsuits were filed challenging the

(continues)

Box 4.2 Continued

---

government's actions. Ultimately, in a series of decisions, the US
Supreme Court ruled that (1) the Constitution's due process rights
existed to restrict the government from abusing its powers anywhere, not to give full or partial rights to citizens and no rights
to noncitizens being held in foreign locations; (2) detainees had to
be provided some access to due process of law through appropriately constituted tribunals; and (3) Congress should authorize
such tribunals. Congress subsequently passed legislation authorizing military tribunals for this purpose, but only a limited number of such cases against detainees were expected, as many of
the detainees have since been repatriated to other countries.

Unquestionably, determining right and wrong here is difficult
after the events of 9/11. How would a realist explain the Bush
administration's actions? How would a liberal interpret these
events? Would constructivists see these events differently? Does
idealism figure into any of these explanations? In your view,
what's right and what's wrong here?

Source:

Linda Cornett and Mark Gibney, "The Rights of Detainees: Determining
the Limits of Law," in Ralph G. Carter, ed., *Contemporary Cases in U.S.
Foreign Policy: From Terrorism to Trade,* 5th ed. (Washington, DC: CQ
Press, 2014), pp. 409–434.

Conclusion

As should now be clear, many different governmental officials and
organizations participate in the making of US foreign policy. The
individuals provide crucial information on issues, concerns, opportunities, and challenges; they help identify and analyze options and
possibilities for action; they make the key decisions needed for the
government to act; and they implement the decisions made.

In fact, there are so many potential governmental actors involved
that tracing who the actual decision makers are can be difficult at
times. Further, other societal and external actors get involved as
well. This is the subject of Chapter 5.

Suggested Reading

Carter, Ralph G., and James M. Scott. *Choosing to Lead: Understanding Congressional Foreign Policy Entrepreneurs.* Durham, NC: Duke University Press, 2009.
Fowler, Linda L. *Watchdogs on the Hill: The Decline of Congressional Oversight of U.S. Foreign Relations.* Princeton: Princeton University Press, 2015.
Milner, Helen V., and Dustin Tingley. *Sailing the Water's Edge: The Domestic Politics of American Foreign Policy.* Princeton: Princeton University Press, 2015.
Preston, Thomas. *The President and His Inner Circle: Leadership Style and the Advisory Process in Foreign Affairs.* New York: Columbia University Press, 2001.
Rudalevige, Andrew. *The New Imperial Presidency: Renewing Presidential Power After Watergate.* Ann Arbor: University of Michigan Press, 2005.

Notes

1. See *United States v. Curtiss-Wright Export Corp.,* 299 U.S. 304 (1936).
2. For more on the power to persuade, see Richard A. Neustadt, *Presidential Power: The Politics of Leadership* (Cambridge, MA: Harvard University Press, 1960).
3. For more on Henry Reuss as a foreign policy maker, see Ralph G. Carter and James M. Scott, *Choosing to Lead: Understanding Congressional Foreign Policy Entrepreneurs* (Durham, NC: Duke University Press, 2009).
4. For more on this, see Patrick Cox, "John Nance Garner on the Vice Presidency—In Search of the Proverbial Bucket," Dolph Briscoe Center for American History, University of Texas at Austin, http://www.cah.utexas.edu/news/press_release.php?press=press_bucket.
5. For more on the role of Dick Cheney, see Bob Woodward, *State of Denial* (New York: Simon and Schuster, 2006), and *The War Within: A Secret White House History 2006–2008* (New York: Simon and Schuster, 2008); John W. Dean, *Worse Than Watergate: The Secret Presidency of George W. Bush* (New York: Grand Central, 2005); and Ivo H. Daalder and James M. Lindsay, "America Unbound: The Bush Revolution in Foreign Policy," *Brookings Review* 21 (Fall 2003): 2–6.
6. For more on Dulles, see Townsend Hoopes, *The Devil and John Foster Dulles* (Boston: Little, Brown, 1973). For more on Acheson, see Robert L. Beisner, *Dean Acheson: A Life in the Cold War* (New York: Oxford University Press, 2009).
7. See Woodward, *State of Denial.*

8. See David Halberstam, *The Best and the Brightest* (New York: Random House, 1989); and Woodward, *State of Denial,* respectively.

9. See Table 8.8 "Outlays for Discretionary Programs in Constant (FY 2009) Dollars: 1962–2021," https://obamawhitehouse.archives.gov /omb/budget/Historicals.

10. See Curt Tarnoff and Larry Nowells, "Foreign Aid: An Introductory Overview of U.S. Programs and Policy," *Congressional Research Service Report for Congress,* April 15, 2004, https://digital.library.unt .edu/ark%3A/67531/metacrs5904.

11. See Winslow Wheeler, "Correcting the Pentagon's Distorted Budget History," *Time,* July 16, 2013, http://nation.time.com/2013 /07/16/correcting-the-pentagons-distorted-budget-history/.

12. For more on this notion, see Andrew J. Bacevich, *The New American Militarism: How Americans Are Seduced by War* (New York: Oxford University Press, 2005).

13. Julian E. Barnes, "Defense Chief Urges Bigger Budget for State Department: Beyond Guns and Steel, the U.S. Should Build Up Diplomacy and 'Civilian Instruments of National Security,' Gates Says," *Los Angeles Times,* November 27, 2007, http://articles.latimes.com/2007/nov /27/nation/na-gates27.

14. See the DNI website, https://www.dni.gov/index.php/who-we-are /history.

15. "Intelligence Budget Data," Intelligence Resource Program, Federation of American Scientists, http://www.fas.org/irp/budget/index.html; "The Black Budget," *Washington Post,* http://www.washingtonpost.com /wp-srv/special/national/black-budget/.

16. Greg Miller, "CIA's Secret Agents Hide Under a Variety of Covers," *Seattle Times,* July 25, 2005, https://www.seattletimes.com/nation -world/cias-secret-agents-hide-under-a-variety-of-covers/.

17. See the NSA/CSS (Central Security Service) website, http://www .nsa.gov/.

18. See "Intelligence Agency Budgets: Commission Recommends No Release but Releases Them Anyway," Federation of American Scientists Intelligence Resource Program, http://www.fas.org/irp/commission /budget.htm.

19. James Bamford, *Body of Secrets: Anatomy of the Ultra-Secret National Security Agency from the Cold War Through the Dawn of a New Century* (New York: Doubleday, 2001).

20. James Bamford, *The Shadow Factory: The Ultra-Secret NSA from 9/11 to the Eavesdropping on America* (New York: Anchor Books, 2009)

21. Harold Koh, *The National Security Constitution: Power Sharing After the Iran-Contra Affair* (New Haven: Yale University Press, 1990).

22. William G. Howell and Jon C. Pevehouse, *While Dangers Gather: Congressional Checks on Presidential War Powers* (Princeton: Princeton University Press, 2007).

23. For more on congressional caucuses, see Susan Webb Hammond, *Congressional Caucuses in National Policymaking* (Baltimore: Johns Hopkins University Press, 2001).

24. Maggie Master, "Got an Issue? Congress Has Your Caucus," *Hill,* November 28, 2007, http://thehill.com/capital-living/23977-got-an -issue-congress-has-your-caucus.

25. For examples of congressional caucuses, see ibid. and the website of Representative Albio Sires (D-NJ), https://sires.house.gov/about /committees-and-caucuses.

26. Melissa D. Ho and Charles E. Hanrahan, "U.S. Global Food Security Funding, FY2010–FY2012," *CRS Report for Congress,* April 28, 2011, http://www.fas.org/sgp/crs/row/R41812.pdf.

27. "Department of State's Report to Congress and U.S. Oversight of Civilian Assistance to Pakistan Can Be Further Enhanced," *GAO Report,* GAO-11-310R, February 17, 2011, http://www.gao.gov/products/GAO -11-310R.

28. For more on this point, see Frans Bax, "The Legislative-Executive Relationship in Foreign Policy: New Partnership or New Competition?" *Orbis* 20 (1977): 881–904.

29. For more on these avenues of influence, see Carter and Scott, *Choosing to Lead,* Chapter 1.

30. For more on these congressional foreign policy entrepreneurs, see ibid.

31. For more on congressional war powers, see Howell and Pevehouse, *While Dangers Gather.*

32. For more on this example, see George Crile, *Charlie Wilson's War: The Extraordinary Story of the Largest Covert Operation in History* (New York: Atlantic Monthly Press, 2003), or watch the movie by the same title.

33. Again, see Carter and Scott, *Choosing to Lead.*

34. See David R. Mayhew, *America's Congress: Actions in the Public Sphere, James Madison Through Newt Gingrich* (New Haven: Yale University Press, 2000).

35. See *U.S. v. Curtiss-Wright Export Corp.,* 299 U.S. 304 (1936).

36. See *Youngstown Sheet and Tube v. Sawyer,* 343 U.S. 579 (1952).

37. See Gordon Silverstein, *Imbalance of Powers: Constitutional Interpretation and the Making of American Foreign Policy* (New York: Oxford University Press, 1997).

38. See *Goldwater v. Carter,* 444 U.S. 996 (1979).

39. Stephen Koff, "Dennis Kucinich Files Lawsuit Against President Obama, Says Libya War Violates the Law," *Cleveland Plain Dealer,* June 15, 2011, http://www.cleveland.com/open/index.ssf/2011/06/dennis _kucinich_files_lawsuit.html.

5

How Decisions Are Made

Learning Objectives

- Explain the difference between individual and small group decision making.
- Illustrate the types of situations that favor individual versus small group decision making.
- Define a rational actor approach to decision making.
- Evaluate the roles and relevance of cognitive shortcuts and decision heuristics.

The image is iconic: a lonely individual sitting at a big desk, perhaps staring out a window while pondering a momentous decision that could impact millions of lives around the globe. Manifested by Harry Truman's claim that "the buck stops here" and George W. Bush's self-proclaimed title of "Chief Decider," the notion of presidents making the decisions that shape US foreign policy is commonplace in US political culture. But how accurate is it? Is this how US foreign policy is typically made?

The simple answer is no. Although presidents may be the ultimate foreign-policy decision makers in many cases, it is unusual for them to act alone or make decisions without the face-to-face

input of others. Richard Nixon was perhaps one of the few exceptions to this rule. He was reputed to take input in the form of one-
page memorandums into his private office, close the door, and
later emerge with a decision on what the US foreign policy
should be. Early reports from the Donald Trump administration
also suggest that he has made some foreign policy decisions with
little input from others, but such solitary decision making is far
from the norm.

When foreign policy decisions are made, a number of formal
or informal presidential advisers tend to also be in the room. Thus,
rather than the president acting as the "lone ranger" in foreign
policy making, more often such decision making is the product of
small group decision processes. This chapter covers the processes
of small group decision making and the roles played by the president and others in the administration.

Small Group Decision Making

Presidents and Their Staffs

Presidents have considerable staff assistance when making foreign
policy decisions. As noted in Chapter 4, the president may call on
the vice president, the national security adviser, intelligence community officials, cabinet secretaries, and a host of other personal
and National Security Staff aides and administration officials for
information and policy input.

The goal for decision-making teams is simple: make good
decisions. Luck always helps, but a good decision is usually pred-
icated on having good information as well as a good grasp of the
relevant options. Even with all the help available to the president,
getting both good information and adequate knowledge of the
available options when needed can be challenging at times.

As president in the 1950s, former general Dwight Eisenhower
relied on his military background and used his cabinet officials as
he had previously used his military staff officers. He pressed them
for whatever relevant expertise they could bring to bear on the
problem at hand, and cabinet meetings became real foreign policy
decision-making settings. President Eisenhower was followed by
the much younger John Kennedy, whose relative inexperience might

have initially led him to be too impressed with "experts," as was demonstrated in the events of 1961, described below.

Upon entering office, Kennedy inherited a CIA covert operation to invade Cuba, an initiative long past its final planning stages and about to go operational. Before making the "go or no-go" decision to topple Cuba's new Communist leader Fidel Castro, Kennedy listened to the rosy predictions of success from top CIA officials. Essentially, their message to the new president was, "We've done this before" (in places such as Iran and Guatemala) and "we know what we're doing." However, the other participants in the decision-making group failed to question the tenuous assumptions on which the operation was based, stifled any doubts of their own, and were apparently very concerned with "fitting in" and maintaining the goodwill of the others in the group. Thus, difficult questions were not asked, possible flaws in the plan were not discussed, and the resulting Bay of Pigs invasion was a fiasco in which seemingly everything that could go wrong did. Such decision-making behavior in a concurrence-seeking group is now called **groupthink**, and though it does not guarantee a bad decision, it makes one far more likely.[1]

Another example might be the Trump travel ban. According to published reports, the original executive order was largely drafted by presidential advisers Steve Bannon and Stephen Miller to implement President Trump's campaign pledge to ban Muslims from entry into the country. The traditional interagency vetting process—which would have included affected organizations such as the Departments of State and Homeland Security as well as representatives from US Citizenship and Immigration Services and US Immigration and Customs Enforcement from the beginning—was not followed. Some affected agencies did not even get to read the executive order until a day after it had been implemented. As a result, the travel ban had to be revised twice before the Supreme Court approved it. The fact that those initially involved in the drafting of the order saw the issue in exactly the same way meant that either they did not anticipate the problems posed by the original draft of the order or perhaps did not care. Had the arbitrariness and capriciousness of the order (to paraphrase several federal court judges) been recognized, perhaps the travel ban would have been better written and implemented from the start, which might have avoided the chaos that erupted at the border.

To be fair, it is not unusual for people who meet regularly to try to minimize or put aside their differences in an attempt to get along. The downside to such behavior may be negligible in many settings, but when making decisions that potentially affect the lives of over 329 million people, the costs of such decision-making mistakes may be catastrophic. Thus, it is hard not to conclude that a decision-making group's emphasis should be on getting the decision right, not just getting along with the others in the room or avoiding looking foolish. Full and free discussion of the situation, of all the assumptions involved, and of the pros and cons of the relevant options should have been encouraged.

One way to promote such a dynamic discussion would be to use a **rational actor model (RAM)** of decision making. Following the RAM would require the president to ask the staff to identify all the options available in the situation, list each option's strengths and weaknesses, and then discuss all the options, seeking to find the one that is optimal—the overall best option, the one promising the best possible outcome in light of the incurred costs, or the overall least bad option if all options are bad.

What's the downside of such an approach? Even if it is humanly possible to identify all options and determine their strengths and weaknesses, it takes lots of time. Presidents may feel they have neither the time nor the inclination to invest so much effort in the particular decision at hand. With more decisions still to be made, more official duties still to perform, and more position papers still to read in preparation for the days ahead, they often turn to any available shortcuts to make the decision faster and easier.

One way to do this is to use a **multiple advocacy** approach in which members of the decision-making group are tasked with the responsibility to become advocates for different options and find the flaws in the options under consideration. If done well, all major sides to controversial issues should be fairly presented to the president or other top foreign policy decision makers before a decision is made, thus increasing the chances of making a good decision.[2] Although such an approach may produce discord among the participants, particularly for decisions made under stressful conditions, the president can try to promote an environment in which the decision makers can "disagree without becoming disagreeable."[3] However, this approach may still require a lot of time.

A more practical alternative may be to ask an influential adviser to play the role of "devil's advocate." Vice President Joe Biden was often asked to play this role by President Obama, so his job in decision-making groups was to ask tough questions, challenge assumptions, and otherwise "think outside the box."

Of course, one of the concerns here involves hierarchical authority; the president has a lot more influence than the others in the room. Therefore, if presidents don't want others to simply agree with the boss, they would be well-advised to keep their policy preferences under wraps—at least at first. That way, others are encouraged to say freely what they think, so as to get the best ideas out for consideration. Even then, presidents should be mindful of the personalities and responsibilities of those in the room, knowing that some forceful personalities might need to be kept in check and some more-reticent advisers might need additional prompting, particularly if they possess good judgment or the expertise needed in the situation. On the other hand, if presidents express their preferences early in the process and don't like disagreement from advisers, the efficacy of small group decision making breaks down and the odds of poor policy choices increase.

We have to keep in mind that presidents and other top administration foreign policy makers are like the rest of us. They often don't want to work any harder than necessary to make a good decision. To make things easier, they often look for ways to simplify decision making.

Cognitive Shortcuts

There are many ways foreign policy makers can simplify their thinking in order to make easier and faster decisions. Some officials come into office with a relatively fixed image of how the political world works, which they rely on to point them in the right direction. Such an **operational code** provides a blueprint for the decision maker by specifying what is important, what motivates others, and what tends to work best in solving foreign policy problems.[4] President Jimmy Carter's operational code told him what was most important in international politics was how governments treated their citizens, and thus he made human rights the central focus of US foreign policy during his administration. He was followed in office by President Ronald Reagan, who saw the world through Cold War lenses, who felt the Soviet Union was the source of all evil in the world, and who believed the spread of communism should be contested at every opportunity. Not surprisingly, the foreign policy directions of these two administrations were quite different. The operational codes for Presidents Obama and Trump seem to be quite different as well, as shown in Box 5.1.

Box 5.1 The Worldviews of Barack Obama and Donald Trump: Christian Realism Versus Transactionalism?

What made Barack Obama and Donald Trump so different as presidents? Part of the difference has to be the way they respectively see the world, in other words, their operational codes. Obama once professed agreement with what Reinhold Niebuhr, a Christian theologian, called "Christian realism." From Niebuhr's writing, Obama said, "I take away the compelling idea that there's serious evil in the world, and hardship and pain. And we should be humble and modest in our belief we can eliminate those things. But we shouldn't use that as an excuse for cynicism and inaction." In his December 2009 acceptance speech for the Nobel Peace Prize, Obama said, "We must begin by acknowledging the hard truth: we will not eradicate violent conflicts in our lifetimes. There will be times when nations—acting individually or in concert—will find the use of force not only necessary but morally justified . . . Whatever mistakes we have made, the plain fact is this. The United States of America has helped underwrite global security for more than six decades with the blood of our citizens and the strength of our arms." Regarding ends, Obama pressed the idea that we should improve things where we can, and that partial victories are better than no victories at all. Regarding means, Obama stressed that we should not abandon our moral values when fighting evil, for to do so is to become evil ourselves.

Donald Trump's early speeches suggested a darker and more foreboding worldview. He said America was at a crisis point. In his speech accepting the Republican presidential nomination, he said that at home, runaway crime and illegal immigration made Americans less safe. Abroad, he decried the Iran nuclear deal as a giveaway with nothing in return, which made the United States less safe, and he said Obama's unenforced red lines in Syria humiliated the United States. He reiterated these themes in his presidential inaugural speech, and he added that bad deals had plagued US foreign policy—giving wealth away to others, protecting allies but not protecting US borders, losing the battle of foreign trade, and so on. Regarding ends, Trump's professed goal—reiterated from his campaign—was to make America great again. The means to do this involved a transactional approach to foreign policy. Every deal was seen as zero-sum. The United States either won or lost, and Trump wanted to renegotiate many—if not most—of the agreements his recent predecessors had reached so as to "win" on each of them.

Does it seem this simple to you? Given the visible differences in style and operation by these two presidents, are their differences in policy and approach the result of seeing the world in very different ways?

Sources:

David Brooks, "Obama's Christian Realism," *New York Times,* December 14, 2009; Politico staff, "Full Text: Donald Trump 2016 RNC Draft Speech Transcript," June 21, 2016, https://www.politico.com/story/2016/07/full-transcript-donald-trump-nomination-acceptance-speech-at-rnc-225974; David Sanger, "Memo from Washington: A New Nobel Laureate's Pragmatic Approach to 'the World as It Is,'" *New York Times,* December 12, 2009; Jeff Zeleny, "Accepting Peace Prize, Obama Offers 'Hard Truth,'" *New York Times,* December 10, 2009; Full Text of President Donald Trump's Inauguration Speech, *Fox News,* January 20, 2017, http://www.foxnews.com/politics/2017/01/20/full-text-president-donald-trumps-inauguration-speech.html.

Some presidents rely more on instinctive approaches to decision making. President Trump said he could "read" other people very quickly. George W. Bush said he relied on his "gut" (i.e., his intuition) in making decisions or reacting to others, and he did not question those decisions thereafter.[5] On the other hand, his father, President George H. W. Bush, appears to have been more instinctively guided by **prospect theory**. This theory holds that when things are going well, decision makers tend to act prudently and become more risk averse, so as not to upset a status quo that is favorable. When things are not going well, decision makers become prone to risky strategies as they seek to change that unacceptable status quo. Thus, George H. W. Bush failed to reach out with much aid to Russia after the Soviet Union collapsed—when you are the only superpower left, why aid a potential enemy that might rise again?—but chose to go to war with Iraq in 1990 rather than accept its occupation of neighboring oil-rich Kuwait, even though at the time the Iraqi army was the fourth largest in the world. In the first instance, he was risk averse, but he was risk prone in the second.

Another instinctive way for presidents to make decisions easier is to compare them with prior situations. Sometimes, they use metaphors. Thus, when George H. W. Bush called Saddam Hussein a "Hitler" following the 1990 Iraqi invasion of Kuwait, that metaphor tilted a US response away from any conciliatory behavior toward Iraq and instead toward a more robust US response to the invasion. After all, how can you compromise with someone like Hitler? Other times, presidents say they apply the lessons of history. President Harry Truman explained his quick reaction to North Korea's 1950 invasion of South Korea by saying that the "lessons of Munich" showed that appeasing aggressors did not work. After all, Adolf Hitler demanded and gained the German-speaking part of Czechoslovakia at a meeting in Munich in 1938, but instead of being satisfied, Hitler went on to order the invasion of Poland the next year. During his administration, whenever President Bill Clinton contemplated the use of force to stop the genocide in Rwanda or the ethnic cleansing in the former Yugoslavia, he and his advisers kept remembering the images of dead US servicemen being dragged through the streets of Mogadishu, Somalia, in 1993. That image prevented any serious discussion of putting "boots on the ground" to protect civilians from genocidal violence.

Decision Heuristics

Beyond psychological shortcuts, decision makers often rely on what they might call "common sense" or "rules of thumb" to make decision making easier and faster. Psychologists call such guidelines **decision heuristics**.[6] One such heuristic is **incrementalism**—making only minor changes from what has been done before or from one's current policy position. Such approaches avoid the investment of time and effort that finding an optimal solution requires.[7] In line with this thinking, when the Vietnam War was not going well and the military asked for more troops, President Lyndon Johnson complied and ordered that more troops be deployed. With each small escalation went the hope that perhaps this new troop level would produce a victory, thereby avoiding any painstaking reevaluation of the US role in that war.

Implicit in most incremental approaches is the notion of *satisficing,* the idea that the goal is not to discover the optimal or best solution but rather to hit on one that is "good enough" to be satisfactory or sufficient.[8] Any solution that can be portrayed as satisfactory or sufficient to meet the policy need is particularly attractive to an administration when it is under public pressure to "do something" regarding an issue. If such a satisficing solution can be marketed as a "success" by the administration, so much the better. For example, when the Obama administration chose to let Congress largely write the details of an economic stimulus package in 2009, it got a satisficing response. While the results may not have been ideal to many, they did largely quell the public's demands to "do something" about the Great Recession, and the administration could claim that a worse depression had been avoided.

Another decision heuristic requires a bit more thought on the part of administration actors. A **poliheuristic** approach envisions decision making as a two-step process. The first step is to eliminate as many options as possible, using whatever reasoning makes sense in the situation. The second step is to devote whatever time is left to carefully evaluating the few remaining options with the goal of maximizing benefits and minimizing risks.[9] The 1962 Cuban Missile Crisis decision—resulting in a decision to deploy a naval blockade to force the Soviets to remove their missiles from Cuba—illustrates this approach. Options such as appealing to the United Nations, directly approaching Cuban president Fidel Castro, and invading Cuba were quickly discarded, leaving the majority of the analysis devoted to only two options—a naval blockade or an air strike. These two options were considered carefully before the air-strike option was discarded (as it could not guarantee that all missiles would be rendered inoperative), and thus the blockade option was chosen.[10]

More recently, the Obama administration appears to have used such an approach in making the decision to deploy a troop surge in Afghanistan in December 2009, as shown in Box 5.2. Although a poliheuristic approach to decision making is potentially a faster process than the RAM, it is still not a quick way to make a decision, as this box illustrates. The meaningful question is whether the result of any process was a good decision.

Box 5.2 Deciding on the Afghan "Surge":
Poliheuristic Decision Making or Indecisiveness?

On December 1, 2009, President Barack Obama announced a long-anticipated policy shift in a speech at the United States Military Academy at West Point, New York. He said he would increase the number of US troops in Afghanistan by approximately 30,000 within the next six months. Along with 10,000 more troops that he hoped NATO allies would contribute, the goals of these additional forces would be to beat back the Taliban insurgency against the Afghan government, attack al-Qaeda elements in Afghanistan and weaken their ability to attack the United States and its interests, and strengthen Afghan forces so they could provide for their own national security, thus allowing US and NATO forces to leave sooner rather than later. The goal, he said, was to begin the process of military withdrawal in July 2011.

This decision—to increase the number of troops in Afghanistan to beat back the enemy so that US troops could begin the process of leaving Afghanistan sooner—was more than two months in the making. The question of what strategy to follow in Afghanistan—where US forces had been fighting for over seven years without much to show for their effort—had been hanging over the new administration since it arrived in Washington. Moreover, news reports indicated Taliban forces were getting stronger; something different needed to be done.

On August 30, 2009, the US commander in Afghanistan, General Stanley McChrystal, submitted a classified report asking for more troops. The options he outlined were an 80,000-troop increase to undertake a countrywide counterinsurgency campaign against the Taliban and al-Qaeda forces, which had the greatest hope for a military success; a 40,000-troop increase to take on the Taliban and al-Qaeda in eastern and southern Afghanistan where they were strongest, which might preclude a military failure; or a 10,000–15,000-troop increase to focus on training Afghan forces whose performance could not be predicted.

When considering these options, the president made the ultimate decision, but he was aided by a small group of officials dubbed the "AfPak" national security team. Group members included Vice President Joe Biden; Presidential Chief of Staff Rahm Emanuel; the national security adviser, General James Jones; Deputy National Security Adviser Thomas Donilon, Secretary of State Hillary Clinton; Ambassador to the United Nations Susan Rice; Special Envoy to Pakistan and Afghanistan Richard Holbrooke; Secretary of Defense Robert Gates; the chairman of the Joint Chiefs of Staff, Admiral Mike Mullen; the chief of US Central Command, General David Petraeus; Director of National Intelligence Dennis Blair, and Director of Central Intelligence Leon Panetta. This core group of thirteen people— with additional input at times from Senior Adviser to the President David Axelrod, Ambassador to Afghanistan Lieutenant General Karl Eikenberry, and General McChrystal—met on ten occasions from September 13 to November 29 for a total of twenty-five hours.

Obama had previously read a book on the Vietnam War called *Lessons in Disaster* by Gordon Goldstein. The lesson the president took away from the book was that the US intervention in Vietnam had failed because both Presidents Kennedy and Johnson had not questioned the underlying assumptions on which US military intervention was based. Obama was determined not to make the same mistake, so he asked the AfPak group fundamental questions such as:

- What were the relationships between the Afghan Taliban, the Pakistani Taliban, and al-Qaeda?

(continues)

Box 5.2 Continued

- Could al-Qaeda be defeated without defeating the Afghan Taliban?
- Could the Afghan Taliban be defeated without the defeat of the Pakistani Taliban next door?
- Did the Afghan regime led by Hamid Karzai have sufficient strength and legitimacy to participate in a counterinsurgency war, or would such a US effort be wasted?
- If the Taliban took control of Afghanistan, would Pakistan be next?

The "do nothing" option was a nonstarter, and the president also eliminated the 80,000-troop increase option as too much to consider. From that point on, he listened and encouraged the others to debate the various pros and cons of the remaining options. Proponents of a 40,000-troop increase included Generals Petraeus and McChrystal and Secretary Clinton. Director Panetta pressed for more covert operatives and Predator unmanned drone aircraft to be assigned to Pakistan. Vice President Biden pushed for a more limited military operation directed solely at al-Qaeda operatives. Ambassador Rice, Ambassador Holbrooke, Chief of Staff Emanuel, Ambassador Eikenberry, and Adviser Axelrod expressed doubts about any military surge because of the human and financial costs involved or the reliability of the Afghan government.

The president's goal was to give the Karzai regime a chance to prevail against the Taliban and al-Qaeda without locking US forces into an indefinite commitment. Secretary Gates came up with the 30,000-troop option, arguing that NATO could be pressed to put up the remaining 10,000. Admiral Mullen came up with the idea of beginning a withdrawal by July 2011.

Unfortunately, someone leaked General McChrystal's classified report to the media in mid-September. Thus, as the weeks went by, the public question became: When will someone make a decision? The president and his supporters stressed that the decision was too important to be rushed without sufficient consideration of all the relevant facts and factors. Critics led by former vice president Dick Cheney argued that the delay in announcing a decision amounted to indecisiveness, a dangerous trait in a commander in chief.

When the decision was finally announced on December 1, some thought it was a judicious decision that balanced the various concerns that motivated the president. Others were less sure of the decision's wisdom. Some Americans wanted to initiate a US troop withdrawal from Afghanistan, not a surge. Others wanted a targeted operation against al-Qaeda, not a surge. Some thought a 30,000-troop increase was clearly insufficient for the task and, thus, a waste of effort, resources, and lives. Others thought the idea of publicizing a withdrawal date in advance gave the enemy a huge tactical advantage; the enemy would think it just had to wait for eighteen months and the Americans would begin to leave.

Was this a sound poliheuristic process leading to a wise decision, or was it an indecisive response—designed primarily to try to please as many different audiences as possible—and thus, likely to fail? Did it produce a good decision?

Source:

Peter Baker, "How Obama Came to Plan for 'Surge' in Afghanistan," *New York Times,* December 12, 2009, http://www.nytimes.com/2009/12/06/world /asia/06reconstruct.html?_r=3&scp=19&sq=afghan%20surge&st=cse.

Perhaps the approach involving the least effort is **cybernetic decision making**, literally making decisions with a minimum of thinking or analysis. Here, the decision makers ask questions such as: "Can we do anything? If so, try it." A good example of cybernetic decision processes came when Britain, France, and Israel invaded Egypt in the 1956 Suez Crisis. To force the British out of Egypt, President Eisenhower asked his cabinet, "What can we do?" When told that the United States had sufficient British currency reserves in its treasury to bankrupt Britain (if all that currency were dumped on global money markets at the same time), Eisenhower threatened the British with just such an action.

The British promptly withdrew their troops from Egypt. Who would have guessed that input from the secretary of the treasury would be the key to ending a military invasion?

However, as most decisions are made by small groups, there is one other factor to consider. As situations vary, so do the inputs facing policy makers and the amount of stresses they experience in seeking policy answers. The nature of the situation thus needs to be considered as well.

Types of Situations

Not all foreign policy decisions are the same. Administrative foreign policy decisions that involve easy choices or routine matters tend to be made elsewhere in the administration (see Chapter 6 on bureaucratic decision making). As President Obama once observed, the only decisions that got all the way to his desk were the tough ones. Yet not all tough decisions are the same. The small group dynamics covered up to this point typically apply to noncrisis decision making. As a limited subset of all foreign policy decisions, crises have their own characteristics.

A **crisis** is a situation that represents a significant threat to core values or high-priority goals, requires a quick response, and comes as a surprise to decision makers.[11] Despite the fact that many decision makers are quick to label things as crises, most situations tend to meet only one or two of these criteria. Only a small fraction of the many situations facing foreign policy makers truly fit all three of these criteria, and the combination of these criteria produce some commonalities in decision making.

First, the high level of threat quickly kicks the decision all the way up to the top of the administration, so the highest-level official available will be involved—and that is almost always the president. Second, the short time frame for a response limits the number of others whose input can be sought, so the decision group is typically even smaller than usual. The group may literally be the president with only a few advisers, as fewer experts happen to be available on short notice and there may not seem to be enough time to include more experts or trusted advisers in the decision group. Third, with the element of genuine surprise, the result may be a decision that, to a greater degree than normal, reflects the personal traits and idiosyncrasies of the president. The result may be a quick response that is more extreme than one that policy makers might otherwise choose if they had more time to think things through and consult with more experts.

For example, President Richard Nixon built his early political career on a tough stance against the Soviet Union and the communist threat to the United States, but his almost visceral opposition to whatever the Soviets did seemed to moderate when he became the president. However, the hopes for improving US-Soviet relations in the détente period were seriously jolted in October 1973 when the Soviets suddenly threatened to intervene militarily in the ongoing October War in the Middle East.

In that war, Israeli forces violated a US-Soviet-sponsored UN cease-fire by surrounding the Egyptian Third Army in the Sinai Desert, thereby cutting the army off from food, water, and medical supplies. To deal with this genuine emergency, the Soviets proposed a joint US-Soviet military rescue of the Egyptian forces. When President Nixon rejected that idea, the Soviets declared they would intervene unilaterally to save the Egyptians and began loading troopships in the Black Sea for the short cruise to Egypt. Nixon told the Soviets to stop their actions and then ordered all US military forces around the world to be put on heightened alert status.

By taking the provocative step of ordering a global military alert instead of a regional military reaction, Nixon risked a wider confrontation with the Soviets, thereby going further than other presidents might have gone in similar circumstances. In a decision apparently made with only one other adviser—Henry Kissinger—involved, the US global response may have been a knee-jerk reaction based on Nixon's long-standing opposition to Soviet military expansionism and distrust of Soviet leaders.[12] Luckily, the Soviets backed down, and the Israelis allowed supplies to be brought to the Egyptian forces, thereby defusing the crisis. Yet the point remains: when only a few voices are heard, crisis decision making tends to be quite different than noncrisis decision making, as illustrated in Box 5.2.

Presidents are virtually guaranteed to be involved in crisis decision making. By contrast, the opposite of crises are those occasions for decision when presidents may not be involved at all. There are various reasons for presidents deciding to step out of the decision-making process. Sometimes, presidents feel that their presence in the group may stifle a robust discussion of all alternative options or that any change from their previously announced public schedule would have negative consequences in the situation.

A good example of these concerns came in the 1962 Cuban Missile Crisis. The missiles the Soviets deployed in Cuba would have threatened an arc-shaped area of the United States—stretching roughly from Washington, DC, to Houston, Texas—combined with a possible nuclear attack occurring after only a few minutes' warning. After feeling misled by the "experts" in the 1961 Bay of Pigs debacle, President Kennedy sought to ensure the consideration of a wide array of views. He did so by creating a group of advisers dubbed the Executive Committee of the National Security Council—or "ExComm" for short—which would meet without him present to determine the appropriate response. The ExComm included members from the State, Defense, and Treasury Departments and the director of central intelligence. It also included members personally close to the president: the attorney general (his brother, Robert Kennedy), the national security adviser, and a presidential counsel. The president was kept abreast of the group's deliberations while he maintained his normal schedule of activities so the Soviets would not realize his administration had discovered the missile threat. After days of tense deliberations, the group recommended the blockade of Cuba, which was the course of action the president apparently preferred but did not want to order without the input of the others.[13]

Sometimes, presidents have other reasons to want to be out of the decision-making loop. In some cases, deniability may be desired. For example, in the late 1980s, President Reagan felt the leftist Sandinista leadership in Nicaragua represented a communist threat to the United States. What if Soviet aircraft were based in Nicaragua? Would they be within range of the oil fields in Texas and Louisiana? Correspondingly, Reagan provided US military assistance to the Nicaraguan counterrevolutionaries—the Contras—who were fighting the Sandinista regime. When Congress passed the Boland amendments making such military aid illegal, a National Security Council staff aide—Colonel Oliver North of the US Marines—came up with a plan to sell arms secretly to Iran and divert the proceeds to the Nicaraguan Contras. His boss, the national security adviser Admiral John Poindexter, approved the plan, and it was put into action with the help or at least the knowledge of the CIA. When this illegal operation became public knowledge, Admiral Poindexter resigned, Colonel North was fired, and both were indicted and convicted of federal crimes, though their convictions were later overturned on appeal.[14] More to the point, President Reagan was able to claim no direct knowledge of the matter.[15]

At other times, presidents want to be out of the loop because they want to preserve their time for other policy matters that are simply more important to them. President Bill Clinton entered office with a distinctly domestic policy emphasis and a foreign policy agenda largely limited to promoting free trade. Perhaps as a result of this greater domestic focus, the more benign image of the new Russian regime under Boris Yeltsin, the relatively reduced global role of the Russian Federation that was weakened after the breakup of the Soviet Union, and other such factors, Clinton quickly delegated most issues involving US-Russian relations to Vice President Al Gore. In 1993, this delegation was formalized in the creation of the US-Russian Joint Commission on Economic and Technological Cooperation, cochaired by Vice President Gore and Russian prime minister Viktor Chernomyrdin (hence, the Gore-Chernomyrdin Commission).

The commission's initial goals were to coordinate US-Russian cooperation regarding space and energy issues. Its role soon expanded into a wide array of economic cooperation initiatives, the conversion of defense infrastructure to civilian use, and cooperation in scientific, health, and environmental areas. Thus, key foreign policy decisions affecting US policy toward Russia were being made by Gore and the other US representatives on the commission: the secretaries of the Departments of Agriculture, Commerce, Defense, Energy, and Health and Human Services; the administrators of the Environmental Protection Agency and National Aeronautics and Space Administration; and the director of the President's Office of Science and Technology Policy. These officials were aided by officials from the National Security Council staff, the vice president's national security adviser, and State Department experts on Russia and the other former Soviet republics.[16] Led by Gore, this group of administration officials made most US policy toward Russia, with the president's role confined largely to announcing the policy decisions and representing the United States at US-Russian summit conferences.

Conclusion

To repeat, the image of the president as the sole maker of US foreign policy is largely misplaced. Presidents occasionally make decisions by themselves regarding foreign policy, and they certainly represent the face of the United States to external audiences. However, the foreign policy decisions deemed by presidents to be most significant are almost always the product of small group decision making, in which the president works with a handful of people who are experts on the subjects at hand or whose judgment and advice the president trusts. Far more common are the many foreign policy decisions that are fairly routine in nature or do not rise to the level of importance to compel interest from the White House. For these matters of policy making, the most important decision makers are often bureaucratic officials. They come under discussion in Chapter 6.

Suggested Reading

Gvosdev, Nikolas K., Jessica D. Blankshain, and David A. Cooper. *Decision-Making in American Foreign Policy: Translating Theory into Practice.* Cambridge: Cambridge University Press, 2019.
Hermann, Charles F., ed. *When Things Go Wrong: Foreign Policy Decision Making Under Adverse Impact.* New York: Routledge, 2012.
Janis, Irving L. *Groupthink.* 2nd ed. Boston: Wadsworth, Cengage Learning, 1982.
Mintz, Alex, and Carly Wayne. *The Polythink Syndrome: U.S. Foreign Policy Decisions on 9/11, Afghanistan, Iraq, Iran, Syria, and ISIS.* Stanford: Stanford University Press, 2016.

Notes

1. For more on the groupthink phenomenon and the Bay of Pigs example, see Irving L. Janis, *Groupthink,* 2nd ed. (Boston: Wadsworth, Cengage Learning, 1982).

2. For more on the multiple-advocacy approach, see Alexander L. George, "The Case for Multiple Advocacy in Making Foreign Policy," *American Political Science Review* 66 (1972): 751–785; or his *Presidential Decisionmaking in Foreign Policy: The Effective Use of Information and Advice* (Boulder: Westview, 1980).

3. This phrase is attributable to former US House Speaker Jim Wright (D-TX), who used it often in conversation.

4. The concept of an operational code was initially developed by Nathan Leites in *The Operational Code of the Politburo* (New York: McGraw-Hill, 1951) and reinvigorated by Alexander L. George in "The 'Operational Code' A Neglected Approach to the Study of Political Leaders and Decision-Making," *International Studies Quarterly* 13 (1969): 190–222. For a more contemporary treatment of this approach, see Mark Schafer and Stephen G. Walker, eds., *Beliefs and Leadership in World Politics: Methods and Applications of Operational Code Analysis* (New York: Palgrave Macmillan, 2006).

5. For more on this decision-making style, see Bob Woodward, *State of Denial: Bush at War, Part III* (New York: Simon and Schuster, 2006); or Ron Suskind, *The One Percent Doctrine: Deep Inside America's Pursuit of Its Enemies Since 9/11* (New York: Simon and Schuster, 2006).

6. For more on such decision-making heuristics, see Herbert A. Simon, "Theories of Decision-Making in Economics and Behavioral Science," *American Economic Review* 49 (1959): 253–283; or Daniel Kahneman, Amos Tversky, and Paul Slovic, eds., *Judgment Under Uncertainty: Heuristics and Biases* (Cambridge: Cambridge University Press, 1982).

7. See Charles E. Lindblom, "The Science of 'Muddling Through,'" *Public Administration Review* 19 (1959): 79–88.

8. Simon, "Theories of Decision-Making."

9. Alex Mintz, "How Do Leaders Make Decisions? A Poliheuristic Perspective," *Journal of Conflict Resolution* 48 (2004): 3–13.

10. See Graham T. Allison and Philip Zelikow, *Essence of Decision: Explaining the Cuban Missile Crisis*, 2nd ed. (New York: Longman, 1999).

11. Charles F. Hermann, "Some Issues in the Study of International Crisis," in Charles F. Hermann, ed., *International Crises: Insights from Behavioral Research* (New York: Free Press, 1972).

12. For more on this crisis from the inside, see Henry Kissinger, *The Anatomy of Two Major Foreign Policy Crises: Based on the Record of Henry Kissinger's Hitherto Secret Telephone Conversations* (New York: Simon and Schuster, 2003).

13. For more on this, see Allison and Zelikow, *Essence of Decision.*

14. They had been granted immunity and forced to testify before Congress about the Iran-Contra Affair. The court ruled that their convictions would not have occurred without the information revealed in their testimony before Congress.

15. For more, see Bob Woodward, *Veil: The Secret Wars of the CIA, 1981–1987* (New York: Simon and Schuster, 1987).

16. "The Gore-Chernomyrdin Commission," https://www.revolvy.com/page/Gore%252DChernomyrdin-Commission.

6

The Role of Bureaucratic Politics

Learning Objectives

- Explain the typical motivations of bureaucratic actors.
- Illustrate which stages of the input-output process favor bureaucratic participation.
- Distinguish between the types of issues that favor bureaucratic influence.
- Assess the advantages and disadvantages of bureaucratic participation in foreign policy making.

For many issues, foreign policy making involves doing today what has been done before in similar circumstances. Policy making by inertia, as this has sometimes been called, is fairly commonplace and tends to feature the bureaucratic organizations identified in Chapter 4.[1] A focus on the bureaucracy raises intriguing questions about these actors as foreign policy makers. Thus, it is important to examine what motivates them, the phases of the policy-making process where their impact is greatest, the types of issues that best lend themselves to bureaucratic policy making, the processes by which bureaucratic actors make their foreign policy decisions, and the advantages and disadvantages bureaucrats bring to the policy-making arena.

Bureaucratic Motivations

Over half of the 1.4 million civilian employees of the US government work in the foreign policy/homeland security/national security arena, and the uniformed military adds nearly 1.4 million more.[2] There is an array of professional motivations for these individuals.

One way of understanding the motivations of bureaucratic actors comes from the idea of a **principal-agent model**. In this view, bureaucratic personnel are the agents who are assigned tasks by their principals—the president and members of Congress.[3] By being responsive to elected officials, these bureaucratic actors are responding indirectly to the needs of the broader voting public.

Two potential difficulties arise from the principal-agent perspective. First, these bureaucratic agents typically know far more about their professional subject matter than do either the principals to whom they report or the people who elected those officials. Obviously, this knowledge gap causes tensions at times, particularly when what is popular with the public or elected officials does not coincide with what bureaucratic experts think is good for the country or for their agency or department. This happens more often than one might think. What is the bureaucratic official to do in such circumstances? Second, elected officials come and go (particularly in the White House), but the vast bulk of federal bureaucrats stay for a very long time—often, for their entire careers. In such situations, bureaucrats may be motivated by more parochial goals that make sense to them, such as:

- equating what is in their bureaucratic organization's interest with what is in the national interest,
- putting their organization's success and survival ahead of broader national interests, or
- putting their personal career goals ahead of national interests.

Literally, what a president may think is best for the country may not be what the organization most directly affected thinks is best for the country—or for itself.[4] Perhaps the president and administration experts may not even agree on what the facts are. A contemporary example came in early 2019 when the director of national intelligence and the director of central intelligence testified to the Senate

Select Committee on Intelligence that ISIS had not been defeated, Russia and China were the greatest threats to the country, and North Korea could not be expected to give up its nuclear weapons. President Trump dismissed these comments as naïve, as they contradicted his prior statements. As one can imagine, policy-making problems quickly arise when national and organizational perspectives or goals do not align with each other. This will be illustrated later with fuller discussion of the 1962 Cuban Missile Crisis.

Bureaucratic motivations become important whenever bureaucratic actors play significant roles in making US foreign policy; such participation may be found in various phases of foreign policy making.

Phases of Policy Making

Elected foreign policy makers such as the president and members of Congress are heavily reliant on bureaucratic actors. The first phase of the policy-making process involves information collection, analysis, and the identification of policy-making options. With the exception of what they already know or glean from the news media, elected officials typically depend on bureaucratic actors for such information and analysis. For example, most presidents rarely make final decisions on diplomatic issues without consulting with relevant State Department personnel first. Members of Congress routinely consult with Defense Department officials and top military officers before making national security policy changes. Such bureaucratic actors have the specific expertise these elected policy makers need to make good decisions, so they are important in the policy making phases that precede decision making.

Bureaucratic actors often help shape US foreign and national security policy decisions in more direct ways during this input phase of the policy-making process. When they tell elected leaders what is possible in a situation, they are structuring the options decision makers consider, and they may do so in such a way that their preferred option seems to be the only prudent choice.

For example, in 1949, the Soviet Union detonated its first atomic bomb and the Chinese Communist Party took control of mainland China. Thus, the inputs from the international context seemed sharply more negative than they had been just months earlier.

Paul Nitze, leader of the State Department's policy planning staff, was convinced that the United States was not spending enough on defense to contain the threat posed by what he saw as a global communist menace. He therefore persuaded the National Security Council to authorize a broader examination of US strategic policy. That NSC study was largely written by Nitze's staff, *because they volunteered to do the work.*[5] The resulting document, **NSC-68**, outlined a global communist threat and identified four options: doing nothing, engaging the Soviets with diplomatic approaches, launching a preemptive war against the Soviets, or undertaking a massive rearmament campaign to build up US military capabilities. The document recommended massive rearmament as the optimal choice.

Following the invasion of South Korea by North Korean Communist forces in 1950, options such as doing nothing and engaging the Soviets diplomatically seemed to fall far short of what was needed. President Truman and other top officials embraced massive rearmament as the only prudent option, and US defense spending virtually tripled.[6] Nitze got the decision he wanted, at least in part because of the way the options were structured.

Sometimes bureaucratic actors dominate the decision-making phase of the policy process. State Department travel warnings are one example of bureaucratic actors making decisions that directly affect US relations with other countries. In 2018, dozens of countries found themselves on the State Department's Travel Advisories list.[7] Although the potential impact of fewer Americans traveling to Afghanistan, South Sudan, and Iran (all on the Do Not Travel list) might be negligible, travel warnings to other destinations (such as Haiti, Honduras, and Turkey—all on the Reconsider Travel list) can have more far-reaching consequences. Haiti's presence on the list affected its economic recovery following the 2010 earthquake by slowing the flow of the few tourist dollars that normally come into the Haitian economy through the stops made by cruise ships. Turkey responded to its placement on this list by issuing its own travel warning, advising Turks not to visit the United States because of the danger posed by terrorist threats there.

A more controversial example of bureaucratic decision making came in the mid-1980s. While Iran and Iraq were fighting a war, Iran secretly sought to purchase arms from the United States. Despite the presence of economic sanctions against Iran, President Ronald Reagan was persuaded by the then national security adviser Robert McFarlane to proceed with the arms sale to Iran secretly, because such a sale might improve US relations with both Iran and Lebanon and might contribute to the release of seven Americans being held in Lebanon. Once the "arms-for-hostages" deal was uncovered, the public outcry led to an internal investigation during which Attorney General Edwin Meese discovered that $18 million of the $30 million Iran paid for the weapons was missing. As noted previously, NSC staff member marine lieutenant colonel Oliver North diverted the missing money to supply the Contras, the counterrevolutionaries who were fighting the leftist Sandinista regime in Nicaragua. North had done so with the approval of newly appointed national security adviser admiral John Poindexter but apparently without the knowledge of the president or higher elected officials. The resulting Iran-Contra scandal damaged the credibility of the Reagan presidency and tainted the image of the United States in Latin America, but it was the product of decisions by bureaucratic actors who thought they were acting in line with the president's interpretation of the US national interest.[8]

Far more often, bureaucratic actors are heavily involved in the last phase of the policy-making process: implementation of the decision. How they implement policies matters. Following the September 11, 2001, terrorist attacks, much of the world was sympathetic to the United States and supported the US military effort to go after al-Qaeda units in Afghanistan and the Taliban forces protecting them. However, that global support eroded quickly when military and intelligence personnel went too far in interrogating detainees captured on the battlefields of Afghanistan and, later, Iraq. Leaked photographs revealing the torture and humiliation of detainees at Iraq's Abu Ghraib prison scandalized the international community, the United States lost the moral high ground, and many Muslims around the world began interpreting US policy as a war on Islam.

In another example, US-Chinese relations were severely damaged in 1999 when the Chinese embassy in Belgrade was bombed as part of NATO's campaign against Yugoslavia in the war over Kosovo. The Clinton administration maintained that the bombing of the embassy compound, in which several Chinese government personnel were killed and others were wounded, was a tragic mistake based on the use of an out-of-date map by the mission's planners. The official explanation was that the embassy compound had previously been a headquarters and communications facility for the Yugoslav army (and thus, a legitimate military target) and that the CIA-supplied map had not been updated to show that the Chinese had purchased the site for their embassy.

However, a subsequent investigation by the British news media reported that the CIA knew at the time it was the Chinese embassy and that the building was targeted intentionally, because the Chinese were electronically tracking US and NATO cruise missile attacks and allowing the Yugoslav army to use the embassy's radio transmitter to communicate with Yugoslav army and air defense units in the field.[9] Two interpretations of this event thus seem possible. First, the bombing mission may have been an implementation mistake, which was the product of human or organizational error. Second, the CIA and military planners were acting to protect US and NATO aircraft and crews and did so either on their own without the knowledge of President Clinton or in such a way that Clinton could later claim that the bombing was an accident. Whichever interpretation is chosen, the result of this implemented action was the deaths of several Chinese government employees, days of anti-US rioting in China, and considerable harm to US-Chinese relations.

If implementation of governmental decisions can be problematic when the implementers are government employees, what happens when they are not? Increasingly, and for a variety of reasons, governmental bureaucracies turn to private contractors to handle certain aspects of US foreign policy. These choices to "outsource" policy implementation carry risks as well, as is illustrated in Box 6.1.

Just as some phases of the policy-making process are more open to significant bureaucratic input and roles (notably the input and implementation phases), some types of issues also lend themselves to bureaucratic input.

Issues and Organizational Roles

Certain types of issues just lend themselves to increased bureaucratic involvement. Bureaucracies typically handle routine or recurring issues reasonably well, usually creating standard operating

Box 6.1 Bureaucratic Outsourcing: Private Contractors and US Foreign Policy

The use of private contractors to perform functions otherwise handled by governmental employees can be very attractive. Cost savings are involved. Because contractors are paid by the project, the government is not required to keep those employees on the payroll on a permanent basis; when the contract ends, so do the government's payments. The result can be money saved. Further, full-time government personnel are freed up to do other things. Finally, the use of private contractors can create some distance between the government and what these contractors do, thus potentially reducing the government's direct responsibility for actions that go awry.

The "poster child" for poor behavior by a private security contractor is Academi (now part of Constellis Holdings but formerly known as Xe Services and before that as Blackwater USA). A billion-dollar defense contractor, Blackwater was started by Erik Prince, the brother of Trump administration Secretary of Education Betsy DeVos. In 2007, Blackwater personnel providing security for US diplomats in Baghdad killed seventeen Iraqi civilians. In 2015, a US federal court convicted four lower-level Blackwater employees in the deaths, sentencing one to life in prison and three others to thirty-year prison terms. A fifth employee pleaded guilty to manslaughter charges and testified against the others. In 2009, a State Department audit found Blackwater had overbilled the government by tens of millions of dollars for providing security to diplomatic personnel. Following a raid on its corporate headquarters, in 2010 five former top Blackwater executives (including the former president of Blackwater Worldwide) were indicted on federal weapons charges and making false statements to investigators. In 2018, Erik Prince proposed replacing US troops in Afghanistan with private military contractors. The idea was rejected by Defense Secretary James Mattis, who said: "When the Americans put their nation's credibility on the line, privatizing it is probably not a wise idea."

(continues)

Box 6.1 Continued

Yet, Blackwater/Xe Services/Academi is not the only private contractor to cause problems for its governmental employer. One incident occurred at the US embassy in Kabul, Afghanistan, among members of the ArmorGroup (a subsidiary of Wackenhut, which in turn is owned by the British firm G4S), who participated in lewd and drunken hazing rituals. ArmorGroup settled with the US government by paying a $7.5 million fine. For other contractors, paying off the Taliban with US-supplied dollars not to attack their trucking business was literally "the cost of doing business," but that meant that US dollars were going to the Taliban. Some estimates are that contracts by Afghan businesses were increased 10–20 percent just to pay Taliban protection money.

Incidents like the above point to recurring problems with private contractors. These problems include poor contract job descriptions, lack of accountability by contractors, lack of oversight of contractors, overpricing and fraud in billing, other financial mismanagement, contractors performing functions that are inherently governmental, and even terrorism-related acts by contract personnel. To some extent, the question thus becomes: Who is actually conducting US foreign policy? Who should be doing so? Would the implementation of US foreign policy be improved if government employees resumed many of these roles, or would the financial costs seem too high at a time when the national debt is rising?

Sources:

Matt Apuzzo, "Ex-Blackwater Guards Given Long Terms for Killing Iraqis," *New York Times,* April 13, 2015, https://www.nytimes.com/2015/04/14/us/ex-blackwater-guards-sentenced-to-prison-in-2007-killings-of-iraqi-civilians.html; Lee Ferran and Jack Cloherty, "Partying Security Contracting Group Pays $7.5 M Fine," *ABC News,* July 7, 2011, https://abcnews.go.com/Blotter/armorgroup-kabul-contractor-group-settles-75-fine/story?id=1402045; GlobalPost, "Who Is Funding the Afghan Taliban? You Don't Want to Know," *Reuters,* August 13, 2009, http://blogs.reuters.com/global/2009/08/13/who-is-funding-the-afghan-taliban-you-dont-want-to-know/; Ellen Mitchell, "Mattis Rejects Plan to Privatize

Military Effort in Afghanistan," *Hill,* August 28, 2018, https://www
.msn.com/en-us/news/politics/mattis-rejects-plan-to-privatize-military
-effort-in-afghanistan/ar-BBMzfA0; James Risen and Mark Mazzetti,
"U.S. Indicts 5 Blackwater Ex-Officials," *New York Times,* April 16,
2010, https://www.nytimes.com/2010/04/17/world/17XE.htm; Justin Rood,
"Audit: U.S. Overpaid Blackwater," *ABC News,* June 16, 2009, https://abc
news.go.com/Blotter/Blackwater/story?id=7851018.

procedures (SOPs) for that purpose. SOPs are patterns of steps learned (and possibly perfected) over time that allow the organization to produce a coordinated response to a situation, thereby freeing the individuals in the organization from having to come up with new responses each time a similar occasion for decision or action arises. In other words, the wheel does not have to be continually reinvented. For example, when the US Agency for International Development (USAID) funds a public-health program involving prescription drugs abroad, it can rely on SOPs that have been developed for drug management in laboratories and for different types of diseases and recipients.[10] SOPs exist for other recurring actions, such as how to administer the transfer of military weaponry to allied states or how to handle routine diplomatic negotiations.

On the other hand, issues that are nonroutine or that require creative solutions each time they arise do not lend themselves to bureaucratic SOPs. Given that bureaucratic organizations exist primarily to handle repeated tasks well, it is hard to order bureaucrats to be innovative. When faced with such challenges, bureaucratic actors may often create ad hoc task forces or interagency teams to deal with them or send those issues up the chain of command for resolution by higher officials.

The latter is certainly the case with crisis situations. In crises, bureaucracies may be highly involved in gathering relevant information or identifying options for decision makers, and they are often involved in implementing those decisions. However, they rarely play a significant role in the actual decision-making process in a true crisis (i.e., a surprise situation that threatens core values and demands a response). As noted in Chapter 5, crisis decision making heavily favors the president and a small number of other executive branch actors. But when they do get heavily involved in making policy, how do bureaucratic actors typically perform?

Bureaucratic Policy Making

When bureaucracies engage in the decision phase of policy making, they may have neither the time nor the inclination to follow the idealized decision-making steps of the rational actor model—that is, identifying all possible options, evaluating them, and choosing the optimal one. Just as important, bureaucratic officials operate in a specific organizational context that conditions both how they approach policy making and the policies that they choose. The operative phrase usually is, "Where you stand on an issue depends upon where you sit." In other words, bureaucratic officials tend to view occasions for decision based on the face of the issue they see, and the face of the issue seen is a function of how that issue typically affects their own bureaucratic organization. Depending on which face of the issue they see, the officials will take whatever stand they feel is appropriate. Then, the question of who prevails in the decision-making game may not be who has the best response to the situation but may depend upon who has more influence, who has more formal or informal power, who has the ear of more powerful officials, who can be the most stubborn, and so on.

A variety of examples of bureaucratic organizations in action can be found in the well-chronicled 1962 Cuban Missile Crisis.[11] In September 1962, there were reports coming in to the CIA that the Soviet Union might be placing missiles in Cuba. On September 19, officials in the Intelligence Community (represented at that time by the US Intelligence Board) made the determination that enough indicators were present to justify a reconnaissance overflight, specifically to look for evidence of missiles in Cuba.

From that point, it took fourteen days to get authorization from another bureaucratic entity—the Committee on Overhead Reconnaissance—to send a high-flying U-2 spy plane over Cuba to take the pictures. This delay resulted for several reasons. First, the State Department was worried about the diplomatic costs if a U-2 aircraft were shot down over Cuban airspace. Not only had a U-2 been shot down over the Soviet Union just two years before, but on September 9, a US-made U-2 operated by the Taiwanese regime had been shot down over the People's Republic of China, so the risks of losing a very expensive aircraft and its pilot were quite real. Moreover, each prior incident had resulted in considerable negative diplomatic fallout.

Second, there was the obvious question of where exactly in Cuba to look. Cuba is an island, but at 760 miles long by 55 miles wide, it is not exactly small. The CIA had to sift through all the available bits of information to determine the most likely locations for such missiles, and analysts also had to guess where they would put missiles if they were the Soviets. That took time, too'.

Third, how to conduct the flight was another decision. Flying directly over the areas in question might result in the best pictures but also might put the pilot at the greatest risk of being shot down. Instead, it was decided to fly along the periphery of the areas in question so the pilot would be in a position to evade any surface-to-air missiles that might be launched against him by leaving Cuban airspace as quickly as possible.

Once the authorization was made, *another ten days* were consumed in determining who would conduct the flight. Both the CIA and the air force operated U-2 aircraft. Both wanted the mission, and each thought it was better suited than the other to conduct it. The Defense Department pressed the case for the air force, noting that if the plane were shot down, it would be better to have the pilot wearing a military uniform. The penalty for a uniformed military officer might be prisoner-of-war status, whereas a civilian-attired CIA pilot might be considered a spy and be executed. The CIA countered with the argument that this was an intelligence mission and that was its primary jurisdiction. The CIA claimed more experience and possibly better equipment for such a mission, whereas the air force claimed that its pilots were unsurpassed. Ultimately, a compromise was reached; an air force pilot would fly a CIA aircraft.

Once the presence of the missiles in Cuba was confirmed by U-2 photographs, how to respond to them depended on who was asked at the meeting. Not surprisingly, in the decision-making phase of the process, the State Department pressed for a diplomatic response. Whether it was a diplomatic appeal to the Soviets, the new Castro regime in Cuba, or the United Nations, this option would give the State Department the mission, and all bureaucratic organizations want appropriate missions to justify their continued existence, budgets, and importance. Further, the State Department argued that if diplomacy should fail, more forceful options could still be used later.

Defense Department representatives responded that, in the time needed for a diplomatic approach to be attempted, the missiles might become operational. If they became operational, the entire southeastern United States would be at risk of a nuclear attack, with only a couple of minutes of warning. Air force officials argued instead for an air strike to take out the missiles. After all, removing the threat was the real goal. Bombing could do that.

However, others at the meeting raised objections to air strikes. First, could air strikes guarantee success? For an air strike to be successful, all the missiles had to be destroyed. If just one missile with a nuclear warhead survived the attack, it might be launched against the United States. When pressed, air force representatives acknowledged that an air strike had only a 90 percent chance of getting all the missiles. Their 90 percent figure was based on their estimates, given that Intelligence Community reports said the missiles were mobile. If they were mobile, they might have moved in the interval between the last overflight photo and the actual bombing mission. With antiaircraft batteries and surface-to-air missiles firing at them, the bomber pilots might not be able to linger in the area looking for missing missiles to bomb. Only later did air force representatives learn that the missiles were mobile in the same way as a small house was mobile; they could be moved, but it was a slow and difficult process.

When asked what an air strike might involve, air force officials said it might take 500 bombing sorties against Cuba to get the missiles. What political officials had assumed would be a "surgical" strike with limited damage now looked like "saturation" bombing instead. Might such air strikes run the risk of starting World War III? A heavy bombing attack would surely kill Soviet and Cuban military personnel and possibly any Cuban civilians living near the bombing area. How might the Soviets or Cubans respond? Would the Soviets attack US missile installations near the Soviet border in Turkey? Would they retaliate against West Berlin, a noncommunist enclave deep inside communist East Germany? Where and how would the Soviets respond to such an attack?

Shared values also came into play. After being the victims of a Japanese surprise attack on the US naval fleet at Pearl Harbor in 1941, did US officials want to do that to someone else? Was the moral high ground being abandoned with such an approach? The president's brother, Attorney General Robert Kennedy, thought so.

Based on a variety of factors, a mid-range approach advanced by the navy was chosen. Rather than the diplomatic option that seemed too timid or the air strike option that might start a world war, decision makers chose to impose a naval blockade against Cuba. That option would convey a strong message (after all, a military blockade was traditionally considered an act of war), but it would not necessarily initiate a shooting conflict. The next decision would then be back in the hands of Soviet leaders. Although a naval blockade did nothing to remove the threat of missiles already in Cuba, it would stop additional Soviet cargo ships from delivering more military supplies to Cuba, and it would buy time for the Soviets to reconsider their decision to base offensive missiles in Cuba.

A bureaucratic factor that helped this option was that a naval blockade against Cuba was well within US organizational capabilities. The United States had a large navy, whereas the Soviet Union did not. Moreover, the operation would occur practically in the US backyard; the East and Gulf Coasts had multiple naval and air bases from which a blockade and air support could be launched, and Soviet personnel in Cuba were very far from any home base.

Once the blockade option was announced, bureaucratic actors were called upon to implement it. Per its usual SOP, the navy positioned its ships 500 miles off the Cuban coast. That distance was not by chance. At 500 miles from Cuba, the ships were considered safe from attack by Cuban aircraft, which did not have the combat range to attack the ships and return to land without running out of fuel and ditching in the ocean.

When the president decided to give his Soviet counterparts more time to decide whether to try to run the blockade with their cargo ships, the secretary of defense ordered the navy to pull the blockade line back closer to Cuba. When the crisis was over, officials learned that naval commanders had ignored that order, because the order put their ships and crews in danger. Here was a case of insubordination, where military officers were sure that they knew better how to run this operation than did the commander in chief or his designated defense secretary. The navy also took another action that was in its bureaucratic interest. It used this opportunity to show off its antisubmarine warfare capability, for which it had been requesting additional funding. Without authorization from higher officials, the navy engaged Soviet submarines and forced some to surface, thereby risking a deadlier confrontation and possibly the start of World War III.

The Cuban Missile Crisis thus shows the many ways in which bureaucratic actors become important in all phases of foreign policy making. Policy makers typically rely on bureaucratic organizations for what they know and on bureaucratic expertise for what it means. They often ask bureaucratic actors for advice in determining options to consider and sometimes request that they get involved in the decision-making phase. And they almost always have to rely on bureaucratic actors to implement the decisions made. These are the ways in which bureaucratic actors can be important players in making US foreign policy. Is that a good or a bad thing?

Bureaucratic Advantages and Disadvantages

Bureaucratic involvement in foreign policy making and implementation carries with it both advantages and disadvantages. Advantages include expertise, competence, and consistency over time.

Expertise is a fairly obvious advantage. Bureaucracies developed in the first place to have the same people handle a similar set of issues repetitively, thereby using SOPs to make governmental responses to similar issues a matter of routine. In this way, different officials did not have to waste their time relearning how to do the same thing. By being immersed daily in a restricted range of issues, bureaucratic actors come to know those issues well, expertise is developed, and more rational policy making should be the result.[12] Thus, for example, if presidents want to evaluate the nuclear programs of states such as Iran or North Korea, there are multiple sources of expertise to tap within the administration. Experts on various aspects of nuclear weapons—including their research and development, production, testing, and maintenance—can be found within the various members of the Intelligence Community, the National Security Staff, and the Departments of

Defense (air force; navy; Joint Chiefs of Staff; international security affairs), Energy (the National Nuclear Security Administration), State (Bureau of International Security and Nonproliferation; Bureau of Arms Control, Verification, and Compliance; Bureau of Intelligence and Research), and Commerce (the National Technical Information Service). For virtually any foreign policy issue, there are bureaucratic officials with expertise in that subject matter.

The added value of expertise is competence. By building their expertise, bureaucratic officials come to know what works and what does not. By doing something repeatedly, officials can get better at the task—whether that involves tracking international financing for suspected terrorist organizations, analyzing how other regime leaders tend to act, conducting military operations, or distributing foreign aid in developing countries. Take diplomatic negotiations, for example. Diplomats who are calm, patient, and unrelenting in their efforts to get what they desire may often simply wear down their counterparts, who may lack such patience or need to move on to other issues. According to a story told about Warren Christopher, the secretary of state for Bill Clinton, Christopher was highly respected by Foreign Service officers at the State Department because of something that had happened early in his career. Apparently, Christopher was an accomplished negotiator, and at one point he wore down a counterpart in a negotiating session by sitting at the table—without getting up for any reason—for hours and hours, thereby refusing to stop negotiating until he got what he desired.

Consistency over time is another advantage provided by bureaucracies. Humans like order, and other regimes appreciate knowing what to expect from the United States in certain circumstances. By relying on competent experts for policy guidance, policy making, or policy implementation, administrations gain the benefit of consistency over time. It is a given in international affairs that national policies may need to change occasionally, but others in the international system respect or appreciate those changes if they result from changed circumstances and not just from the personal whims of policy makers. The negative reaction from US allies to President Trump's surprise decision in 2018 to pull US troops out of Syria illustrates how others come to expect such order and dependability. Thus, the vast majority of foreign policy actions by an administration for any particular issue tend to be constant, and at least in part, that is a result of bureaucratic participation.

Nonetheless, bureaucracies come with some clear disadvantages as well. As noted earlier, there is a tendency for bureaucratic officials to see issues from the perspective of their specific organization (**parochialism**) and their personal role in it, (**careerism**). Thus, what is good for the organization or the officials personally may come to be more important than what is good for the United States. An example of parochialism comes from the experience of the air force and army. For years, the culture of the air force stressed the importance of strategic bombardment, the idea of carrying the fight to the heartland of the enemy.[13] Thus, the army seemed unable to get the air force to devote sufficient resources (at least from the army's perspective) to the low-altitude, close-air support mission that troops on the ground required, because that mission was not in line with air force culture. Finally, the army chose to develop its own close-air support capability, and it now possesses a large close-air support capability with hundreds of attack helicopters as well as other aircraft for its use. On the other hand, careerism can be seen when those with a twenty-five- to thirty-year career in a particular department or agency say, "Presidents come and go every four or eight years, but my department will always be here." Such thinking can easily color their judgment.

As suggested earlier, different parts of the bureaucracy often do not cooperate well with each other. Parochialism suggests they typically compete to get the most desirable missions, the largest budgets, the ear of the president, and so on. Such rivalries can spawn bureaucratic empire building, with bureaucratic organizations seeking to become bigger (in personnel or budgets) at the expense of their rival organizations.

A classic instance of this was seen in the investigations that followed the September 11, 2001, terrorist attacks on the United States. In the years leading up to the attacks, various officials knew Osama bin Laden and his al-Qaeda group were threats to the United States. In the months before the attacks, various parts of the Intelligence Community, the Defense Department, the Immigration and Naturalization Service, and the Federal Bureau of Investigation knew the names of some al-Qaeda members, that some of them were in the United States, that aircraft could potentially be used as terrorist weapons, that some Saudis were taking flying lessons in the United States but were unconcerned about learning to take off or land, and that something "big" was about to happen.[14] Yet these individual bits of information were not shared with others in a way that allowed these dots to be connected so that the threat of using commercial aircraft as weapons against buildings could be foreseen. In a bureaucratic environment where "information is power," sharing information is *not* the norm.

Another disadvantage of bureaucracies comes from rigidity in both thinking and actions. As noted earlier in this chapter, organizations designed to do certain things repetitively and well are not structurally suited to creativity or innovation. A good example of this occurred at the end of the Cold War. For two generations, intelligence officers had been tasked with helping to prepare the United States to deal with its superpower rival, the Soviet Union. When one's rival has thousands of nuclear weapons and its leader has publicly declared, "We will bury you," it is only prudent to assume worst-case scenarios when planning. Thus, the strengths of the Soviet Union were stressed while its weaknesses, to the extent they were known, tended to be underestimated. Signs that the Soviet Union was weakening by the mid-1980s, particularly in its economic performance, were either totally missed or misinterpreted. Analysts were so focused on the smaller details of the Soviet military threat that they missed the bigger picture of a superpower in serious decline. As a result, most members of the Intelligence Community were just as surprised as anyone else when the Soviet Union abruptly fell apart in 1991.[15] In short, bureaucratic structures reflect organizational assumptions, those assumptions are not checked at the door by those who work there, and such shared assumptions or attitudes can limit creativity.

Both rigid thinking and a failure to cooperate across agencies can be seen in the 2018 enforcement of a Trump administration "zero tolerance" policy toward illegal immigration that resulted in the separation of parents from their children, as described in Box 6.2.

Further, speed is not a hallmark of bureaucratic organizations. The more complex the organization and the greater the number of administrative layers reflected in its organizational chart, the slower it tends to operate. Most information flows from the bottom of an organization up, and important decisions or actions flow from the top down as they require high-level authorization.

Box 6.2 Family Separations in the Trump Administration

One of the earliest campaign pledges by then presidential candidate Donald Trump was to stop illegal immigration into the country. Within two weeks of Trump's inauguration, a Department of Homeland Security official suggested separating families to deter illegal immigrants from trying to enter the country. On April 6, 2018, Attorney General Jeff Sessions announced a Department of Justice "zero tolerance" policy, whereby all illegal immigrants referred to the Justice Department by the Department of Homeland Security would be prosecuted. The consequence of this zero tolerance policy was that all adults suspected of entering the country illegally would be arrested and prosecuted, which meant that if they had children with them, the families would be separated. In a subsequent series of news interviews, John Kelly, secretary of homeland security and later presidential chief of staff, said he thought family separation would be a "tough deterrent" but that the children would be "well cared for." Attorney General Sessions later also confirmed that the policy was meant as a deterrent.

In the spring and early summer of 2018, nearly 3,000 children were separated from their parents. Once separated from their families, the children were referred to the custody of the Office of Refugee Resettlement in the Department of Health and Human Services, where they were often housed in hastily arranged shelters that were sometimes hundreds, if not thousands, of miles away from their parents and were operated by for-profit corporations. The horror stories quickly began. Lawyers and other advocates for the families reported children being kept in cages with no toys, educational materials, or access to meaningful medical care. Some Immigration and Customs Enforcement officers reportedly told parents they were taking their children for a bath, without letting them know they wouldn't see them again. One story suggested a father in custody committed suicide when he realized he had lost his child. Multiple children later died in US custody.

The public outrage at this policy was sharp and immediate, catching administration officials by surprise. A lawsuit filed on behalf of the families by the American Civil Liberties Union resulted in a federal judge's order to stop the practice and reunite the families within thirty days. Meeting that deadline proved impossible. The combination of poor record-keeping in the transfer of children from control of the Department of Homeland Security to the Department of Health and Human Services, as well as the difficulty later in locating parents who had since been released from custody, prevented the reunification of at least several hundred children.

Immigration policy has international ramifications, and the international reaction to the family separation policy was swift. Pope Francis, British prime minister Theresa May, Canadian prime minister Justin Trudeau, Guatemalan president Jimmy Morales, Iranian supreme leader Ayatollah Ali Khamenei, and even Marine Le Pen, the leader of France's National Front anti-immigration party, condemned the policy, which contributed to the image of President Trump as out of step with international norms. As this example shows, shared assumptions, rigid thinking, and the challenges of interdepartmental bureaucratic cooperation can tarnish US foreign policy.

Sources:

Philip Bump, "Here Are the Administration Officials Who Have Said That Family Separation Is Meant as a Deterrent," *Washington Post,* June 19, 2018, https://www.washingtonpost.com/news/politics/wp/2018/06/19/here-are-the-administration-officials-who-have-said-that-family-separation-is-meant-as-a-deterrent/?utm_term=.80cdef3e6a92; Chico Harlan and William Branigin, "Trump's Family-Separation Policy Faces International Condemnation from Pope Francis, Theresa May and Others," *Washington Post,* June 20, 2018, https://www.washingtonpost.com/world/pope-francis-criticizes-trumps-family-separation-policy-on-migrants-says-populism-is-not-the-solution/2018/06/20/65c15102-7472-11e8-9780-b1dd6a09b549_story.html?utm_term=.731a9281cc19; Dara Lind, "The Trump Administration's Separation of Families at the Border, Explained," *Vox,* June 15, 2018, https://www.vox.com/2018/6/11/17443198/children-immigrant-families-separated-parents; Office of Public Affairs, "Attorney General Announces Zero-Tolerance Policy for Criminal Illegal Entry," Office of the Attorney General, Department of Justice, Friday, April 6, 2018, Press Release Number 18-417, https://www.justice.gov/opa/pr/attorney-general-announces-zero-tolerance-policy-criminal-illegal-entry.

Take this hypothetical example. Several relatively new Foreign Service officers posted at the US Embassy in Paris get what they think is a great idea for improving US-French relations. They write a memo and send it to their supervisor. The supervisor tweaks it a bit, approves the memo, then sends it up the embassy's food chain. At some point, the embassy's chargé d'affaires (its top career Foreign Service officer) has to approve it, after which it goes to the ambassador. If the ambassador approves it, the memo then goes to the French desk at the State Department back in Washington, DC. If the desk officer approves it, it goes up the organizational chart at headquarters until someone with an appropriate level of authority can formally approve it. That might be the assistant secretary for European and Eurasian affairs, the undersecretary for political affairs, the deputy secretary of state, or finally even the secretary of state. Assuming the memo gets final approval and goes back to those junior Foreign Service officers who first drafted it, considerable time has probably elapsed, and the approved memo may only bear a slight resemblance to the one originally drafted.

This hypothetical example is drawn from real life. Within the State Department, there are multiple administrative layers, and each of the offices indicated are really smaller organizations in their own right, with multiple people of multiple ranks working there and reporting to their superiors, who then have to deal with their own superiors, and so on. The Department of Defense is similarly complex, as is the Intelligence Community and the Department of Homeland Security, each with components containing many subcomponent organizations.

The pace of bureaucratic behavior slows even more when multiple organizations are involved. Consider again the Cuban Missile Crisis example. Once a determination was made to check to see if nuclear-capable missiles were only ninety-five miles from Florida, it still took twenty-four days to get the U-2 flight implemented because multiple bureaucratic actors were involved—and that was considered a *crisis.*

Finally, although expertise is an advantage, it can be a disadvantage as well, at least from the president's perspective. What happens when bureaucratic actors—or other expert policy advisers—choose to act on their expertise rather than on the president's wishes? That occurred in the Cuban Missile Crisis with the actions of the navy mentioned earlier. More recently, some White House officials in the Trump administration actively tried to thwart the president's wishes when they believed his inclinations were not in the national interest. Although policy experts might be correct in their concerns, the president was elected by the public, and they were not.

Conclusion

Bureaucratic organizations are essential actors in US foreign policy making. They are instrumental in collecting the information needed by policy makers to understand external threats and opportunities; they are normally involved in formulating and then evaluating the possible options for US actions; at times they are involved in the actual decision-making process; and they are almost always involved in the implementation of whatever policies are chosen. Thus, bureaucratic actors—and their strengths and weaknesses—are interwoven in the process of foreign policy making.

Suggested Reading

Allison, Graham T., and Philip Zelikow. *Essence of Decision: Explaining the Cuban Missile Crisis.* 2nd ed. London: Pearson, 1992.
Art, Robert J. "Bureaucratic Politics and American Foreign Policy: A Critique." *Policy Sciences* 4 (1973): 467–490.
Halperin, Morton H., and Priscilla A. Clapp, with Arnold Kanter. *Bureaucratic Politics and Foreign Policy.* 2nd ed. Washington, DC: Brookings Institution, 2006.
Hilsman, Roger. *The Politics of Policy Making in Defense and Foreign Affairs: Conceptual Models and Bureaucratic Politics.* 3rd ed. Upper Saddle River, NJ: Prentice Hall, 1993.

Notes

1. For more on this idea of inertial policy making, see Barbara Hinckley, *Less Than Meets the Eye: Congress, the President, and Foreign Policy* (Chicago: University of Chicago Press, 1994).
2. Stephen Dinan, "Federal Workers Hit Record Number, But Growth Slows Under Obama," *Washington Times,* February 9, 2016,

https://www.washingtontimes.com/news/2016/feb/9/federal-workers-hit-record-number-but-growth-slows/.

3. See, for example, Terry M. Moe, "The New Economics of Organization," *American Journal of Political Science* 20 (1984): 734–749; and B. Dan Wood and Richard W. Waterman, "The Dynamics of Political Control of the Bureaucracy," *American Political Science Review* 85 (1991): 801–828.

4. See Christopher M. Jones, "The Foreign Policy Bureaucracy in a New Era," in James M. Scott, ed., *After the End: Making U.S. Foreign Policy in the Post–Cold War World* (Durham, NC: Duke University Press, 1998).

5. See Graham T. Allison, *Essence of Decision: Explaining the Cuban Missile Crisis* (Boston: HarperCollins, 1971), 161.

6. See "NSC-68, 1950," U.S. Department of State, Timeline of U.S. Diplomatic History, 1945–1952, https://history.state.gov/milestones/1945-1952/NSC68.

7. See U.S. Department of State, "Travel Advisories," https://travel.state.gov/content/travel/en/traveladvisories/traveladvisories.html/.

8. For a concise history of this affair, see "The Iran-Contra Affair," PBS *American Experience,* http://www.pbs.org/wgbh/americanexperience/features/reagan-iran.

9. John Sweeney, Jens Holsoe, and Ed Vulliamy, "NATO Bombed Chinese Deliberately: Nato Hit Embassy on Purpose," *Observer,* October 17, 1999, http://www.guardian.co.uk/world/1999/oct/17/balkans.

10. "Pharmaceutical Management—Assuring the Quality and Safety of Medicines," *USAID Impact,* http://blog.usaid.gov/2011/01/pharmaceutical-management-%E2%80%93-assuring-the-quality-and-safety-of-medicines/.

11. For more on this example, see Allison, *Essence of Decision.*

12. For more on this subject, see Max Weber, *Economy and Society,* ed. Guenther Roth and Claus Wittich (Berkeley: University of California Press, 1968).

13. See Lynne E. Vermillion, "Understanding the Air Force Culture," Air War College, Air University, Maxwell Air Force Base, Report AU/AWC/RWP/258/96-04, April 1, 1996, http://www.dtic.mil/cgi-bin/GetTRDoc?AD=ADA393915&Location=U2&doc=GetTRDoc.pdf.

14. See Thomas H. Kean and Lee H. Hamilton, *The 9/11 Report: The National Commission on Terrorist Attacks upon the United States* (New York: St. Martin's Paperbacks, 2004).

15. See John Diamond, *The CIA and the Culture of Failure: U.S. Intelligence from the End of the Cold War to the Invasion of Iraq* (Stanford: Stanford University Press, 2008).

7

The Role of Congress

Learning Objectives

- Identify the types of congressional actors most often involved in foreign policy making.
- Explain the motivations of members of Congress who participate in foreign policy making.
- Differentiate between four distinct processes of congressional influence.
- Evaluate the impact of Congress on foreign policy making.

News reports often begin with something along this line: "Today the administration announced." This implies that the president and administration officials are the only foreign policy makers who matter. They matter tremendously, but as noted in Chapter 4, the Constitution provides Congress with more foreign policy roles and powers than it allots to the presidency. Day in, day out, Congress is the second-most-significant foreign policy maker in the United States, only trailing the presidency. Moreover, at certain times and for some selected issues, Congress, and not the president, makes US foreign policy. The congressional role in foreign policy making should therefore not be underestimated. Discussion in this chapter thus centers on the congressional actors most likely to become highly involved in making foreign policy, the inputs that motivate Congress and its members, the avenues or processes through which Congress influences (if it does not make) foreign policy, and the overall congressional record in terms of foreign policy outputs.

Who in Congress Makes Foreign Policy?

All of the 435 members in the House of Representatives and the 100 members in the Senate present and voting make foreign policy, at least when dealing with issues that result in floor votes in their respective chambers. However, not all issues are handled in such ways, and the number of members of Congress highly active on issues of foreign policy is usually considerably smaller. Still, this smaller subset often acts in the name of the larger Congress. Those who tend to act in the name of Congress are typically elected party leaders, members of congressional caucuses, members of relevant committees and their subcommittees, and congressional foreign policy entrepreneurs. Each of these actors are discussed in turn.

Elected Party Leaders

Some of those active in foreign policy making are the elected party leaders in each chamber—the House and Senate majority and minority leaders and the Speaker of the House. The Speaker schedules business for the House floor and decides who can speak on the House floor during debate on an issue. These elected leaders also canvass their party members so the leaders know how others are likely to vote on an issue. This allows the House Speaker and Senate majority leader to schedule floor votes appropriately—either when support is greatest for bills they support or when opposition is greatest for bills they oppose. Although the leaders of the president's party in each chamber can generally be expected to support the president's foreign policy agenda, the leaders of the nonpresidential party will often find partisan reasons to disagree with the administration's position on foreign policy issues. When the nonpresidential party is the majority party in a chamber of Congress and thus controls it, that party leader—the Speaker of the House or the Senate majority leader—often emerges as a focal point of opposition to the president's foreign policy agenda.

Many examples of House Speakers' positions come to mind: Jim Wright (D-TX) pressing the Reagan administration to assist the peace process in Central America in the 1980s; Newt Gingrich (R-GA) pressing the Clinton administration for national missile defense (NMD) and covert operations to undermine the Iranian regime; Nancy Pelosi (D-CA) pushing for global climate change legislation against the wishes of the George W. Bush administration or for more humane immigration policies from the Trump administration; and Paul Ryan (R-WI) opposing the Obama-backed Iran nuclear deal. In the Senate, Majority Leader Bob Dole (R-KS) was a constant critic of the Clinton administration regarding what he saw as too little US support for Bosnians facing the threat of ethnic cleansing from the Serbs in the 1990s; and his successor, Trent Lott (R-MS), challenged the Clinton administration over additional funding for the International Monetary Fund during the Asian financial crisis of 1997–1998. In 2016, President Obama was stopped from publicly revealing the extent of Russian interference in the US presidential election campaign by Majority Leader Mitch McConnell (R-KY). In a bit of a surprise, in 2017 Republican leaders in both the House and Senate challenged the president from their own party by passing new sanctions on Russia for intervening in the 2016 presidential election. Thus, elected party leaders can become foreign policy makers as they swing considerable weight with their own party members in Congress.

Congressional Caucuses

Members of congressional caucuses can also become significant players in foreign policy making at times. These informal groups are composed of members who care about an issue, a set of related issues, US policy toward another country or part of the world, and so on. Some of the caucuses deal with foreign policy issues on the basis of their constituents' economic interests (e.g., the Congressional Pro-Trade Caucus or the Congressional Steel Caucus). Others focus on the link between constituents' identity interests and another country or region (e.g., the Congressional Asian Pacific-American Caucus, the Congressional Czech Caucus, or the Congressional Caucus on Turkey and Turkish Americans). Others focus on specific policy issues (e.g., the Congressional Coalition on Adoption or the Out of Iraq Caucus).

A good example of how a caucus can mobilize members of
Congress on an issue came in the late 1980s and early 1990s. The
marine corps needed a new vehicle to replace its aging fleet of
CH-46 helicopters, but the United States was in a recession and the
George H. W. Bush administration was trying to hold down government spending. Boeing and Bell Helicopter proposed their
jointly built V-22 aircraft to meet the needs of the marine corps—
a tilt-rotor, vertical takeoff and landing aircraft that could fly faster
and farther and carry more troops or cargo than the helicopters it
would replace. The marine corps wanted the aircraft badly, but the
Bush administration wanted to save money by buying cheaper helicopters instead. Led by Representatives Curt Weldon (R-PA),
whose district included a Boeing plant, and Pete Geren (D-TX),
whose district included a Bell plant, the Congressional Tilt-Rotor
Caucus was formed. It pooled the efforts of those members of
Congress who believed in this new technology, whose districts
benefited from the contracts and subcontracts the V-22 project
would bring, or who were pro–marine corps in their orientation.
These members of Congress played a major role in protecting the
V-22 from the administration's budget cutters—led by President
Bush and Secretary of Defense Dick Cheney—who wanted to terminate the program. Based on the success of the Tilt-Rotor Caucus
in convincing other members of Congress to support funding for
the project, the marine corps got its new aircraft.

Another, more recent example can be found in the efforts of
the bipartisan Congressional Caucus for Effective Foreign Assistance. The members of Congress in this caucus recognize the value
of foreign assistance in both improving the lives of people in
developing countries and improving the image of the United States
abroad. However, caucus members insist that foreign assistance
programs be implemented with greater transparency, in terms of
program means and goals, which would allow better congressional
oversight of these programs. Given the early efforts by the Trump
administration to reduce the foreign aid budget, time will tell
whether this caucus is as successful as the V-22 caucus was.

Committees and Subcommittees

Structurally speaking, the places where most members of Congress
get actively involved in foreign policy issues are the congressional

committees and subcommittees that deal with foreign policy, but those committees and subcommittees include far more than the obvious ones such as armed services or foreign relations. House and Senate committees dealing with foreign policy matters include agriculture (promoting exports of agricultural products), appropriations (funding foreign policy), armed services (authorizing national security spending), banking and financial services (pushing international financial policy), commerce (regulating foreign trade), energy (decreasing reliance on foreign oil suppliers and providing for the safety of nuclear weapons), environment (addressing global climate change and promoting pro-environmental policy), foreign relations (overseeing foreign policy and authorizing foreign aid spending), homeland security (protecting Americans at home from foreign threats), intelligence (learning what others may be planning or doing), and science and technology (promoting global competitiveness).

Most committee members typically develop expertise on the subject matter of their committees or subcommittees. Those who serve for long periods on their respective committees and subcommittees often come to know as much or more about their subject than do the administration's own officials, and if they do not, they will be able to identify others who do. Consequently, such committee members often put their mark on US foreign policy by relying on such expertise and political power. A very early example came in the 1960s when senators such as Edward (Ted) Kennedy (D-MA), Stuart Symington (D-MO), John Sherman Cooper (R-KY), and Philip Hart (D-MI) got tired of the Johnson administration's experts telling them that they did not sufficiently understand the technical details of nuclear weapons issues to justify their opposition to a proposed anti-ballistic missile (ABM) defense system. Undeterred, the senators identified their own group of rocket scientists whose expertise could not be discounted and who also questioned the expense and performance of an ABM system. By continuing to attack the ABM proposals of Johnson's successor, Richard Nixon, these senators ultimately led Nixon to seek a negotiated limit with the Soviets on ABM systems. In another example, Senator William Fulbright (D-AR) used his chairmanship of the Senate Foreign Relations Committee to hold televised hearings questioning the wisdom of American involvement in the Vietnam War, including testimony from nonadministration experts who could credibly challenge the assumptions of Defense Department officials testifying on behalf of continued US participation in the war.

A well-known example of such committee power being lodged in just a couple of people can be seen in the movie *Charlie Wilson's War.* Representative Charles Wilson (D-TX) served on the House Appropriations Committee and, even more important, on its Defense and Foreign Operations Subcommittees. When he chose to help the Afghan mujahedin acquire the weaponry they needed to defeat the Soviet invaders of their country, he was in the right place to do it. All he had to do was to convince Representative Clarence "Doc" Long (D-MD), the chairman of the Foreign Operations Subcommittee, that the Central Intelligence Agency needed to get more arms to the mujahedin, and then Long could get the other subcommittee members to go along. Then the entire Appropriations Committee would go along with what the subcommittee had recommended. He was successful in that effort. Wilson was able to send millions of dollars' worth of weapons to the mujahedin, including portable anti-aircraft missiles that could shoot down the Soviet helicopter gunships that the Afghans particularly feared. The good news is that his efforts turned the tide in Afghanistan in the 1980s and helped to hasten the end of the Soviet Union. The bad news is that he was unable thereafter to get members of other appropriations subcommittees to provide the funding to build the schools in Afghanistan that might have prevented the rise of the Taliban there.[1]

Congressional Foreign Policy Entrepreneurs

As the earlier anecdotes suggest, some members of Congress care more about foreign policy than others do. Those who are willing to invest their time and energy to act on their own foreign policy agendas, rather than to await administration action on those issues, can be considered congressional foreign policy entrepreneurs.[2] These policy innovators are a source of significant congressional initiative and innovation regarding foreign affairs. They can be found most often on the foreign policy–related committees of Congress, because their foreign affairs interests typically lead them to ask to be placed on those committees, and as their seniority in the chamber rises, they stand a better chance to get those wishes fulfilled. However, those who do not serve on such relevant committees can still be entrepreneurs; they just have to use other forums for their activity. A forum available to all members of Congress is their respective chamber floor, where they can introduce legislation, introduce amendments carrying their substantive message, make speeches, and build coalitions in support of their policy views. All such entrepreneurs also have access to the media and interest groups, and they can use these contacts to press their policy concerns. Those entrepreneurs who are elected party leaders have another bit of leverage they can bring to bear for the issues they champion; they can press their party cohorts in ways other members of Congress cannot.

The examples of Bob Dole, Newt Gingrich, Trent Lott, Nancy Pelosi, William Fulbright, Jim Wright, and Charlie Wilson all illustrate congressional foreign policy entrepreneurs at work. Such entrepreneurs can be found across the entire post–World War II era. Early in the post–World War II era, they were more likely to come from the Senate than from the House, but over time that difference has eroded to the point that they are practically as likely to come from the House now as the Senate. Moreover, their numbers are growing. Over time, more members of Congress are engaging in foreign policy entrepreneurship, and as Table 7.1 shows, their policy impact can be substantial.

What motivates all these members of Congress to try to shape foreign policy? In other words, what are the inputs to the congressional foreign policy process?

What Motivates Members of Congress?

One might think that the inputs to foreign policy making are fairly obvious. Senators and representatives respond to external events that represent either opportunities for advancing US interests or threats to US national interests. However, those events are presumably the same for all, yet not all choose to get involved in foreign policy making. What motivates this smaller group to get involved? The answers can be as diverse as members of Congress themselves, but some patterns seem evident. Core values, the desire to make good policy, the desire for influence in the chamber, partisanship, and the desire for reelection can motivate members of Congress in foreign policy making.

Table 7.1 The Impact of Congressional Foreign Policy Entrepreneurs

Specific US Initiatives with Congressional Roots

The creation of the UN and what later became the European Union
Spain's inclusion in the Western alliance and NATO
Immigration restrictions during the Cold War
Cold War homeland security changes not unlike the more recent
    USA PATRIOT Act
Insistence that the space race with the Soviets be a civilian-run operation
    through the creation of NASA
The Peace Corps
Relaxing the economic embargo on Cuba
Returning control of the Panama Canal to Panama
Improving relations with both the Soviet Union and the People's Republic
    of China
Endorsing reform in UN operations, leading to a reduction in US dues to the UN
Limiting ABM systems
Pressing for an end to the Vietnam War and limiting US participation in other
    Southeast Asian conflicts
Improving US-Mexican relations
Ending private support for the Irish Republican Army
Limiting or in some cases banning US military aid to repressive military regimes
Promoting a regional peace plan for Central America
Encouraging more relief for international refugees
Sponsoring the V-22 tilt-rotor aircraft
Aiding the Afghan mujahedin
Cutting funds for the intervention in Somalia
Pushing for the creation of an International Criminal Court but repudiating it later,
    when its actions would not be subject to UN Security Council authorization
Saving Mexico's economy by finding a formula to bail out the peso
Ensuring the return of looted Jewish artworks by the Swiss government
Promoting World Bank funding of HIV/AIDS programs
Calling attention to Russian-Iranian missile technology trade
Promoting the protection of Bosnian Muslims
Pressing for the recognition of the People's Republic of Vietnam
Making humanitarian relief supplies exempt from economic embargoes
Abolishing the Arms Control and Disarmament Agency and the
    US Information Agency as separate entities and rolling their functions
    into the State Department
Pushing for sanctions on Iran over its nuclear and missile programs
Proposing the enlargement of NATO
Promoting reforms in how the International Monetary Fund operates
Finding the diplomatic formula to end the Kosovo War
Promoting national missile defense
Limiting funding for international agencies that allow the use of abortions
Banning the trade in "conflict diamonds"

Source: Ralph G. Carter and James M. Scott, *Choosing to Lead: Understanding Congressional Foreign Policy Entrepreneurs* (Durham, NC: Duke University Press, 2009).

Core Values

A primary motivator for members of Congress to become engaged in foreign policy making is often their core values. As former House Speaker Jim Wright (D-TX) once noted, members of Congress are motivated because "they have convictions."[3] Such convictions might be based on their political ideology. For example, more conservative members of Congress might press for foreign policy initiatives that emphasize free-market principles in international politics, "peace through strength" approaches to national security, or protection of US national sovereignty whenever it seems threatened. More liberal members of Congress might press for more cooperative efforts to solving common problems, working with and through international organizations to meet global needs, or spending somewhat less on the defense budget and somewhat more on foreign assistance.

Another aspect of core values involves personal experiences. We are all shaped by our pasts, and members of Congress are no different. As Speaker Wright said in an interview, his generation was shaped by participation in World War II. He noted that many members of Congress who served in combat abroad (as he did) came home with no illusions about how events far from the United States could have profound repercussions back home.[4] Similar life-shaping experiences were shared by Korean War veterans such as Representatives John Conyers (D-CA) and Charles Rangel (D-NY),[5] and the same can be said for such Vietnam veterans as Senators Chuck Hagel (R-NE), John Kerry (D-MA), and John McCain (R-AZ). We have already begun to see Iraq and Afghanistan war veterans—for example, army helicopter pilot and Purple Heart recipient Senator Tammy Duckworth (D-IL) and a former Navy SEAL, Representative Scott Taylor (R-VA), just to name two—elected to Congress. Nineteen military veterans were elected to Congress in 2018 and so the veteran experience will likely grow in shaping foreign policy in the future.

Beyond wartime or other military service, additional personal experiences often shape an interest in, or approach to, foreign policy. For Senator Christopher Dodd (D-CT), serving as a Peace Corps volunteer in the Dominican Republic sensitized him to the needs of Latin Americans. In addition to his Vietnam War service, for Hagel it was his prior career in international telecommunication sales.[6] For then senator Barack Obama (D-IL), it was his career as a community organizer. In addition to his combat service in World War II, for Representative Henry Reuss (D-WI), it was his role as an administrator in occupied Germany after the war. Experiences such as these shape people in ways that become part of their core values.

Family experiences play a similar role in shaping core values. Members of Congress whose families come from immigrant backgrounds often retain an interest in the old country. That was as true for Irish Americans such as former House Speaker Thomas P. "Tip" O'Neill (D-MA) and former senator Ted Kennedy (D-MA) as it was for such Cuban Americans as Representatives Ileana Ros-Lehtinen and Lincoln Diaz-Balart (both R-FL), or Senator Robert Menendez (D-NJ). Former representative and later senator Jacob Javits (R-NY) often noted that his family's history of immigrant status made him more sympathetic to the needs of immigrants and refugees everywhere.[7]

Desire to Make Good Policy

Another motivating factor for members of Congress is their personal desire to make good policy.[8] One might assume that this motivates all members of Congress, but, to be candid, some are more motivated by ensuring their chances for reelection than by engaging in good public policy making (not shocking, but still sad to say). Those who choose to take on foreign policy issues often want to be part of the solution to the country's problems, not part of the problems themselves. To know what policies will be good in a particular situation, members of Congress will rely on their own values, ideas, and predispositions, on the advice of their own or committee staff members, on the cues given to them by other members of Congress known to be expert in that subject area, and on what they learn through the media.[9]

Several of these cue-givers deserve special mention. The views of their own office or committee staff members who have earned a reputation for expertise on that subject will generally be taken seriously by members of Congress, as will some of the "talking head" experts seen on television. Particularly important cue-givers are those other members of the House or Senate who have developed a reputation for their relevant expertise. In foreign policy matters,

Republican senator Richard Lugar of Indiana earned such a reputation. For years, many members from both major parties in both congressional chambers would wait until Lugar announced his position on an issue, then taking their cue from his announcement. That way they had the benefit of his expertise and were spared the effort of becoming more expert themselves.

Desire for Influence in the Chamber

Desire for influence in Congress is another motivating factor for members of Congress. Every legislator who desires to be reelected probably cares about domestic policy, as the public pays close attention to it. Thus, there are potentially 435 domestic policy "experts" in the House and 100 in the Senate. However, fewer members of the public pay close attention to foreign policy, and thus fewer members of Congress generally invest their scarce time resources in developing foreign policy expertise. As shown by the example of Senator Lugar, developing a reputation of expertise gains respect from one's peers in Congress and with it comes broader influence in Congress.

Yet Senator Lugar is far from the only example of such respect given to members of Congress resulting from their command of policy details. Former Senate Foreign Relations Committee chairman John Kerry (D-MA) was widely respected for his general foreign policy expertise (and served several times as a diplomatic messenger for the Obama administration to Afghan president Hamid Karzai; such knowledge and roles helped him get appointed secretary of state, succeeding Hillary Clinton); Senator John McCain (R-AZ) was often looked to for advice on military matters; Chairwoman Ileana Ros-Lehtinen (R-FL) of the House Foreign Affairs Committee was an expert on Cuba-related issues, and her colleague on the committee Christopher Smith (R-NJ) was well known for his knowledge of international adoption and abortion-related issues.

Partisanship

Another important motivator of members of Congress is the push and pull of partisanship. Congress is a highly partisan body because the control of its chambers and its formal distribution of power are based on party membership. The party with the most members in each chamber—the majority party—controls that chamber, which means it has more of its members on every committee and subcommittee, its members serve as the chairs of all committees and subcommittees, and its elected party leaders control the chamber's agenda and schedule. Therefore, members of the majority party in both the House and the Senate are structurally well positioned to advance their own policy agendas. In the House, they have the potential votes to accomplish any goal they set, if all the majority party members vote together. In the Senate, they may need some help from the other side of the aisle if they don't have a sixty-seat majority. Still, as long as they can convince their fellow co-partisans to go along (which is not always as easy as it may sound), they can usually pass legislation and otherwise act in the name of the chamber.

Partisanship matters in another practical way as well. There is the president's party label to consider. Of course, members of Congress desire to get things done, but there is an additional partisan motivation to help a president who is a member of their political party. If the president and the legislator are from the same party, then by acting together they can help each other look good to the American public. At least to some degree, they may share electoral fortunes. Popular presidents may help get other members of their party elected to Congress, and the power of this factor was seen in the number of members of Congress who initially expressed doubts about Donald Trump as a presidential candidate but then moved in the direction of his policy agenda once he was elected.

Conversely, being a member of the nonpresidential party matters as well. Although one might hope that some objective measure of the national interest overrides all other considerations when members of Congress are deciding how to act on a foreign policy matter, history shows that the bipartisan era—when members of Congress put aside their partisanship and worked closely with the president to present a united front to the rest of the world—largely ended in the 1950s. Since then, members of Congress from the nonpresidential party tend to be quicker to oppose a presidential initiative in foreign policy than is the case with members of Congress from the president's own party. Even when opposition party members of Congress share a president's foreign policy goal, they may prefer other means by which to achieve it than the course of action the president recommends. For most issues in Congress, the best predictor of how members of Congress will vote is whether they share the president's party label.

Beginning in the 1990s, partisanship became so pronounced in Washington, DC, that cooperating with members of the other party was often seen as a sign of disloyalty by some elected officials. Although this development has sometimes proven toxic to effective government, often leading to legislative gridlock when Congress and the presidency are controlled by different parties, partisanship need not necessarily be a bad thing. By carefully scrutinizing a president's foreign policy requests and initiatives, the opposition party may be in a position to uncover any weaknesses or flaws in those proposals. If weaknesses are identified and are corrected, sounder US foreign policies may be the result.

Desire for Reelection

Finally, many would argue that the most important motivator of almost all members of Congress is getting reelected, and attending to the needs of one's constituents is a very good way to help get reelected. Although some members of Congress claim that foreign policy has no natural constituency (as in "Afghanistan is not in my district"), at times clear constituency concerns are evident.

Take foreign aid, for example. Most US foreign aid is conditional in nature. If the United States provides foreign aid to Kenya in the form of loans for agricultural investment and Kenya chooses to purchase farm equipment and fertilizer with those funds, the farm equipment and fertilizer must be purchased from US companies. Such a condition is routinely inserted into foreign aid bills. Thus, for members of Congress with manufacturers of farm equipment and fertilizer in their districts, supporting that foreign aid bill means good business for some constituents back home. Similarly, US food aid means more sales for US farmers, medical aid means more sales for the pharmaceutical and medical-equipment industries, military assistance means more sales for defense contractors, and so on. Members of Congress are well aware of such businesses in their districts or states.

In addition to the many economic groups that might benefit from a US foreign policy decision, some constituents may have a personal interest in US foreign policy toward a particular country, region, or issue. As noted earlier, Americans with immigrant roots might have a continuing interest in the old country, so Irish Americans may care more about US policy impacting Ireland or Northern Ireland than do others in that district. It was not surprising, then, that the lead roles in getting the Irish American community to stop contributing money to the Irish Republican Army, money that allowed it to carry on its war with British police and troops in Northern Ireland, were played by two Irish American members of Congress—House Speaker Tip O'Neill (D-MA) and Senator Ted Kennedy (D-MA). Similar policy connections can be found for Italian Americans, Greek Americans, Armenian Americans, Mexican Americans, Indian Americans, and so on, regarding policies impacting their families' countries of origin. They may care more in general, or they may still have relatives in those countries. More broadly, Latin Americans may have a greater interest in the entire Latin American region, and those originally from Cuba, Haiti, the Dominican Republic, and elsewhere might care more about US policy toward the Caribbean region. Finally, there are some citizens who simply care about a particular issue and press their legislator to act in the direction of their preferences. That issue might be AIDS/HIV relief in Africa, the proliferation of nuclear weapons globally, the environment, protecting the rights of women and children, ensuring religious freedom abroad, or global monetary policy, to name a few such issues.

These constituency influences on members of Congress can work in several ways. The norm of representation suggests that members of Congress should care to act on the interests of the public back home. Those local concerns are often articulated and conveyed to members of Congress by representatives of that concerned group of citizens—via personal contacts; phone, fax, email, Facebook and Twitter communications; letters; and more indirect methods such as advertisements in or letters to the editor of the local paper. Sometimes political advertising is used. Years ago, there was a very prominent billboard on the side of the highway leading out of the Des Moines, Iowa, airport. It simply read "Get the United States Out of the UN!" Obviously, someone cared enough to pay for such a sign placed where elected officials who fly in and out of that airport could not fail to see it. If members of Congress know that a group back home cares about a particular issue, they may anticipate the positions likely to be taken on those issues by their constituents and move in that preferred direction without waiting to receive such a request. In that way, they have anticipated the reaction of constituents even before the constituents have acted. Even if members of Congress do not always share their constituents' views, they do care about reelection. That provides another motivation to be responsive to the desires of organized groups back home.

How do these inputs turn into policy outputs on Capitol Hill? There are multiple processes used by members of Congress in this regard.

Processes of Congressional Influence

How does Congress actually make foreign policy? The most obvious way is to dictate foreign policy through legislation, but that is only one means Congress has at its disposal. There are four broad processes or avenues members of Congress use to make or influence foreign policy.[10] Think of it this way: First, congressional action can be direct or indirect. Direct actions are specific to a particular issue; indirect actions are less specific but seek to impact the broader policy context involved. Second, actions can be legislative or nonlegislative. Legislative actions seek to pass a particular piece of legislation—a bill or an amendment—whereas in the short run, nonlegislative actions do not. Combining these dichotomies produces four different avenues of congressional activity: direct-legislative processes, direct-nonlegislative processes, indirect-legislative processes, and indirect-nonlegislative processes. Direct-legislative processes involve passing bills that could include authorizations to act, appropriations of money, Senate approval of treaties, and so on. Direct-nonlegislative processes involve holding hearings, engaging in oversight activities, communicating with other policy makers in the executive branch, or even filing lawsuits in court. Indirect-legislative processes involve passing procedural legislation or passing nonbinding legislation to indicate the will of Congress on an issue, senators approving foreign policy personnel appointments, and so on. Indirect-nonlegislative processes involve trying to set the government's agenda, framing the debate regarding a substantive issue, making contacts with foreign officials, and other such actions.

Direct-Legislative Processes

Direct-legislative processes are the most obvious way members of Congress make foreign policy. Congress passes bills that make or shape foreign policy, such as authorizing the use of force, imposing economic sanctions, changing immigration laws, changing laws to improve homeland security, dictating import and export policies, and approving or not approving treaties. Members of Congress attend to these matters as political circumstances in the international or domestic environments dictate or as opportunities arise.

Presidents at times take credit for the legislative initiatives that members of Congress undertake. A good example concerns the Peace Corps, through which US civilians volunteer to help people in other countries, thereby improving the local quality of life while improving the reputation and image of the United States in the process. The idea for the Peace Corps came from Henry Reuss, a Wisconsin Democrat representing Milwaukee who introduced a bill in the House of Representatives to establish a civilian volunteer agency. A journalist told the then-presidential candidate John F. Kennedy about Reuss's idea, and Kennedy later proposed it in a campaign speech. After being elected president, Kennedy created the Peace Corps by an executive order, but Reuss and Minnesota Democratic senator Hubert H. Humphrey got the necessary legislation passed, authorizing the Peace Corps as an ongoing entity with a regular budget.[11] The president got the political credit for the Peace Corps, but Reuss and Humphrey did the heavy lifting that institutionalized it.

Because of constitutional requirements, some governmental matters dictate a significant congressional role. The greatest of these concerns government expenditures of funds. The president proposes a budget each year, but it is the Congress that first authorizes how much money may be spent for each specific purpose each year and then provides the actual money to be spent. Without such budgeted funds, the government literally cannot function. Employees cannot be paid and programs cannot be implemented without funding. Thus, Congress's "power of the purse" is a tremendously significant direct-legislative process, because by appropriating money, Congress makes things happen, and vice versa.

Members of Congress are opportunistic in using their power of the purse to fund the policies they like and to minimize or end undesired policies by starving them of funds. For example, for years members of Congress appropriated more money for the national guard than what presidents requested. National guard units were based back home, and thus the money was going back to local constituencies in terms of new jobs, new construction projects, better weapons or equipment for those in the guard, and so on. Keeping the folks back home happy was a good way for members of Congress to get reelected. Sometimes, members of Congress just had an idea they wanted to push, as with Newt Gingrich inserting unrequested money into the Intelligence Community's budget to destabilize the government of Iran or Charlie Wilson pushing covert funds for the Afghan resistance to Soviet occupiers. On the other hand, cutting off funding is a sure way to kill an initiative. That is how US participation in the Vietnam War ended. In the early 1970s, Congress made it clear to President Richard Nixon that it would cut off funding for the war. Nixon reluctantly heeded the warning and directed negotiators to sign a peace agreement with the North Vietnamese in early 1973. Several months later, Congress passed the final version of the legislation cutting off funding for the war, thereby preventing any change of heart by the president. Many such presidential initiatives have been killed by Congress, either by refusing to authorize or fund the initiative or by threatening to do so. Time will tell if the extended border wall with Mexico requested by President Trump will be added to this list of things presidents did not get from Congress.

Direct-Nonlegislative Processes

Yet direct-legislative processes are not the only way members of Congress influence foreign policy. By pursuing direct-nonlegislative means, members of Congress influence policy without resorting to legislation. Another example involving President Kennedy illustrates this avenue. One of Kennedy's most iconic moments as president was his "I am a Berliner" speech, made in West Berlin during the 1961 crisis with the Soviet Union. In that speech, he showed solidarity with the beleaguered people of West Berlin and demonstrated to the Soviet Union's leadership that he would not back down in the Cold War. The idea for such a speech, and the general content to be included in it, came from Henry Reuss. Before he went there, Kennedy sought out Reuss for his advice, as a German American, about what Kennedy should stress while in West Berlin. Reuss told Kennedy what he thought the president should say, and the rest is history.[12]

Beyond consulting or advising activities, another example of direct-nonlegislative processes is congressional hearings. Members of Congress in charge of congressional standing committees or their subcommittees often call hearings to set the stage for later policy changes or to pressure the administration regarding current policies. Through the latter half of the 1960s, one of the ways Democratically controlled Congresses kept pressure on the president to end the Vietnam War was to hold hearings on the conduct of the war, what its objectives were, the prospects for victory, and so on. Such hearings became forums in which the arguments for and against continued US involvement in the war could be raised.

Congressional oversight is another type of direct-nonlegislative process. Because they authorize and fund governmental programs and agencies, members of Congress can periodically investigate those programs and agencies to ensure that they are effectively run and doing what Congress intended. Sometimes such investigations can have embarrassing consequences for the administration. For example, in the late 1960s and early 1970s, rumors began to circulate that the Intelligence Community had engaged in a variety of unsavory actions that seemed to contravene traditional US values. Newspaper accounts reported some of what had been rumored, such as assassination plots against foreign rulers, support for military regimes with repressive human rights records, and illegal spying activities conducted in the United States against US citizens. Both the House and the Senate created committees to investigate these reports. The Senate committee produced a record of governmental behaviors that shocked many Americans and led its chairman, Senator Frank Church (D-ID), to compare the CIA to a "rogue elephant on a rampage."[13] The committee's final report called for the creation of permanent intelligence committees in Congress to oversee the Intelligence Community, prior notification to those committees of covert operations, publication of the annual total budget for the Intelligence Community, and an end to support for repressive regimes. A number of these recommendations were later enacted into policy.

More recently during the Trump administration, both the House and Senate intelligence committees held oversight hearings on the nature of the Russian intervention in the 2016 election. The two Republican-controlled committees looked at much of the same material and heard from many of the same witnesses but surprisingly issued differing judgments on whether the intervention had occurred. The Senate committee upheld the judgment of the Intelligence Community that Russia had interfered with the election, whereas its House counterpart questioned that conclusion.

As noted earlier, although they are somewhat rare, lawsuits can be a direct-nonlegislative method of congressional influence on foreign policy making as well. Senator Goldwater's lawsuit against the Carter administration's change of policy regarding Taiwan is a well-known illustration. More recently, 200 congressional Democrats filed a lawsuit against President Trump, arguing that the Trump Organization's operation of the Trump International Hotel in Washington, DC, violated the Constitution's emoluments clause. That clause was meant to keep federal officials from accepting gifts from foreign entities, as such gifts might influence US policies. When traveling to Washington following President Trump's inauguration, numerous foreign governments chose to rent rooms in Trump's Washington hotel rather than in other hotels in the area. The question becomes: were they attempting to gain favorable treatment from the president?

Thus, Congress will use both direct/legislative and direct/nonlegislative means to push and prod presidents, thereby shaping foreign policy, as illustrated in Box 7.1.

Indirect-Legislative Processes

Indirect-legislative processes are available to Congress as well. Sometimes nonbinding legislation sends important signals to the president or other executive branch actors. For instance, in 1997 the Senate put an immediate stop to any serious US consideration of the Kyoto Protocol to the UN Framework Convention on Climate Change, a treaty that would have required the United States to reduce significantly its fossil fuel emissions. A nonbinding "sense of the Senate" resolution was passed, which opposed the treaty because it required developed countries to cut their fossil fuel emissions but exempted developing countries from having to reduce their emissions. Not only did this seem unfair, but sharp cuts in fossil fuel emissions would curtail considerable economic

Box 7.1 The Power to Deny and Compel

In many ways, the easiest power for Congress to utilize is the power to say no in order to prevent presidential overreach. As President Barack Obama learned, such negative power can be manifested in a variety of ways.

Despite reopening diplomatic relations with Cuba, Obama never asked Congress to repeal the economic embargo against that regime. The reason is simple; members of Congress made it clear he did not have the votes. Congressional opposition also forced Obama to agree to climate-control agreements with other countries that were only voluntary—not mandatory—and were executive agreements rather than binding treaties. The Senate refused to consider the Trans-Pacific Partnership agreement, a trade agreement the Obama administration negotiated and strongly endorsed. As noted earlier, Congress refused to authorize military strikes against Syria's use of chemical weapons, and Congress refused Secretary of Defense Robert Gates's request to reshape the defense budget to emphasize the items needed to fight terrorist insurgencies and deemphasize "big ticket" weapons systems.

In his first two years with a Congress totally controlled by his own political party, President Donald Trump rarely got such pushback against his proposals. However, one major congressional initiative was forced upon his administration. President Trump made it clear he thought prior economic sanctions against Russia were a bad idea, and he waited over a year to implement the sanctions that President Obama had initiated via executive order in late 2016. He also did not want Russia further sanctioned for its intervention in the 2016 election. However, many legislators felt that Obama's sanctions did not go far enough, and in 2017, Congress passed the Countering America's Adversaries Through Sanctions Act. This legislation included the sanctions on Iran and North Korea that Trump desired, but it also included new sanctions on Russia that President Trump vehemently opposed and sought to get dropped from the bill. The bill also prevented the president from ending such sanctions without a congressional vote on the matter. The bill passed the House by a 419–3 vote, and the Senate by a 98–2 vote. Because the bill passed with an overwhelming, veto-proof majority in both chambers, Trump was compelled to sign the bill or look weak by having his veto overridden. He angrily signed it but missed the congressionally imposed deadline for its implementation by almost a month. It's also telling that after two years with a Republican-controlled Congress, Trump was unable to get funding for his border wall with Mexico. When he challenged the newly seated Democratically controlled House of Representatives by shutting down the government to get funding for his border wall, Speaker Nancy Pelosi said no. After a thirty-five-day partial shutdown, Trump was forced to reopen the government on conditions congressional Democrats had previously supported. So, although presidents are the single most powerful actors in making US foreign policy, they are far from omnipotent. The typical view from the White House is that Congress either keeps the presidency in handcuffs in terms of what it can and cannot do in foreign policy or it at least tries to do so. Either way, presidents usually see Congress as a formidable obstacle to be surmounted in making US foreign policy, as Congress can both deny and compel most administrative actions if it so chooses.

Source:

Conor Finnegan, "Timeline of Trump's Delays on Russia Sanctions," *ABC News,* October 27, 2017, https://abcnews.go.com/Politics/timeline-trumps -delays-russia-sanctions/story?id=50733408.

activity and harm the US economy. The fact that the resolution passed by a vote of 95–0 indicated that the Kyoto Protocol had *no chance,* as written, to gain Senate approval. The United States still has not joined the Kyoto Protocol. A more recent example came in 2018 when Senator Lindsey Graham (R-SC) introduced a sense of the Senate resolution calling on President Trump to continue US military activities in Syria following Trump's pledge to remove US troops from Syrian battlefields. The resolution effectively died when Senator Rand Paul (R-KY) put a "hold" on it, saying military hawks in the Senate needed to be stopped.

Procedural legislation is another form of indirect-legislative process. Congressional investigations in the 1970s discovered that the Nixon administration had made secret commitments to other governments, often in the form of arms sales that implied a long-term commitment to stand by that customer. Thus, in 1976, Congress passed the Arms Export Control Act. Since then, the act has been amended to keep up with changing times, but it now requires the administration to inform Congress thirty days in advance of any proposed sales of major defense equipment valued at $14 million or more, of defense articles or services valued at $50 million or more, and design and construction services valued at $200 million or more. In this way, Congress has a chance to reject the sales—and the closer ties with that regime—if members so desire.[14]

Trade provides another example. For years Congress mandated that "most favored nation status," or what is now called **normal trade status**, would be granted to the People's Republic of China only on a year-to-year basis. Thus, Congress created a procedure that allowed members of Congress annually to criticize China's economic practices, measures that worked to the detriment of American workers. Such Chinese practices included a currency kept arbitrarily low in value to promote Chinese exports, underpaid workers, poor working conditions, and environmental damage in the name of economic growth. Others broadened the debate to criticize the Chinese Communist regime for its repression of Christians, dissidents, practitioners of Falun Gong/Falun Dafa, use of abortion to control population growth, and so on. In the end, China's most favored nation status got approved each year, but many members of Congress believed the annual outpouring of criticism kept pressure on China and prevented it from pursuing even more reprehensible behavior.[15] This annual process of certifying China's trade status ended with China's 2001 entry into the World Trade Organization, which grants most favored nation status to all members.

A final form of indirect-legislative process involves approving personnel appointments. The Senate is required to approve many top executive branch appointees, for example, cabinet secretaries and ambassadors. Most of the time the Senate approves the president's choices for office, but because some of these appointments carry clear policy implications, the Senate will occasionally say no. In 1989, the Senate rejected the nomination of Senator John

Tower (R-TX) as secretary of defense. Although many senators cited Tower's personal failings as the reason for their negative vote, at least some were concerned that he would have too much influence over his former protégé, President George H. W. Bush, who often noted Tower as his mentor. An even more clear-cut example of policy differences came with the refusal of the Senate to consider John Bolton to be the US ambassador to the United Nations for President George W. Bush, as Bolton was considered by many to be a virtual enemy of the institution in which he would be serving. Rather than totally give up on his nomination, President Bush made Bolton a "recess appointment," which meant he could hold the job on a temporary basis only until that session of Congress ended seventeen months later. In this case, both sides scored a partial victory: The president got Bolton in that role at least for a while, but the Senate prevented Bolton from getting the job for the rest of the president's term of office. Sometimes the Senate confirmation process can preview difficulties to come. As secretary of state nominee, Rex Tillerson's confirmation hearings foretold the future. In those hearings, he expressed views that differed from President Trump's stated views on the need for sanctions for Russia's intervention in the 2016 presidential election, Russia's takeover of Crimea from Ukraine, nuclear proliferation by US allies, and the value of the proposed Trans-Pacific Partnership trade agreement. Not surprisingly, Tillerson lasted only thirteen months in that role before Trump dismissed him.

Indirect-Nonlegislative Processes

The final avenue for congressional foreign policy roles involves indirect-nonlegislative processes. A major effort that fits here is agenda setting. Literally, this involves getting the government to deal with the issues Congress wants addressed. National missile defense provides a good example. The 1995 Republican "Contract with America" called for the establishment of an NMD system, and Republicans in both the House and the Senate pressed the Clinton administration to do more to create a defensive system to protect the United States from missile attack. Following hundreds of speeches and years of pressure on the reluctant administration, Congress was able to muster the votes to pass the National Missile Defense Act in 1999.

Another example concerns climate change. Despite the opposition of President George W. Bush to significant climate change legislation, in 2006 House Speaker Nancy Pelosi (D-CA) vowed to keep the pressure on by forming the House Select Committee on Energy Independence and Global Warming. Led by Representative Ed Markey (D-MA), the committee held numerous hearings on global climate change and its impacts on the United States. As a result of such pressure, before his term ended President Bush was willing to consider legislation that at least set "aspirational" (i.e., nonbinding) goals for reductions in fossil fuel emissions.

However, the record for long-term efforts to set the governmental agenda might go to former senator William Proxmire (D-WI). Beginning in 1967, Proxmire made a speech on the Senate floor virtually every day the Senate was in session, pressing for the US ratification of the Genocide Convention. When it was finally approved twenty years later, he had given over 3,000 floor speeches to ensure that the Senate did not forget about this treaty.[16]

Framing debate is another indirect-nonlegislative process. This refers to casting or "branding" the terms of a debate in ways that help one side over the other. This tactic is well illustrated by the actions of Representative Chris Smith (R-NJ), who continually cast the "most favored nation" debate on China in terms of "supporting baby killers," thus explicitly linking China's abortion policies to a trade issue. Similarly, congressional supporters of military aid for Colombia continually stressed that the aid is part of a "war on drugs" in the United States. As a consequence, those legislators who said the aid strengthened a repressive regime guilty of human rights violations then had to protect themselves back at home from charges of being "soft on drugs," and they lost the debate.

A final example of indirect-nonlegislative processes involves contacts with foreign leaders. By meeting foreign leaders and giving them a favorable audience, members of Congress can push administrations to do more on certain issues. In the 1980s, House Speaker Jim Wright (D-TX) used his contacts with Costa Rican president Óscar Arias to continually press for US support of a Central American peace plan. Arias went on to win the Nobel Peace Prize for his role in ending the conflict in Central America. Multiple presidents have had difficulty pressing Israeli governments to make concessions in return for peace with the Palestinians. Yet when Israeli leaders come to Washington, they are showered with support by members of Congress who tell them, as Speaker Pelosi did in 2010, "We in Congress stand by Israel," which undercuts the administration's position.[17] In 2015, House Speaker John Boehner (R-OH) violated normal protocol by inviting Israeli prime minister Benjamin Netanyahu to come speak to Congress without first clearing the invitation with the Obama administration. Boehner's goal was to use Netanyahu's address as a way to frame the Iran nuclear deal in negative terms and keep the issue on the government's agenda. President Obama signaled his displeasure by refusing to meet with Netanyahu during his visit.

Obviously, some members of Congress prefer some of these four processes of congressional activity more than others, whereas some often move back and forth seamlessly between them. Some issues illustrate multiple processes over time as well, as illustrated in Box 7.2. However, the most interesting question is how much impact Congress and its members have had in shaping US foreign policy.

Congressional Foreign Policy Influence

In the end, then, how much influence does Congress have over US foreign policy making? The short answer is: *as much as its members desire.* As already noted, Chapter 4, Congress has an impressive array of constitutional powers in the realm of foreign policy. Congress can influence almost any aspect of US foreign policy by what it chooses to authorize, to fund, and to mandate the administration to do or by how it chooses to shape the public debate.

Historically, Congress has authorized and funded the basic governmental structures that implement and administer foreign policy—from cabinet departments such as the Departments of State, of Defense, and of Homeland Security, to such agencies as the CIA and the NSA, to presidential advisory bodies such as the National Security Council (and staff) and the National Economic Council (and staff). Just as Congress can create such entities, it can also terminate them, as it did with the US Information Agency, or submerge them in a larger entity, as it did by changing the Arms Control and Disarmament Agency from an independent agency to a subsidiary unit of the State Department, both cases coming at the insistence of one member of Congress—Senator Jesse Helms (R-NC)—in the late 1990s.

Box 7.2 Congressional Pressures on the Trump Administration

Normally, one would assume a new administration entering office, with a Congress controlled by the same party, would have an easier path to making and implementing foreign policy. President Trump generally found support in the Republican-controlled Congress to back away from the Trans-Pacific Partnership trade agreement, withdraw from the Iran nuclear deal, and repudiate the Paris Agreement, just to name a few examples. However, President Trump's stances on Russian relations—and on pushing policy positions favoring Russian interests—generated a variety of resistance measures by members of Congress that featured a mix of congressional approaches.

As noted in Box 7.1, Trump neither wanted to enforce existing sanctions nor accept new sanctions on Russia for its intervention in the 2016 presidential election, but he was pressed by Congress to do so. Direct-nonlegislative pressures were employed, as leading Republicans in Congress warned President Trump not to ignore existing sanctions on Russia, and the passage of new sanctions in 2017 was a direct-legislative means to compel his actions.

Despite continually calling the investigations of Russian intervention in the 2016 election a witch hunt, congressional committees headed by Republicans held hearings on the matter. Although the House Intelligence Committee report said it had found no evidence of Russian involvement, every Democrat on that House committee rejected the report, saying the opposite was the case. Both the Republicans and Democrats on the Senate Intelligence Committee agreed that there had been Russian involvement and interference in the election. Such oversight hearings were direct-nonlegislative means to influence U.S.-Russia policy and served to keep the subject on Congress's agenda.

During the presidential campaign, Trump called the NATO alliance obsolete. When he attended his first NATO summit conference on May 25, 2017, he challenged NATO members over their defense-spending levels and pointedly refused to endorse the responsibility of the United States to come to the aid of other NATO members if they were attacked. He implied that US support would not be automatic but conditional upon the other's level of defense spending. Multiple members of Congress, for example, Senate Foreign Relations Committee Chairman Bob Corker (R-TN) and Senator Lindsey Graham (R-SC), took the direct-nonlegislative step to informally press the White House staff and President Trump to reaffirm such automatic commitment, a step that Trump reluctantly announced fifteen days later. Graham then introduced a resolution in the Senate reaffirming the US commitment to the NATO alliance and to Article 5—the automatic requirement to lend aid to an alliance member if attacked. The vote on the resolution was 100–0, a direct-legislative rebuke of the president.

Finally, President Trump's performance at the 2018 Helsinki summit with Russian president Vladimir Putin suggested a willingness to see things more from Russia's point of view and again to accept Putin's statement that Russia did not interfere in the 2016 presidential election. Trump's apparent greater faith in President Putin than in the US Intelligence Community's unanimous conclusion that Russia had interfered in the election created a political and media firestorm. As CNN reported, the "unprecedented refusal by a US president to believe his own intelligence agencies over the word of a foreign adversary . . . drew swift condemnation from across the partisan divide." After the summit, House Speaker Paul Ryan released a prepared statement noting that "there is no question that Russia interfered in our elections . . . The President must appreciate that Russia is not our ally. There is no moral equivalence between the United States and Russia, which remains hostile to our most basic values and ideals." Senate Foreign Relations Committee Chairman Corker said Trump's statements "made us look like a pushover." As a result of this mounting direct-nonlegislative pressure—often from Republicans—Trump later read a prepared statement claiming he misspoke during the post-summit press conference and that he had complete faith in the US Intelligence Community and its assessments.

Thus, Congress and its members have employed both direct-legislative and direct-nonlegislative means to challenge President Trump's statements regarding Russia. Time will tell if

(continues)

Box 7.2 Continued

this congressional pressure continues, but make no mistake: a Republican president was pushed back into a corner on an issue by a Republican-controlled Congress. It will be interesting to see how President Trump interacts with the Democratically controlled House of Representatives in 2019 and 2020.

Sources:

Jeremy Diamond, "Trump Sides with Putin over US Intelligence," *CNN,* July 16, 2018, https://www.cnn.com/2018/07/16/politics/donald-trump -putin-helsinki-summit/index.html; Pamela Engel, "Congress Is Increasingly Becoming a Counterweight to Some of Trump's More Controversial Foreign Policy Instincts," *Business Insider,* June 17, 2017, https://www .businessinsider.com/congress-trump-foreign-policy-nato-russia-saudi -arabia-2017-6; Jeremy Herb, "Trump Commits to NATO's Article 5," *CNN,* June 9, 2017, https://www.cnn.com/2017/06/09/politics/trump -commits-to-natos-article-5/index.html.

Yet on a day-to-day basis, Congress's greatest structural power is its right to appropriate funds for the programs those departments and agencies administer. As noted earlier, if its members so choose, Congress can limit or put conditions on funds for initiatives it questions (such as limiting military assistance to regimes accused of significant human rights violations), deny funds for initiatives it opposes (e.g., supporting the Contras in Nicaragua, continuing US participation in the Vietnam War, or building a wall along the entire US-Mexico border), and provide funds for causes it champions (e.g., NMD or undermining the Iranian regime). If Congress does not provide the administration with the funding it requests, it is almost impossible for an administration to continue that foreign policy initiative. In such a case, the president might be able to devote some of his limited discretionary funds to that purpose, but each year the amount of discretionary spending he is allowed is set by members of Congress, so this is a route presidents would be wise not to abuse. Alternatively, presidents could ask wealthy US allies such as Saudi Arabia to fund initiatives that Congress rejects, again a course of action presidents prefer to avoid if possible.

Not only can Congress impact the structure of government and what those foreign policy actors do, but it can also help set the basic strategic policy of the United States. In the late 1940s and early 1950s, Congress used economic aid to Spain to push the United States into a relationship with Spain's right-wing regime, a foreign policy position that President Truman opposed. However, that push by Congress helped facilitate Spain's reincorporation into the Western security alliance, which in turn served to encourage the development of a representative democracy in Spain. In the 1960s, Congress chipped away at the policy of containing communist expansion by questioning the Vietnam War, endorsing arms talks with the Soviet Union, and providing support to the communist regime in Yugoslavia. In the 1970s, Congress attacked the US practice of aiding and abetting unsavory dictators and oppressive regimes whose primary value had been that they were reliably anticommunist. In the 1980s, members of Congress supported a nuclear-freeze movement that pushed the Reagan administration closer to arms negotiations with the Soviets, and they also pressed the Reagan administration to end its support of the minority white regime in South Africa. In the 1990s, consistent congressional pressures led the Clinton administration to back away from meaningful participation in multilateral approaches to solve global problems such as prosecution of war criminals or slowing the rate of global climate change. In the 2000s, Congress banned US participation in the trade of so-called blood diamonds, the revenues from whose sale funded violent militias and other terrorist groups. Congress also pushed for deadlines to start the de-escalation of military involvement in both Iraq and Afghanistan, and, when asked by the president, it opposed US military responses to Syria's use of chemical weapons against its own citizens.

Again, the examples in this chapter show that Congress has substantial power to shape and set US foreign policy when its members choose to do so. However, there are three things presidents can do that Congress cannot equal. First, presidents are the only actors who can claim to speak for the nation as a whole. It is difficult for members of Congress to claim to speak for the entire nation when they are elected only by the citizens of their own state or district. Thus, presidents serve as the face and voice of the United States, both at home and abroad. The ability to represent the entire nation gives presidents a "bully pulpit," in the words of President Theodore Roosevelt, to act in the name of the American people.

Second, presidents alone have the sole constitutional ability to grant diplomatic recognition to other regimes, a fact Senator Barry Goldwater (R-AZ) learned when he sued President Jimmy Carter over Carter's decision to end diplomatic recognition of Taiwan and to recognize diplomatically the People's Republic of China (Communist China) instead. The Supreme Court said this constitutional power of the president was clear.

Third, as commander in chief, presidents can send troops into harm's way. Congress can then choose whether to authorize such a use of force, provide or deny funding for that use of force, publicly question the reasons behind the use of force, and perhaps vote on a formal declaration of war again in the future, but those responses typically occur well after the use of force has begun. Thus, presidents have considerable discretion to start wars, and they can create political facts by putting "boots on the ground" or bombs in the air before Congress can react. Once force has been used, presidents may count on a **rally effect**, a short-lived boost in presidential public support that makes many members of Congress reluctant to take any political actions that open them to the criticism that they do not support the troops or are disloyal in time of war.

Yet even in this instance, where presidential policy-making influence is highest, it is not without congressional constraints. A carefully conducted study on congressional checks on presidential war powers offers a powerful conclusion that even war-making decisions are never devoid of political considerations that make Congress relevant. This analysis of presidential use of force since World War II shows that

- presidents who face Congresses controlled by the opposition party send troops into harm's way less frequently than those whose political party controls at least one chamber of Congress;
- the greater the partisan opposition the president faces in Congress, the less likely a crisis is to produce a military response; and
- the greater the partisan opposition the president faces in Congress, the longer the president will wait between the onset of a crisis and an eventual use of force.[18]

The study concludes by stating: "Presidents consistently heed the distinctly political threat posed by large, cohesive, and opposing congressional majorities—a threat that is all too often latent, but that when mobilized, materially affects the president's efforts to rally public support for an ongoing deployment and to communicate the nation's foreign-policy commitments to both allies and adversaries abroad."[19]

Therefore, the degree to which Congresses challenge presidents over foreign policy making in general varies over time, by the type of issues in play, and by the partisan composition of Congress compared to the party of the presidency. Across the entire post–World War II period, the frequency of overall congressional activity in foreign policy making has generally decreased over time but *congressional assertiveness—being willing to question or challenge what the president wants—has increased over time.* From the end of World War II until around 1958, Congress was largely supportive of the president's foreign policy agenda, which was dominated by Cold War issues. From 1958 until 1967, Congress became increasingly likely to challenge the president's foreign policy wishes. Some members of Congress thought presidents were not pressing the Cold War against the Soviets enough, while others began wondering if the Cold War was necessary. From 1968 through the 1980s, Congress was both active in and assertive of its own prerogatives in foreign policy making. Thus, from the height of the Vietnam War to the end of the Cold War, Congress was quite willing to challenge presidential foreign policy initiatives. Since the end of the Cold War until the present, Congress has returned to being less active in foreign policy making but more willing to challenge the president when it decides to act.[20]

Conclusion

In summary, the role of the president in making US foreign policy should never be underestimated, but neither should the congressional role be unnecessarily minimized. Congress routinely sets the legal, financial, and political parameters of what an administration can do in foreign affairs and at times determines the basic direction of the ship of state itself.

Suggested Reading

Carter, Ralph G., and James M. Scott. *Choosing to Lead: Understanding Congressional Foreign Policy Entrepreneurs.* Durham, NC: Duke University Press, 2009.

Fowler, Linda L. *Watchdogs on the Hill: The Decline of Congressional Oversight of U.S. Foreign Relations.* Princeton: Princeton University Press, 2015.

Hersman, Rebecca K. C. *Friends and Foes: How Congress and the President Really Make Foreign Policy.* Washington, DC: Brookings Institution Press, 2000.

Howell, William G., and Jon C. Pevehouse. *While Dangers Gather: Congressional Checks on Presidential War Powers.* Princeton: Princeton University Press, 2007.

Lindsay, James M. *Congress and the Politics of U.S. Foreign Policy.* Baltimore: Johns Hopkins University Press, 1994.

Notes

1. See George Crile, *Charlie Wilson's War: The Extraordinary Story of the Largest Covert Operation in History* (New York: Atlantic Monthly Press, 2003); also, these facts were confirmed in an interview Ralph Carter conducted with Charlie Wilson on September 3, 2008, at the Texas Christian University campus in Fort Worth, Texas.

2. For more on congressional foreign policy entrepreneurs, see Ralph G. Carter and James M. Scott, *Choosing to Lead: Understanding Congressional Foreign Policy Entrepreneurs* (Durham, NC: Duke University Press, 2009).

3. Interview with the author, Fort Worth, Texas, November 20, 2001.

4. Ibid.

5. Nancy Pelosi, "Pelosi Remarks at Congressional Ceremony Commemorating the 60th Anniversary of the Korean War," Nancy Pelosi website, June 24, 2010, https://pelosi.house.gov/news/press-releases /pelosi-remarks-at-congressional-ceremony-commemorating-the-60th -anniversary-of.

6. Carter and Scott, *Choosing to Lead.*

7. Ibid.

8. See Richard F. Fenno, *Congressmen in Committees* (Boston: Little, Brown, 1973).

9. For more on these policy cue-givers, see John W. Kingdon, *Congressmen's Voting Decisions,* 3rd ed. (Ann Arbor: University of Michigan Press, 1989).

10. For more on these four avenues, see Carter and Scott, *Choosing to Lead.*

11. For more on this, see Henry S. Reuss, *When Government Was Good: Memories of a Life in Politics* (Madison: University of Wisconsin Press, 1999).

12. Ibid.

13. Loch K. Johnson, *A Season of Inquiry: The Senate Intelligence Investigation* (Lexington: University Press of Kentucky, 1985), 57.

14. Richard F. Grimmitt, "Arms Sales: Congressional Review Process," *Congressional Research Service Report for Congress,* January 8, 2010, RL31675.

15. See Steven W. Hook and Franklin Barr Lebo, "U.S.-China Trade Relations: Privatizing Foreign Policy," in *Contemporary Cases in U.S. Foreign Policy: From Terrorism to Trade,* 5th ed., ed. Ralph G. Carter (Washington, DC: CQ Press, 2014).

16. For more on these efforts, see Carter and Scott, *Choosing to Lead.*

17. Youtube, https://www.youtube.com/watch?v=dCrjGXb2ekM.

18. William G. Howell and Jon C. Pevehouse, *While Dangers Gather: Congressional Checks on Presidential War Powers* (Princeton: Princeton University Press, 2007).

19. Ibid., 222.

20. James M. Scott and Ralph G. Carter, "Acting on the Hill: Congressional Assertiveness in U.S. Foreign Policy," *Congress and the Presidency* 29 (2002): 151–169.

8

The Role of
Societal Actors

Learning Objectives

- Explain how a pluralist policy process differs from governmental policy processes.
- Name the different types of domestic actors in foreign policy making.
- Identify the ways political culture and public attitudes and opinion can influence policy makers.
- Assess which governmental policy makers may be most open to domestic foreign policy influences.

In a democracy, the consideration of the public's wants and needs takes on considerable importance. But who composes the public, and what shapes people's thinking about foreign policy? These are important questions, and the answers are not always self-evident. Moreover, as members of the public are by definition not government officials themselves, they must find ways to influence those officials who can directly make the decisions that shape foreign policy. The way the public engages in foreign policy making is through pluralist policy processes. Let's first focus on the nature of such processes and then on the types of actors who rely on these processes for a voice in foreign policy making. The next step is to examine the types of inputs that motivate those actors and what such actors bring to the policy process. Finally, it is necessary to examine how societal actors impact foreign policy making and the effects they have on policy—with a particular interest in the types of issues that lend themselves most to public inputs.

Pluralist Policy Processes

Up to this point, this book has concentrated on how government officials use their formal and informal powers to make US foreign policy. But the United States is a democracy, which raises the question of how the public's views are considered in policy making. An idealized vision of democratic foreign policy making can easily be described. Knowing that they are affected by foreign policy (in terms of the external events, threats, and opportunities facing the country), in an ideal world US citizens would care about these matters, think about them, and convey their thoughts to their elected officials, who would then heed the public's input in foreign policy making to do what contributes to the greater good. The question becomes, to what extent does that really happen?

Most observers would say "not often." There are several reasons that this idealized version of public participation is rarely met. First, most Americans are not that informed about foreign policy. At best, perhaps one-fourth of the US public actually keeps up with foreign policy news and events on a consistent basis.[1] Most Americans are too busy focusing on their own lives, interests, and responsibilities to take the time needed to educate themselves on foreign policy issues.

Second, if Americans did take the time to educate themselves on foreign policy issues, the process of communicating their ideas to elected officials is not easy. If they want to go beyond contacting the White House (via mail, phone, fax, email, Facebook, Twitter, and so forth), citizens must identify at least one or more of the three members of Congress who represent them—the two senators and the one representative. They may also decide to contact even more members of Congress to make sure their message gets out. Then they must determine how best to contact these officials—again, by letter, phone, fax, email, Facebook, Twitter, Instagram, the officials' websites, and so on. All this takes time and perseverance. Some will prefer to communicate face-to-face with elected representatives, which means getting appointments either in Washington or when the official is back home in the state or district. Anyone who has sought personal meetings with members of Congress will tell you that it usually takes weeks or even months to get on their schedule, if you can get on it at all. In the twenty-first century, many members of Congress actually refuse to meet with constituents, either in their offices or in town hall meetings. Thus, contacting one's elected representatives is neither easy nor quick, and relatively few Americans go to such effort.

So how do public sentiments get communicated to policy makers? The answer lies in the **pluralist policy process**. Starting in the 1950s, observers began talking about how individuals got their interests and sentiments expressed to relevant policy makers *through the actions of organized groups to which these individuals belonged.*

Although it takes a lot of effort for individuals to go through the steps mentioned to influence their elected representatives, group membership can make that process easier. By joining a group that shares the same interests, group members can pool their resources—for example, through group membership dues— and sponsor the effort of a few of their members (or professional **lobbyists** hired for this purpose) to communicate the group's wishes to policy makers. Thus, governmental policy is shaped through the competition of these groups in gaining the ears of government officials to persuade the officials to act as the groups prefer. If groups are effective in getting their message to the targeted policy makers and are taken seriously by policy makers, then policy makers will take the groups' views into consideration when making foreign policy.[2] Consider this a form of mediated democracy, in which the groups serve as the agents for their members, who are their principals.[3] Therefore, the essence of pluralist policy processes is that groups compete for the attention of policy makers, so that their interests get represented when decisions are made, and *there is a presumption that no one particular group dominates foreign policy decision making all the time.* This last point means that pluralism is the opposite of **elitism**, which is the idea that a small group regularly dominates foreign policy making. Admittedly, not all groups are created equal—this point should be clearly understood—and some will have more influence than others, but no one group is thought to dominate policy making. If no one group dominates foreign policy making, what types of groups get involved in this competition for influence?

Societal Actors

Four sets of societal actors routinely get involved in influencing foreign policy. One type—interest groups—comes immediately to mind. However, think tanks, the mass media, and individual opinion leaders also play important roles. These are illustrated in Figure 8.1, but as you look at it, remember that these multiple interest groups, think tanks, media outlets, and individual opinion leaders also interact with each other as they are trying to influence governmental policy makers.

Interest Groups

When citizens come together around a common interest, they can influence policy makers based on their numbers as potential vot-

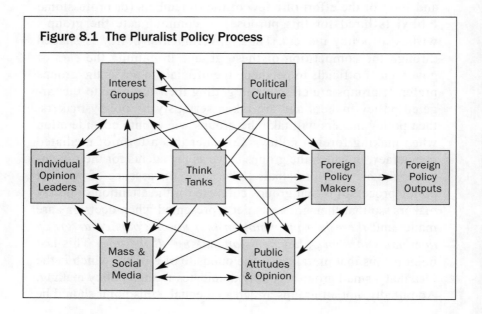

Figure 8.1 The Pluralist Policy Process

ers, the amounts of campaign contributions they may provide, their ability to get the ear of policy makers, and even their ability to get their own members elected or appointed to roles in foreign policy making. Arguably the most influential interest group in shaping US foreign policy has long been the **American Israel Public Affairs Committee (AIPAC)**. Billing itself as "America's Pro-Israel Lobby" on its website (www.aipac.org), for decades AIPAC has courted US foreign policy makers, seeking to strengthen the US-Israel relationship in ways that make each country more secure. AIPAC conducts grassroots organizing of local clubs across the country and on high school and college campuses, it promotes pro-Israeli political activists, it lobbies members of Congress, and though it does not directly contribute campaign funds to like-minded elected officials, it does facilitate the networking of campaign fund-raising activities on behalf of its 100,000 members and other friends of Israel. According to its website, AIPAC has strengthened Israeli security through support for US military assistance and sales to Israel, promoted both US and Israeli homeland security through the sharing of intelligence information, informed Americans about the threat posed by Iran, and promoted a just Middle East peace process. In 2017 alone, AIPAC pushed through Congress a $705-million missile defense system for Israel, advanced legislation targeting Hezbollah and Hamas as terrorist organizations, trained hundreds of student leaders in the United States, got a new Iran sanctions bill passed by Congress, persuaded all 100 senators to support a resolution urging the UN to end its anti-Israeli bias, and coordinated trips to Israel by fifty-seven members of Congress.

Until recently, it was hard to identify a significant foreign policy issue where AIPAC was on the losing side in Washington. However, that happened in 2015 when the Iran nuclear deal was approved over Israel's and AIPAC's objections. AIPAC spent tens of millions of dollars in television advertising against the nuclear deal, sent members of Congress to Israel to learn why the deal was flawed, and organized grassroots town hall meetings and demonstrations against the deal. However, all this effort could not overcome the Obama administration's support for the Iran nuclear deal, and the administration was aided by the efforts of a newer Jewish American lobbying group—J Street—which supported the deal. Over time, AIPAC has had its share of critics as well. Some members of Congress claimed that they were voted out of office at the insistence of AIPAC because the members of Congress were not seen as sufficiently pro-Israel. Other critics argue that AIPAC supports morally unacceptable Israeli security policies, makes the United States indirectly complicit in war crimes, disenfranchises the Palestinian people, and suggests that any criticism of Israel represents a victory for terrorism.

Despite such criticism, there seems little doubt that AIPAC wields considerable influence in Washington, so much so that J Street was created to attempt to offset it. Still, AIPAC has served as a model organization for others seeking similar influence. For example, leaders in the Indian American community sought to model the US-India Political Action Committee on AIPAC as much as they could. Surely, others have as well.

In a democracy where all have the legal right to petition their government for the redress of grievances, well-organized and well-funded interest groups may be important players in shaping US foreign policy. They become even more influential when they informally form alliances with bureaucratic agencies and members of Congress who share their interests. When you get a bureaucratic agency that wants to implement a program, an interest group or set of interest groups that want to benefit from that program, and members of Congress who want to authorize and fund it, this combination is called a **subgovernment**, or iron triangle, and it can be very difficult to oppose it over the long term.[4]

An interesting example of an iron triangle comes in the area of agricultural sales. US agribusinesses continually desire new markets for their products, a desire shared by the members of Congress who represent farming constituencies and bureaucrats at the Department of Agriculture's Foreign Agricultural Service (FAS) who want to promote US agricultural sales. An underserved market for US food products can be found just ninety-five miles south of Key West, Florida. Beginning in the early 1960s, US companies were barred from doing business with Fidel Castro's Communist regime in Cuba. Yet Cuba has to import food, and watching other countries sell food to Cuba over time became painful to the US agribusiness industry. Led by agribusiness giants such as Archer Daniels Midland (ADM), US food producers began asking members of Congress and officials at FAS why these corporations had to stand idly by and watch their international competition make profits by selling food to Cuba. Consistent pressure from groups such as ADM and the officials at FAS led the largely Republican representatives and senators from such areas as the Great Plains and the Midwest in general to question why the Cuba economic embargo should apply to *humanitarian* goods like food sales. If Cuba were going to buy food from someone anyway, why should US food producers be denied a chance at this market? The Trade Sanctions Reform and Export Enhancement Act of 2000 was the result, which allowed food and other humanitarian aid to be exempted from economic sanctions.[5]

In 2001, ADM became the first US company to sign a contract with the Cuban government since the embargo began.[6] Since then, hundreds of millions of dollars in US food sales to Cuba have resulted.[7] In this case, the combined efforts of big business, consistent pressure from the FAS, and the large number of farm-state members of Congress were able to overcome the active resistance of Cuba's detractors. More generally, business-backed interest groups typically triumph over ideologically based interest groups when their positions come into direct conflict, and interest groups that are components of a subgovernment generally prevail over interest groups that are acting without such strong congressional and bureaucratic support. But interest groups are not the only types of groups active in shaping US foreign policy. Think tanks often play key roles as well.

Think Tanks

Privately funded research organizations, commonly referred to as **think tanks**, are another societal source of foreign policy input. For years, entities such as the Council on Foreign Relations, the Business Roundtable, the Brookings Institution, and the Center for Strategic and International Studies have conducted research and issued reports, and their representatives have testified before Congress and gone out into local communities to try to educate the public and policy makers on their preferred foreign policy positions. In extreme cases, think tanks can have profound influences, as shown in Box 8.1.

The number of think tanks has proliferated over time; however, focusing on just one can help illustrate the ways these entities can influence foreign policy. Perhaps the think tank with the

Box 8.1 The Project for the New American Century and the War in Iraq

Possibly the most controversial think tank influencing US foreign policy in the last half century was the **Project for the New American Century (PNAC)**. Founded in 1997 by William Kristol (editor of the *Weekly Standard* and former chief of staff for Vice President Dan Quayle) and Robert Kagan (a senior associate at the Carnegie Endowment for International Peace and a writer for the *Weekly Standard* and the *Washington Post*), it brought together a group of neoconservatives who believed the twenty-first century represented a unique opportunity. Since the United States was no longer opposed by a superpower such as the Soviet Union, PNAC members felt the United States should use its power to spread its values abroad, in short, to do good.

All think tanks benefit from getting their members placed in policy-making positions, but PNAC was extremely successful in that regard. A number of the original signers of its statement of principles went on to important policy-making posts in the George W. Bush administration. They included presidential Special Assistants Elliott Abrams and Zalmay Khalizad (who also later became ambassador to Iraq, ambassador to Afghanistan, and ambassador to the United Nations) as well as Vice President Dick Cheney and his chief of staff, Lewis ("Scooter") Libby and Deputy Assistant for National Security Affairs Aaron Friedberg. Those who moved on to the Defense Department included Secretary Donald Rumsfeld, Deputy Secretary Paul Wolfowitz, and Assistant Secretary Peter Rodman. Those who entered the State Department included Undersecretary Paula Dobriansky and State Department Counselor Eliot Cohen. Even presidential brother Jeb Bush was an original signatory of PNAC's statement of principles. Thus, members of PNAC were well placed to press their views on US foreign policy.

One of their foremost views advocated the overthrow of the Iraqi regime of Saddam Hussein. In 1998, they wrote an open letter to President Clinton calling for the removal of Saddam Hussein's regime from power in Iraq, noting that the costs of leaving him in power and accepting the risks of his regime acquiring weapons of mass destruction were greater than the costs of removing him from power by any means necessary. In addition to Rumsfeld, Wolfowitz, Rodman, Abrams, Khalizad, and Dobriansky, other signatories to that letter who would become officials in the George W. Bush administration included Richard Armitage (deputy secretary of state), Jeffrey Bergner (assistant secretary of state), John Bolton (US ambassador to the United Nations), Robert Zoellick (US trade representative and deputy secretary of state), and Richard Perle (chair, Defense Policy Board Advisory Committee). A similar open letter was also written to House Speaker Newt Gingrich (R-GA) and Senate majority leader Trent Lott (R-MS).

Given that PNAC members were so open in calling for the removal of Saddam Hussein from power and that they later assumed high-level positions in the George W. Bush administration, it seems hardly surprising that the administration would undertake the overthrow of that regime. Admittedly, President Bush could have overruled all these voices had he disagreed with their policy preferences, but he did not disagree. Bush had his own reasons for wanting Saddam Hussein removed from power, once noting that Saddam Hussein tried to have Bush's father assassinated. Still, he brought these individuals into his administration in high positions knowing what their preferences were, and their policy preferences seemed to reinforce—not challenge—his own.

Given how publicly the PNAC was associated with the war in Iraq and how that war did not go according to PNAC's predictions (never finding the weapons of mass destruction thought to be there), the resulting breakdown of societal order following the US invasion, the long military occupation and difficult insurgency campaign that resulted, the challenges of rebuilding Iraq with insufficient planning, and so on—the Project for the New American Century did not survive. By December 2006, it had essentially shut down.

So, what do you think? Should one think tank have its fingerprints all over a policy issue as important as going to war, or is the apparent influence of this group simply the result of a series of personnel appointments that presidents have every right to make?

(continues)

Box 8.1 Continued

Sources:

CNN *Saturday Edition,* October 12, 2002, http://transcripts.cnn.com/TRANSCRIPTS/0210/12/tt.00.html; Project for the New American Century, http://www.sourcewatch.org/index.php?title=Project_for_the_New_American_Century; Paul Reynolds, "End of the Neo-Con Dream: The Neo-Conservative Dream Faded in 2006," *BBC News,* December 21, 2006, http://news.bbc.co.uk/2/hi/middle_east/6189793.stm.

longest history of influence in US foreign policy is the Council on Foreign Relations (CFR). As noted on its website (www.cfr.org), it was formed in 1921 as a nonpartisan advocate of the need for Americans to better understand the world beyond their borders. CFR employs both resident scholars and former government officials to study the foreign policy issues of the day. Its president has been Richard Haass since the early 2000s. Haass previously served as a Senate aide, an official in both the State and Defense Departments, director of policy planning for the State Department, and principal adviser to the secretary of state, special assistant to the president, and senior director for Near East and South Asian affairs on the National Security Council, and as an ambassador leading negotiations in both Afghanistan and Northern Ireland. Among the sitting members of the 2018 board of directors of CFR are many former government officials. These include special assistants to the president, cabinet secretaries (Departments of the Treasury and Homeland Security), retired military flag officers (an army general and two navy admirals), a national security adviser, a director of the Office of Management and Budget, a deputy secretary of defense, a CIA deputy director, and a former member of Congress. Many more such former government officials are included in its 5,000+ membership, including former presidents Jimmy Carter, George W. Bush, and Bill Clinton.

As a think tank, CFR has over seventy researchers—full-time, adjunct, and visiting scholars. CFR supports research on a vast array of foreign policy issues. It has centers and programs that are regionally focused: on Africa, Asia, Europe, Latin America, and the Middle East. It also has centers and programs on topical issues such as civil society, markets, and democracy; digital and cyber-space policy; energy security and climate change; geoeconomic studies; global health; international institutions and global gover-nance; national security and defense; preventive action; renewing America; US foreign policy; and women and foreign policy. CFR disseminates this research through its journal *Foreign Affairs* and through the publication of many books, special reports, memoran-dums, and the testimony of its experts before government bodies. Today, in the internet age, it also publishes fifteen blogs.

Finally, as a think tank, CFR has served as a recruiting pool for new administrations. In the past, transition teams for presidents-elect combed through its membership ranks to find ambassadors and other diplomats, cabinet officials, and national security staffers. With the end of the Cold War and the increasing polarization of American politics, CFR members may be somewhat more likely to be recruited to serve in Democratic administrations in the future, as more conservative think tanks such as the American Enterprise Insti-tute or the Heritage Foundation seem to be popular with Republican administrations. All these think tanks perform similar roles in seek-ing to shape foreign policy.

But again, they are not the only influential societal actors shap-ing foreign policy. There is also the mass media to be considered.

The Mass Media

You might think of the mass media like a public utility; it is there to serve the greater good. However, the US mass media also acts much like an interest group in what news it chooses to cover and how it presents that news. Here, the mass media includes news media organizations such as the major national newspapers, wire services, television and radio networks, internet sites, and social-media sites. At times it can also include the entertainment media, for example, movies or television programs that bear on specific topics related to foreign policy.

For the news media, the challenge is choosing what news to cover. It's hard to get original news stories unless there are reporters nearby or available to cover those events. Historically, America's major newspapers spent the money to station reporters in other countries, but that's changing. Foreign correspondents and offices are expensive. Most major US newspapers are cutting back on their foreign coverage. Of the daily newspapers, the *New York Times* is probably in the best shape in this regard. It has 200 foreign correspondents located in two major hubs (Hong Kong and London) or dispersed around the world. For example, it has four bureaus in the Middle East and three bureaus in Africa. However, some of these foreign bureaus consist of just one reporter.[8] Much the same can be said for major US television news networks. In short, major US news media companies try to cover the world with relatively few people. If those news outlets don't have someone nearby, news events may not get reported at all or may be "old news" by the time they are reported.

But then there's the question of what should be covered. Let's use an example to illustrate the dynamic of news coverage. The Middle East is one of the regions of the world best covered by US news media outlets. Middle East news stories routinely appear on the front page of the *New York Times* and often lead the international news segments of network broadcast news. Still, what someone chooses to cover makes a difference. Consider, for example, the government of Iran.

Because of its past history, Iran looms large among US foreign policy concerns. During the Eisenhower administration, the CIA played an important role in overthrowing a democratically elected regime there in 1953 and installing Iran's young monarch—Shah Mohammad Reza Shah Pahlavi—in control of an oil-rich country in a strategic location. Over the years, US support for the shah continued even as his regime became increasingly corrupt and developed a reputation for widespread human rights abuses. Following Iran's 1979 Islamic Revolution, Iranian students stormed the US embassy in Tehran and held fifty-two American diplomats hostage for over a year. Even after the 2015 diplomatic breakthrough in which Iran agreed to reduce its nuclear fuel enrichment program and allow international inspections of its nuclear facilities in return for a limited lifting of some economic sanctions by the United States and the EU, Iran's Islamic leaders and elected officials continued to refer to the United States as "the Great Satan."

Of particular interest to the news media was the former mayor of Tehran, Mahmoud Ahmadinejad, who was elected to two terms as president, serving from 2005 until 2013. Like other world leaders, he came to the United States every fall to attend the opening session of the UN General Assembly. His speeches were typically included in the daily US news, because of his tendency to make controversial statements. On several occasions at least, he questioned whether the Holocaust had really occurred during World War II, and in 2010, he asserted that the 9/11 attacks on the World Trade Center and Pentagon were the work of the United States itself—a "false flag" operation so as to have a justification to wage war on Islam. As is the case virtually every year, news coverage then showed other diplomats getting up and walking out of the room rather than listening to his heated rhetoric. Then there were the controversies surrounding his reelection in 2009. Official election results named Ahmadinejad the winner without even a runoff, and all three major opposition candidates rejected the results as rigged. Thousands of Iranians took to the streets to protest what many saw as the "stealing" of an election, and Iranian security forces used lethal force to break up the demonstrations.

Based on this news coverage, many Americans may know that Iran has long had a controversial regime that may have been—or possibly may still be—pursuing the development of nuclear weapons. Many think its former leader said "crazy" things, even if they cannot remember his name, and they may think he stole an election. Not surprisingly, they may perceive Iran to be a very anti-American place.

However, what many Americans may not know is that Iran represents a civilization that is 3,500 years old, that its citizens are highly nationalistic, that Iran's president is not the most powerful official in the country, and that its young people—who make up the majority of its population—tend to be pro-Western, if not actually pro-American, in their personal attitudes. Because of the way news is covered, many Americans know a fair amount about Iran's government, but that does not mean what they know about Iran or Iranians is totally accurate.

And then there's the issue of potential media bias. Many Americans feel the media—particularly television news—is biased in its coverage of presidents and their administrations. To some degree, some bias exists, as television network and cable news programs are staffed by humans like us with all of our potential flaws. But how does that bias play out? Can elected officials take advantage of it? Box 8.2 examines the directionality and potential impact of media bias.

**Box 8.2 Presidents and Television News:
Who Leads in This Dance?**

The relationship between presidents and television news programs is a complex one. Perhaps the key element in the president's political power is the power to persuade the public to see things in a preferred way. What better way to do so than through the reach of nationally broadcast television news programs?

For those in charge of TV news programs, several factors traditionally have to be balanced against each other. First, there is the desire to accurately report the news of the day, whether positive or negative to the president and administration. In that sense, the news programs are like a watchdog, continually assessing the wisdom or truthfulness of administration statements. On the other hand, reporting that seems too aggressive— or even seems hostile—in the eyes of those in the White House could have bad repercussions for the broadcasters. Presidents or White House press secretaries could stop calling on a network's reporters in press conferences and press briefings. Some networks have been temporarily shunned, and others given privileged access to policy makers. Thus, network executives might not want their reporters and news anchors to go too far in questioning the administration's policies and motivations, lest they lose their access to such policy makers. Carried to an extreme, acting on these concerns could result in the news programs becoming the administration's lapdog rather than its watchdog.

This question of bias in the news has been a prominent concern for years. The advent of Fox News Network was attributed to the need to get "fair and balanced" news—in other words, news that wasn't suffering from a perceived liberal bias. At least one study reported that, to some degree, ABC, CBS, and NBC news programs presented the news somewhat more favorably to Democratic administrations and more negatively to Republican ones, whereas Fox News Channel was more favorable to Republican administrations and less favorable to Democratic ones. Another study showed that after a Fox News affiliate station had been broadcasting in a viewing area for several years, members of Congress from those areas began shifting their policy statements in a more conservative direction.

So, who is leading whom here? Presidents can now derive a benefit either directly by reaching out to partisan news networks to carry their messages or indirectly by pitching the tone of their messages to fit the ideological slant of more partisan news networks such as MSNBC, CNN, or Fox News Network, knowing that such messaging will more likely get reported favorably on those networks.

We've seen examples of these dynamics in the last two administrations. President Obama famously broke with Fox News Network, saying it had become a forum for the Republican Party and was no longer a journalistic entity. By contrast, President Trump watches Fox News daily, often tweeting about the issues in the stories Fox broadcasts just minutes after those broadcasts are aired. President Trump has publicly called the *Fox and Friends* program the best news program on television. Moreover, he regularly takes weeknight phone calls from Fox News's host Sean Hannity. Hannity reportedly encourages the president to stand tall against his adversaries; he notes that Trump never gets enough credit; and he praises Trump for his many accomplishments. It would seem this works for President Trump and for the network's ratings as well.

Yet this approach can backfire. In December 2018, President Trump signaled his willingness to accept less than a border "wall" to get funding to prevent a government shutdown only to find his decision derided on Fox News by conservative pundit Ann Coulter as gutless. The next day, Trump reversed his prior willingness and demanded millions for a wall and allowed the government to shut down operations over the issue.

So, what do you think? Are news networks supposed to be neutral purveyors of news content or echo chambers for presidential messages consistent with the network's ideology? At what point does making money intersect with the network's public responsibilities? Do networks have public responsibilities anymore? Viewers of network news can now select their news à la carte, favoring the news broadcasts that reinforce their beliefs and values. Is that a good or a bad thing, or does it matter?

(continues)

Box 8.2 Continued

Sources:

Joshua D. Clinton and Ted Enamorado, "The National News Media's Effect on Congress: How *Fox News* Affected Elites in Congress," *Journal of Politics* 76 (2014): 928–943; Matthew Eshbaugh-Soha, "Presidential Leadership of Partisan News," *Presidential Studies Quarterly* 48 (2017): 27–48; Matthew Eshbaugh-Soha and Christopher Linebarger, "Presidential and Media Leadership of Public Opinion on Iraq," *Foreign Policy Analysis* 10 (2014): 351–369; Tim Groeling, "Who's the Fairest of Them All? An Empirical Test for Partisan Bias on ABC, CBS, NBC, and Fox News," *Presidential Studies Quarterly* 38 (2008): 631–657; Olivia Nuzzi, "Donald Trump and Sean Hannity Like to Talk Before Bedtime," *New York Magazine,* May 14, 2018, http://nymag.com/daily/intelligencer/2018 /05/sean-hannity-donald-trump-late-night-calls.html.

Another way that the mass media may influence policy making is through films—both documentary and entertainment. Any film that informs and educates the public about a foreign policy–related issue can impact policy makers or those who have their ear. A good documentary example is *An Inconvenient Truth,* the Oscar-winning film about former vice president Al Gore's effort to get people to take global climate change seriously. Based on viewing this film, many Americans came to accept the premise that global climate change is occurring, that it is impacted by human activity, and that it should be on the foreign and domestic policy-making agendas.

There are far more examples of entertainment films that have impacted the public about foreign policy issues and the way the United States engages others beyond its borders. A number of films were made after the US withdrawal from the Vietnam War, and most of them presented negative portrayals of engaging in counterinsurgency warfare or intervening in other people's civil wars. Movies such as *Platoon, Apocalypse Now,* and *Full Metal Jacket* made Americans question not only their country's foreign policy but also their country's military. Then movies such as *First Blood* (the first of the *Rambo* series), *Top Gun,* and *An Officer and a Gentleman* made many Americans feel better about their military and its role in society. Many college students learned something about Somalia and the US role there by seeing the film *Black Hawk Down.* They may also have learned about the Rwandan genocide from the film *Hotel Rwanda,* and about the war in Iraq from films such as *The Hurt Locker* and *The Green Zone.* Those interested in the world of intelligence and covert operations might have been attracted to films such as *The Good Shepherd, Syriana, Zero Dark Thirty,* or the films in the *Bourne* series.

Television also has an informative role for many Americans. Some years ago, many Americans got their ideas about the modern presidency from NBC's television series *The West Wing.* More recently, they might derive impressions from Netflix's *House of Cards* or *Designated Survivor.* TV viewers might assume the world of US counterterrorism operations resembles that depicted in the series *24,* or they might have seen counterterrorism operations more realistically portrayed in *N.C.I.S.—Naval Criminal Investigative Service,* or in its spinoff, *N.C.I.S. Los Angeles,* or in Showtime's *Homeland.* The issue of "spies among us" was highlighted in FX's *The Americans.*

In recent years, many in the public have turned to social media outlets for their news. President Trump has relied extensively on Twitter to take his messages directly to the public, which has motivated many members of Congress to do the same. With fewer and fewer people subscribing to newspapers, foreign policy stories that originate in the print media often get found and read on Twitter. Facebook has also become a very important source of news for many. Similarly, Facebook posts serve as a form of "public square" where one can mobilize like-minded individuals on behalf of a foreign policy agenda. Both elected officials and covert foreign operatives use such social media outlets to get their messages out to the public. In short, a number of different mass media outlets provide some information on the external challenges and opportunities that US foreign policy makers must address, and these sources also push specific foreign policy agendas. But individual opinion leaders also try to shape foreign policy, and thus they must be considered important societal actors as well.

Individual Opinion Leaders

Select individuals can influence public opinion in ways that shape policy. Celebrities can at times leverage their fame to bring attention to an issue. Actor George Clooney is a good example. Although he has pushed a number of issues, two in particular stand out. The first was the relief effort for the survivors of the January 2010 earthquake in Haiti. Within days of the earthquake, Clooney had lined up dozens of entertainment celebrities to appear on a two-hour telethon that raised millions of dollars for Haitian relief. Clooney's efforts added public weight behind the efforts of the US government to respond to the Haitian catastrophe.

However, Clooney may be better known for his long-term efforts to bring peace to Sudan. Initially, his efforts were to stop the genocide in the Darfur region of western Sudan. To that end, he appeared at rallies in the United States, went to Chad and Sudan, made a television documentary about the conflict, and appeared before the UN Security Council with Nobel Peace Prize–winner Elie Wiesel to ask for UN intervention to stop the genocide. He also went to Egypt and China to ask their governments to put more pressure on Sudan to stop the genocide. For his efforts, he was appointed by the UN as a "Messenger of Peace."

In 2010, Clooney turned his attention to the vote in Sudan to separate the country by allowing the southern portion to become independent. He traveled to southern Sudan with Ann Curry of the NBC *Today Show,* where he talked to the people about the 2011 vote on splitting the country. Fearing the violence that might result from the vote, he returned to the United States and tried to spread the message that a diplomatic intervention prior to the vote could save countless lives. He appeared on the *Today Show,* he spoke at a meeting of the Council on Foreign Relations, and he briefed President Obama at the White House. In short, many Americans—particularly those who follow celebrities and so-called soft news but not hard news—know something about Sudan and the events there because of the efforts of George Clooney and his colleagues.

However, one does not have to be a celebrity to have potential foreign policy influence. Greg Mortenson was a mountain climber who was rescued and aided by Pakistani villagers when he fell ill and got lost on an expedition. He repaid them and others by building schools in very remote areas of both Pakistan and Afghanistan, and he was later sought out to give briefings at the Pentagon to military commanders involved in counterinsurgency operations on how to win the hearts and minds of Pakistanis and Afghans. Another example is Armand Hammer, an American businessman who lived in the Soviet Union from 1921 until 1930. Because he had known Vladimir Lenin and Josef Stalin personally during those years, he came to know other, later Soviet leaders as well. During the Cold War, he served as an informal adviser to multiple US presidents regarding what the Soviet leaders might be thinking. As these examples suggest, anyone who can get the ear of significant foreign policy makers has a chance to influence foreign policy, but the more important question is, what ideas do such societal actors introduce into the pluralist policy process? What motivates them to get involved?

Motivating Inputs

Two very broad sets of societal motivations provide inputs that help shape US foreign policy making. There is considerable impact from both political culture and public attitudes and opinion.

Political Culture

Political culture describes the idea that most people in a country share an identifiable set of values or beliefs. One element of US political culture is the belief in American exceptionalism, an idea actually older than the United States itself. As noted in Chapter 3, American exceptionalism holds that *the United States is not only different from other countries, it is better than other countries.* This idea originated with the first European colonists who came to the New World and marveled at the temperate climate and abundant resources. Luckily, from the colonists' perspective, the indigenous Native Americans were relatively few in number and often friendly. Those who were unfriendly could not withstand the numbers of colonists who kept arriving or the firearms that those colonists brought with them.

In a nutshell, the colonists' perspective was that such a wonderful land available for their use must be a gift from God, and thus they must be very special people to deserve such a divine gift. Given their material success in this New World, they took it for granted that what worked for them would also work elsewhere, and so they took it as a God-given obligation to share what they had learned with others.

Many Americans still feel they have an obligation to lead and help others in the world by sharing their values and wisdom. As Secretary of State Hillary Rodham Clinton told the Council on Foreign Relations in 2010: "The world is counting on us. . . . After years of war and uncertainty, people are wondering what the future holds, at home and abroad. So let me say it clearly: The United States can, must, and will lead in this new century."[9]

As it leads, the values the United States wants to share with others generally come from liberalism. As suggested in Chapter 2, traditional liberalism holds that the most important thing in society is the freedom and liberty of each individual. Therefore, governments may be necessary to do the things individuals cannot easily do for themselves, but governments should be kept as small as possible so as not to trample on individual liberties. Because liberalism values the individual so highly, democracy is the preferred form of government, as democracy gives free individuals a means to directly participate in choosing who governs them. Finally, liberalism also holds that free-market capitalism is the best economic system, as it enables free individuals to pursue whatever activity they desire to make a living, with the corresponding opportunities to succeed or fail. These values also shape US policy preferences. US foreign policy proposals that do not fit within the parameters of American exceptionalism, individual rights, limited government, democracy, and capitalism become very hard to defend in the public sphere. But political culture is largely static. It has set the boundaries of acceptable policies. Nonetheless, public attitudes and opinions also play important and at times more dynamic roles.

Public Attitudes and Opinion

In a democracy, what the public thinks matters. Such public inputs can either be broad attitudes that do not quickly change or the public's opinion on specific issues at a given point in time, which may change more quickly.

For broad public attitudes to be relatively stable over time, they must be based on fundamental concerns. Some will talk about Americans being liberal or conservative, but the meaning of those labels is hard to pin down. "Liberal" compared to what? "Conservative" compared to what? A more precise way to capture fundamental attitudes about foreign policy is to ask two more specific questions: How do you feel about the use of military power (thus militant internationalism), and how do you feel about cooperating with others (thus cooperative internationalism)?

As Figure 8.2 shows, dichotomies on these two fundamental dimensions create four major attitudinal orientations to foreign policy: *internationalists,* who support both cooperative and militant internationalism; *accommodationists,* who support cooperative internationalism but oppose militant internationalism; *hard-liners,* who oppose cooperative internationalism but support militant internationalism; and *isolationists,* who oppose both cooperative and militant internationalism.[10] Although US leaders tend to be overrepresented in the internationalist and accommodationist categories and are rarely found in the isolationist category, the distribution of the public's attitudes is far more dispersed across all four of these attitudinal categories. A reasonable number of Americans fall into each one, with the

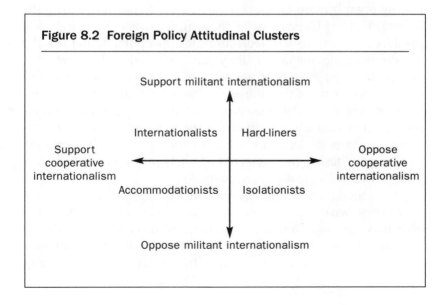

Figure 8.2 Foreign Policy Attitudinal Clusters

smallest category being isolationists, who still account generally for 18–20 percent of the public.[11] Thus, even though not as internationally oriented as their leaders, typically around 80 percent of Americans favor some form of international engagement. They just disagree on the nature of that engagement: Should it emphasize cooperation, the use of force, or both? These attitudes tend to be reasonably stable over time, and when they change, they generally change in incremental stages and in response to changes in the external policy environment. These findings are supported by surveys published by the Chicago Council on Global Affairs that show that from 1974 until 2017, more than 60 percent of Americans thought the United States should "take an active part in world affairs."[12]

In contrast to such broader attitudes, what Americans think on specific, short-term issues is called **public opinion**. Appointed officials may choose to ignore it, but elected officials normally give it at least some consideration when dealing with foreign policy problems and options. There are two important policy-making questions to consider here: whose opinions are considered, and how much weight are they given?

Public opinion polls are a good starting point for measuring what the mass public thinks. For the president, the polls that matter most are national polls, which the national news media and polling organizations conduct regularly, as well as statewide polls in key Electoral College states thought necessary for a first-term president to carry to win reelection. If those polls do not ask the questions presidents desire, they can commission their own private polls to get a better sense of what the public thinks. By contrast, for members of the House and the Senate, the polls that matter most are those that measure what the people think in their districts and states, respectively. If the local news media or university researchers back home do not conduct the polls members of Congress desire, those elected officials may commission their own private polls, just as presidents do.

Yet general public opinion—whether local, state, or national—may not be what matters most for elected officials. Elected officials may care most about the opinions of those who consistently vote for them (their political base) and those who contribute money to their political campaigns. In the past, keeping track of these key audiences involved not only trips back home but fairly constant monitoring of phone calls, letters, visitors to the office, letters to the editor or editorial opinion columns in the newspapers back home, and so on. With electronic media, now elected officials monitor the opinions of those who care most about certain issues by tracking their incoming email messages as well as messages posted on their websites and Facebook pages. Many members of Congress also still travel home frequently—some virtually every weekend—to keep in touch with what their constituents think.

Not only are elected officials at times clearly responsive to public opinion but they also actively try to shape it in preferred directions. If successful, they can then cite the resulting public opinion as justification for their policy position. So, for example, if members of Congress oppose deeper US military engagement in Yemen in the fight against religious extremism, then they may talk up the issue every chance they get with local opinion leaders back home— such as university audiences, the editorial staffs of the local newspapers, local "talk radio" hosts, civil society organizations such as Rotary or Kiwanis Clubs or such groups as the American Association of University Women, and meetings of their local political party organizations. Then if their public responds, they can say that the public wants what they want, thereby justifying their political stance on the issue.

In a democracy, it is a given that public attitudes and public opinion do matter. The more interesting questions are how much they matter and whether they should matter. For the former, how much public opinion and public attitudes matter varies considerably by issue. Americans care a lot about certain foreign policy issues, particularly issues they see impacting them directly: for instance, homeland security concerns or whether they lose their jobs to foreign competitors. They appear to care less about those issues they do not see impacting them as directly, such as global climate change, human rights abuses in Myanmar (Burma), or poverty in North Korea. For issues that many in the public do not care about, the task for groups and individuals that do care about them is to make those issues meaningful to other Americans. That often means putting a human face on them. So, for example, promoting economic development in Pakistan may not move many

Americans to action, but providing schools for Pakistani girls has resonated with many in the United States.[13]

But *should* public attitudes and public opinion play a role in foreign policy making? This may seem like an odd question in a democracy. However, since the days of such philosophers as Aristotle and Plato, some have questioned trusting the public with important decisions. In the nineteenth century, France's Alexis de Tocqueville questioned whether democracy was the best form of government for conducting foreign affairs, considering that the mass public was largely ignorant.

Public opinion polls in the twentieth century continued to demonstrate there was still considerable public ignorance about foreign affairs. In the 1990s, 20 percent of American adults could not name a European country. Fourteen percent of American adults could not find the United States on a blank map.[14] In a 1994 study, adults in eight countries were sampled on four current-events questions. In terms of their average correct scores, Germans were placed first, Italians second, French third, British fourth, Canadians fifth, Spanish sixth, Americans seventh, and Mexicans eighth.[15] In another study from that decade, 41 percent of Americans thought the US foreign aid program constituted the largest single item in the federal budget, at about 15 percent of the total federal budget. When asked how much it should be, a majority said 5 percent. They were probably surprised to learn that foreign aid spending actually represented only 1 percent of the federal budget.[16] More recently, in a 2016 survey of Americans age eighteen to twenty-six who had attended at least two years of college, the average score on a global literacy quiz was only 55 percent, which most of us would consider a failing grade.[17]

As noted by the **Almond-Lippmann consensus**, such public ignorance was cited for years as a reason for officials to ignore public opinion when making foreign policy decisions.[18] Yet, do such facts—that many in the public do not know where countries are on the map or who the Kurds are or how much the foreign aid budget may be—mean the public has no sense when it comes to foreign policy? Some would answer no to this question. The lack of factual knowledge of international affairs does not necessarily preclude the public from having a reasoned point of view—or perhaps some wisdom—regarding the major foreign policy issues of the day. The question thus can be rephrased: if the public has such points of view on the issues facing the country, are their views reasonable guides to policy makers? More careful studies suggest that they are.

Whether looking at narrower issues such as use-of-force decisions or broader aspects of foreign policy, studies have shown that over time, public opinion is rational, prudent, and purposive regarding such issues. Contrary to the Almond-Lippmann consensus, public opinion regarding the use of force seems neither volatile nor unstructured. Instead, it seems purposive and rational, moving in reasonable directions based on international events and the inputs of the media and experts. Further, public opinion can provide a check against risky choices. Over time, public opinion tends to move foreign policy away from extremist positions and back to the center of the policy spectrum, thereby possibly lessening the chances of major foreign policy mistakes.[19] Put normatively, policy proposals that do not pass the public's "common sense" test may not deserve to be pursued or need to be better explained to the public by policy makers and opinion leaders.

The pluralist policy process is composed of all these societal actors and motivating factors. This process is depicted in Figure 8.1. But how do such societal actors influence foreign policy?

Influencing Foreign Policy

As indicated by the specific illustrations discussed earlier, the US government's foreign policy–making system is unusually open to societal influences, and there are a variety of ways societal actors influence US foreign policy. As already noted, public attitudes and political culture set broad parameters around the acceptable options and choices for foreign policy makers. Public opinion also pushes policy makers in certain directions on specific foreign policy issues. If that direction is not what those policy makers desire, they may try to redirect public opinion more in line with their own preferences. Sometimes they are successful in shaping public opinion, and sometimes the effort does not work.

Interest groups, think tanks, the mass media, and individual opinion leaders also try to shape foreign policy options by framing the debate in certain ways. Interest groups and think tanks push policy makers to move in their preferred policy directions. The mass media's coverage of an issue can push that matter onto the government's agenda, and how that issue is covered can shape how the matter is seen by the public and by elites. For example, a Clinton administration official once said that his position on the Kosovo conflict crystallized when his daughter asked how the United States could stand idly by and allow Kosovo's men to be killed and its women to be raped. The daughter got her information by watching television news. Individuals who have the ear of governmental policy makers or who can bring media attention to foreign policy issues can also influence foreign policy, whether they are presidential confidants like Armand Hammer or celebrities like George Clooney. Finally, interest groups, think tanks, and individual opinion leaders take stands on specific issues and convey those to policy makers in every way they can—publicly, privately, in person or through the media, and through campaign assistance or opposition.

Conclusion

In short, domestic preferences often shape US foreign policy or create the parameters within which policies can find public support. When public opinion, interest groups, mass media outlets, think tanks, and individual opinion leaders give mixed signals regarding an issue, foreign policy makers are freer to pursue the policies of their choice. However, when domestic inputs to policy making tend to coalesce around a common view regarding an issue, it becomes harder and harder for foreign policy makers to ignore that view, and in a democracy, that should be expected. As George Washington Plunkitt of New York's Tammany Hall political machine remarked in the nineteenth century, going as an individual to City Hall to get something changed is not likely to be successful. However, if you go and say you represent fifty voters who care as you do, your message is more likely to be heard by someone who has some power.[20] The same thing can happen in the realm of foreign policy making. The presence of societal pressures does not guarantee that policy makers will do what these domestic actors want. However, policy makers—and particularly elected ones—will take what societal actors want into consideration when making their foreign policy choices, and the degree to which policy makers do so depends on the importance of the specific societal actors to them and/or the degree to which those actors' preferences coalesce around a common viewpoint.

Suggested Reading

Baum, Matthew A., and Philip B. K. Potter. *War and Democratic Constraint: How the Public Influences Foreign Policy.* Princeton: Princeton University Press, 2015.
Gries, Peter Hays. *The Politics of American Foreign Policy: How Ideology Divides Liberals and Conservatives over Foreign Affairs.* Stanford: Stanford University Press, 2014.
McCormick, James M., ed. *The Domestic Sources of American Foreign Policy.* 7th ed. Lanham, MD: Rowman and Littlefield, 2017.
Milner, Helen V., and Dustin Tingley. *Sailing the Water's Edge: The Domestic Sources of American Foreign Policy.* Princeton: Princeton University Press, 2015.
Terry, Janice J. *US Foreign Policy in the Middle East: The Role of Lobbies and Special Interest Groups.* Ann Arbor: Pluto, 2005.

Notes

1. Gabriel Almond, *The American People and Foreign Policy* (New York: Praeger, 1965); Ralph B. Levering, *The Public and American Foreign Policy, 1918–1978* (New York: William Morrow, 1978).

2. These observers of the pluralist policy process included, for example, David B. Truman, *The Governmental Process* (New York: Knopf, 1951) and Robert Dahl, *Who Governs?* (New Haven: Yale University Press, 1961) and *Pluralist Democracy in America: Conflict and Consent* (Chicago: Rand McNally, 1967).

3. For more on agents and principals, see James D. Fearon, "Signaling Foreign Policy Interests: Tying Hands Versus Sinking Costs," *Journal of Conflict Resolution* 41 (1997): 68–90, and Walter Carlsnaes, "The Agency-Structure Problem in Foreign Policy Analysis," *International Studies Quarterly* 36 (1992): 245–270.

4. Gordon Adams, *The Iron Triangle: The Politics of Defense Contracting* (Piscataway, NJ: Transaction, 1981).

5. "Trade Sanctions Reform and Export Enhancement Act of 2000 (TSRA) Program," Department of the Treasury, https://www.treasury.gov/resource-center/sanctions/Programs/Pages/tsra.aspx.

6. "ADM Shakes Hands in Cuba," NUTRA Ingredients-USA, updated July 19, 2008, https://www.nutraingredients-usa.com/Article/2002/09/27/ADM-shakes-hands-in-Cuba#.

7. Marc Frank, "US Food Sales to Cuba Seen Boosted by Pending Law," *Cuba Journal,* February 26, 2009, https://cubajournal.blogspot .com/2009/02/us-food-sales-to-cuba-seen-boosted-by.html.

8. Kelly Virella, "How Do We Cover News for the World? Jodi Rudoren Answers Readers' Questions," *New York Times,* December 1, 2017, https://www.nytimes.com/2017/12/01/reader-center/how-many-foreign -bureaus-does-nyt-have.html.

9. Mark Landler, "In a Speech on Policy, Clinton Revives a Theme of American Power," *New York Times,* September 9, 2010.

10. See Eugene R. Wittkopf, *Faces of Internationalism: Public Opinion and American Foreign Policy* (Durham, NC: Duke University Press, 1990), especially Chapter 2.

11. Eugene R. Wittkopf, "What Americans Really Think About Foreign Policy," *Washington Quarterly* 19 (1996): 91–106.

12. Dina Smeltz, Ivo Daalder, Karl Friedhoff, and Craig Kafura, "What Americans Think About America First," The Chicago Council on Global Affairs, https://www.thechicagocouncil.org/sites/default/files /ccgasurvey2017_what_americans_think_about_america_first.pdf.

13. For more on this, see Greg Mortenson and David Oliver Relin, *Three Cups of Tea: One Man's Mission to Promote Peace . . . One School at a Time* (New York: Penguin, 2007).

14. *U.S. News and World Report,* May 29, 1995.

15. *Time,* March 28, 1994.

16. Barbara Crossette, "Foreign Aid Budget: Quick, How Much? Wrong," *New York Times,* February 27, 1995.

17. Becky Little, "Most Young Americans Can't Pass a Test on Global Affairs: Can You?" *National Geographic,* https://news.nationalgeographic .com/2016/09/survey-geography-foreign-relations-americans-students/.

18. Ole R. Holsti, "Public Opinion and Foreign Policy: Challenges to the Almond-Lippmann Consensus," *International Studies Quarterly* 36 (1992): 439–466.

19. See Bruce W. Jentleson, "The Pretty Prudent Public: Post Post-Vietnam American Opinion on the Use of Military Force," *International Studies Quarterly* 36 (1992): 49–73; Bruce W. Jentleson and Rebecca L. Britton, "Still Pretty Prudent: Post–Cold War American Public Opinion on the Use of Military Force," *Journal of Conflict Resolution* 42 (1998): 395–417; and Benjamin I. Page and Robert Y. Shapiro, *The Rational Public: Fifty Years of Trends in Americans' Policy Preferences* (Chicago: University of Chicago Press, 1992).

20. William L. Riordan, *Plunkitt of Tammany Hall* (Lawrence, KS: Digireads.com/Neeland Media LLC, 2010, originally published 1905).

9

The Role of
International Actors

Learning Objectives

- Illustrate the types of international organizations, nongovernmental organizations, and foreign individuals who may shape US foreign policy.
- Describe the circumstances that can allow foreign individuals to play roles in the process of US foreign policy making.
- Interpret the roles played by these various international actors when viewed through the lenses of realism, liberalism, idealism, and constructivism.
- Evaluate the openness of US foreign policy making in light of traditional notions of national sovereignty.

An oft-heard phrase during the Cold War years was "politics stops at the water's edge." That sounds good, but it was rarely true then and, as the preceding chapters have demonstrated, it is certainly not true now. Many domestic actors—government officials, bureaucratic components of the administration, members of Congress, occasionally the courts, public opinion, think tanks, the media, domestic groups, individual opinion leaders, and so on— vie for influence in shaping US foreign policy, but others outside

189

the United States also seek to shape the contours of US foreign policy. They seek to take advantage of a policy-making system that is very open to influence—even external influence. These external actors may include international organizations, non-governmental organizations (NGOs), and individuals representing their states, other international groups, or themselves. Each of these types of external actors deserves consideration.

International Organizations

International organizations figure prominently in US foreign policy. They often provide the stimulus to which foreign policy makers respond. Examples can be found in the UN effort in the early 1990s to lead a humanitarian intervention to safeguard the delivery of relief supplies to refugee camps in Somalia. That well-intentioned effort resulted in the United States being pulled largely against its will into a civil war. In 2011, US allies within the North Atlantic Treaty Organization (NATO) pressed for a collective response to safeguard the Libyan people demonstrating against the repressive Qaddafi regime. Libya's government went to war against its own people, and Libyan refugees fled the violence by illegally entering Europe through Italy. The decision was made to use limited US military assets—largely to take out Libyan air defense and communications links—so other NATO forces could carry out more robust attacks in defense of the Libyan rebels.

However, not all examples involve the military. In 1992 at the Earth Summit in Rio de Janeiro, delegates agreed to the UN Framework Convention on Climate Change, which sought to stabilize greenhouse gases in the atmosphere and limit rising global temperatures. In 1997, the Kyoto Protocol called for developed states to make mandatory reductions in their fossil fuel emissions. To date, the United States has refused to accept mandatory reductions in its fossil fuel emissions. This refusal is based either on fairness issues (developed countries are forced to cut their emissions but developing countries that also pollute have so far been exempted from mandatory restrictions) or on the expected negative economic impact on the United States that would result from a slowdown of its fossil fuel–based economy. In 2015, President Obama signed the Paris Agreement, which called for *voluntary* state actions to cut emissions to preclude a two-degree Celsius increase in global mean temperatures. However, in 2017 President Donald Trump pulled the United States out of the Paris Agreement, citing the damage it would do the US economy. This refusal to agree to any significant emission reductions puts the United States on a collision course with many friends and allies that agreed to make such cuts at Kyoto in 1997, as well as those—for example, China—that agreed to make voluntary reductions in Paris in 2015.

Just as international organizations can create the need for a foreign policy output, they can also be the means through which the United States tries to accomplish its foreign policy goals. For example, the UN's **International Atomic Energy Agency (IAEA)** is the means by which the members of the international system monitor the nuclear programs of other countries. The Nuclear Nonproliferation Treaty and the IAEA have combined to create the **nuclear nonproliferation regime** that governs the acceptable uses of nuclear technologies. These rules and expectations can be used to promote US foreign policy initiatives toward both those that seek to develop nuclear weapons outside the framework of the agreed rules (e.g., North Korea and Iran) and those that seek to develop nuclear energy for peaceful uses within those rules (e.g., Brazil and Japan).

The use of such international organizations as a means to achieve US foreign policy goals is not restricted to just the national security arena. Following the Asian financial crisis of 1997, the G20 was formed to bring together representatives of the twenty largest market-based economies for financial planning and policy coordination. The forum was particularly important in coordinating responses to the Great Recession of 2008–2010, but the Bush and Obama administrations had mixed success in persuading the other members to agree to their preferred economic responses to the recession. US leaders were able to get others to coordinate their policies and somewhat increase their own economic stimulus packages to spur economic recovery, but those other nations (primarily led by the EU) were unsuccessful in their efforts to get the United States to tighten its regulations on the operations of the financial and banking sectors of the economy.

Such mixed success in economic initiatives is also illustrated by US interactions with the **World Trade Organization (WTO)**, as discussed in Box 9.1. However active international organizations are in trying to shape US foreign policy, NGOs are arguably even more frequent participants in US foreign policy making.

Box 9.1 Trump's Tariffs Versus the World Trade Organization

As the *Wall Street Journal* notes, Donald Trump "forged his ideas on trade in the 1980s—and never deviated." On the Oprah Winfrey television show in 1988, he said, "It's not free trade. If you ever go to Japan right now and try to sell something, forget about it. Just forget about it. It's almost impossible . . . . They come over here, they sell their cars, their VCRs, they knock the hell out of our companies." President Trump has long seen trade on a transactional basis: "We buy this from you so long as you buy that from us." In his eyes, a winning trade deal comes from the United States selling more to another country than it buys from that country. However, this view ignores at least three twenty-first-century realities. First, businesses now rely on global supply chains. US firms import many of the components of the products they produce in the United States. Thus, trade restrictions ratcheting up the costs of those imported components hurt US businesses and their workers. Second, macroeconomic factors impact trade balances. If the global economy is slowing down compared to the US economy, other countries don't have as much money to purchase US goods and services. Thus, trade imbalances are not solely the result of bad bilateral negotiations. Third, a large part of the US economy is composed of companies that provide services to others, not goods. The value of exported services is rarely mentioned in discussions of trade imbalances.

Given Trump's emphasis on trade in manufactured goods, it was not surprising that in his campaign stops in the industrial Midwest in 2016 he stressed that the United States needed to restore manufacturing jobs. Not only did he promise new tariffs if elected, he also tweeted that tariffs were good and trade wars could easily be won. His sole focus seemed to be on restricting imports, but that meant bumping up against the rules set by the World Trade Organization, an organization Trump has described as "a disaster."

In his first year in office, Trump increased tariffs on imported steel by 25 percent and on imported aluminum by 10 percent. Given his campaign rhetoric, these tariffs could easily be seen as protectionist measures, which the WTO prohibits. However,

WTO rules allow an exception for tariffs enacted on the basis of national security. So, in order to lessen the chances of the WTO authorizing retaliatory tariff increases on US goods exported abroad, President Trump justified the tariffs on national security grounds. In essence, the administration was stressing that imported steel and aluminum were necessary to make many weapons-system components.

This national security exception would be easier to justify if the United States imported steel and aluminum primarily from potential adversaries. However, the top three sources of imported steel in the United States are, respectively, Canada, Brazil, and South Korea—all friendly regimes. The situation regarding aluminum imports is only slightly different; the top three sources of imported aluminum in the United States are Canada, Russia, and the United Arab Emirates. Canada and the United Arab Emirates are friendly regimes, but Russia is a potential adversary.

WTO rules forced the Trump administration to justify these tariffs in the name of national security. At the request of the European Union and China, in November 2018, the WTO initiated an investigation into whether the tariff increases were justified or merely domestic protectionism. Time will tell if the WTO agrees with the Trump administration's position. What do you think? What's really at stake here?

Sources:

Bryce Baschuk, "WTO Starts U.S. Tariffs Probe, Crossing Trump's Red Line," *Bloomberg News,* November 21, 2018, https://www.bloomberg.com /news/articles/2018-11-21/trump-s-steel-aluminum-tariffs-to-be-investigated -by-wto-panel; Matthew Bey, "How to Understand Trump's Trade Policy: It's About Restricting Imports," *Market Watch,* July 25, 2018, https://www .marketwatch.com/story/how-to-understand-trumps-trade-policy-its-about -restricting-imports-2018-07-25; Conor Friedersdorf, "When Donald Trump Became a Celebrity," *Atlantic,* January 6, 2016, https://www.theatlantic .com/politics/archive/2016/01/the-decade-when-donald-trump-became-a -celebrity/422838/; Phil Levy, "Global Economic Slowdown Will Expose Trump's Trade Ignorance," *Hill,* November 19, 2018, https://thehill.com /opinion/finance/417379-global-economic-slowdown-will-expose-trumps

(continues)

Box 9.1 Continued

-trade-ignorance; Jacob M. Schlesinger, "Trump Forged His Ideas on Trade in the 1980s—and Never Deviated," *Wall Street Journal,* November 15, 2018, https://www.wsj.com/articles/trump-forged-his-ideas-on-trade -in-the-1980sand-never-deviated-1542304508; Bryan Schonfeld, "Why the U.S. Needs the World Trade Organization," *Washington Post,* September 20, 2016, https://www.washingtonpost.com/news/monkey-cage/wp/2016 /09/20/would-the-u-s-be-better-off-without-the-wto-not-when-the-wto -guides-98-percent-of-global-trade/?utm_term=.35bce41f6a3c; Voice of America, "Top US Import Sources of Steel, Aluminum," March 1, 2018, https://www.voanews.com/a/top-us-import-sources-steel-aluminum /4277212.html.

Nongovernmental Organizations

International NGOs often play important roles in US foreign policy making. They are particularly active in an array of humanitarian issues. For example, NGOs often get involved in monitoring human rights situations and generating political pressure on human rights abusers. The case of Saudi journalist Jamal Khashoggi illustrates how that can happen.

First, some background is needed. Jamal Khashoggi was a Saudi who became a prominent Middle East journalist and an insider in Saudi elite circles. After his writings became increasingly critical of the Saudi royal court, he went into exile in the United States, became a permanent US resident, and was a regular contributor to the *Washington Post.* He lost even more favor in Riyadh when he began to single out Crown Prince Muhammad bin Salman (known as MBS) for criticism by name. In October 2018, Khashoggi went to the Saudi consulate in Istanbul to pick up a form needed to marry his Turkish fiancée. He never came out, and the Turkish government issued a statement that said audio and video evidence confirmed Khashoggi had been interrogated, quickly executed, and then dismembered inside the consulate by a Saudi hit team. The response from human rights groups was almost instantaneous, led by groups such as Reporters Without

Borders and Human Rights First. Soon thereafter, twenty-two senators—eleven from each party, including the chairman and ranking members of the Foreign Relations Committee and the Appropriations Subcommittee on State, Foreign Operations, and Related Programs—signed a letter to President Trump formally invoking the Global Magnitsky Act, thus giving the president 120 days to report back to Congress on his investigation of the matter and on whether sanctions against Saudi Arabia would be imposed. The Trump administration later acknowledged that the Saudis probably had Khashoggi killed, but that no evidence linked the crown prince directly to the crime. Pressure from eleven human rights organizations (including among others Human Rights First, Human Rights Watch, Freedom House, and the Committee to Protect Journalists) may have influenced the State Department in 2019 to bar sixteen Saudi Arabian nationals from entering the United States due to their ties to the Khashoggi killing. Time will tell whether Saudi Arabia incurs more penalties from the United States or others as a result of this killing.

The role of NGOs in cases such as Khashoggi's is not uncommon. Human rights, humanitarian, and environmental/ecological NGOs put pressure on the US government to intervene in many cases. Sometimes the United States does so—most commonly when there is no other countervailing national security or economic issue at risk or when international NGOs are able to mobilize politically powerful domestic US NGOs to take up the effort. However, when such countervailing pressures or like-minded domestic groups are not present, international NGOs are often disappointed in the US responses to their appeals. Yet no matter how important traditional NGOs are in impacting US foreign policy, international businesses are arguably even more important.

Multinational corporations operating or based in the United States have long swung considerable weight in Washington, DC. In 1953, the CIA overthrew the popularly elected government of Iranian prime minister Mohammad Mossadegh primarily in response to the urging of the British government acting on behalf of the Anglo-Iranian Oil Company, a British oil firm whose assets had been nationalized by Mossadegh's government. For their part, US-based multinational oil corporations hoped to get a slice of the Iranian oil pie with a new, more pro-US regime in charge. In another example, in 1954 the United Fruit Company used its ties to Secretary of State John Foster Dulles and CIA director Allen Dulles (both of these brothers were former lawyers for the law firm representing United Fruit) to persuade the US government to overthrow the Guatemalan government, led by a popularly elected president, Jacobo Árbenz The Árbenz government had angered United Fruit by nationalizing some of its landholdings in Guatemala and then using United Fruit's own estimates of the real estate's value for tax purposes (which were set at unrealistically low levels) to determine the compensation the corporation deserved.

The leaders of some international corporations can take their case directly to the White House or halls of Congress, but for many international firms, hiring lobbyists to get their cases heard by US policy makers is standard operating procedure. One of the most prominent lobbying firms in the United States is the law firm of Akin Gump Strauss Hauer and Feld, better known simply as Akin Gump. Among its 436 current or former clients in 2019 were eight firms based in Japan (including Sony, Nintendo, and Panasonic among others), six from South Korea (such as Samsung and both Hyundai Motors and Kia Motors), five from Canada (including BlackBerry), five from Germany (including Deutsche Bank, Daimler AG, and Siemens AG), four from he United Kingdom (including the Penguin Group and BP), China's Lenovo computers, Taiwan's Foxconn, Finland's Nokia, Russia's Lukoil, and Venezuela's CITGO Petroleum, among others.[1] If lobbyists like the attorneys employed by Akin Gump are successful in stressing how advancing their client's corporate interests intersects with short- or long-term US interests, they can help set government agendas, shape policy options under consideration by policy makers, and possibly set the parameters of acceptable US responses to policy issues.

At times, international firms may use the appeal of campaign contributions to wield influence, but they must do so very carefully so as not to run afoul of US campaign-finance laws that prohibit foreign nationals or corporations from contributing to US political campaigns. In the 1990s, Chinese satellite companies wanted to purchase communications satellites from US-based Loral Space and Communications, but as high-technology military items, sales of such satellites were governed by licenses issued by the State Department. The State Department was required by law to consider the national security impact of such technology transfers before issuing export licenses. Chinese aerospace companies funneled hundreds of thousands of dollars in illegal campaign contributions to the Democratic Party, and later President Clinton issued a waiver to allow the purchase of four Loral satellites by the Chinese. Later, the administration transferred the authority to issue satellite export licenses away from the State Department to the Commerce Department, whose mission is to promote US business at home and abroad and is not required to protect national security. The sales of such satellites thus got considerably easier. It appears the Chinese got what they wanted.

Following the 2016 presidential election, news reports suggested that a variety of Russian sources may have illegally funneled money to Republican congressional candidates. Leonard Blavatnik, a Ukrainian-born oligarch with dual British and American citizenship, reportedly donated $2.5 million to Senator Mitch McConnell's campaign, $1.5 million to Marco Rubio's campaign, $1.1 million to Wisconsin governor Scott Walker's campaign, $800,000 to Senator Lindsey Graham's campaign, $250,000 to Ohio governor John Kasich's campaign, and $200,000 to Senator John McCain's campaign. An additional $1 million went to President Trump's Inaugural Committee. With his business partner Viktor Vekselberg, Blavatnik owns 26 percent of the Russian company RUSAL, the second-largest aluminum company in the world, and until two days after Trump's election, Blavatnik was a member of RUSAL's board of directors. Further, Vekselberg is the largest shareholder in the Bank of Cyprus.[2] Trump's commerce secretary, Wilbur Ross, was also a shareholder in the Bank of Cyprus and once served as vice-chairman of its board of directors.[3] After the 2016 election, the FBI began an investigation to determine whether Alexander Torshin, the deputy governor of the Central Bank of Russia, had funneled money to the Trump campaign through his contributions to the National Rifle Association, which in turn contributed a record $30 million to the Trump reelection effort.[4] Torshin was later added to a list of Russian oligarchs sanctioned by the US Treasury Department for their "malign activities" in support of Russian interests.[5] Given that Trump's first national security adviser, Michael Flynn, pleaded guilty to lying to the FBI about promising to end sanctions on Russia if Trump were elected, Russian businesses had good reasons to want Trump to be elected.

Multinational corporations can also influence policy making by appealing to public and elite attitudes about the issues important to them. Often, multinational corporations will take out full-page newspaper advertisements in national papers such as the *New York Times,* the *Washington Post,* or the *Wall Street Journal* to raise an issue, stress a policy response, or just try to create a more positive image for themselves that might work to their advantage with policy makers at a later date. Another means is to take out advertisements on television programs that elites and the attentive public often watch, such as the Sunday-morning news programs on major television networks such as ABC, CBS, NBC, CNN, and Fox News. However, they are not the only actors to use such methods. Foreign individuals representing many different actors do so as well.

Individuals

Various individuals from outside the United States also get involved in shaping US foreign policy. Not surprisingly, many are heads of their respective governments. As noted previously, Costa Rican president Óscar Arias met repeatedly in the 1980s with House Speaker Jim Wright and other House Democrats to build support for a Central American peace plan, particularly after it became clear that President Ronald Reagan would not meet with him. Given Arias's ability to sway members of Congress of both parties to his point of view, the Reagan administration ultimately realized it had little chance to stop the negotiated peace settlement in Central America and so ended its active opposition to the plan. The resulting peace agreement won Arias the Nobel Peace Prize.

Other examples come to mind as well. British prime minister Tony Blair was a willing partner to George W. Bush in the war in Iraq. When other European leaders criticized the war, Blair not only contributed British forces to the effort but also constantly encouraged Bush to stay the course and be strong in the face of his critics. George W. Bush's broader views on the Middle East may have been shaped by longtime Saudi ambassador to the United States Prince Bandar bin Sultan, who was so close to the Bush family that George W. Bush nicknamed him "Bandar Bush." When George W. began thinking of running for president, his father—former President George H. W. Bush—told him to seek out Bandar's guidance, because Bandar knew "everyone around the world who counts" and would give George W. his views on current foreign policy issues.[6] In 2016, Russian ambassador to the United States Sergey Kislyak met with then senator Jeff Sessions and two other members of the Trump campaign staff at the Republican National Convention. Shortly thereafter and at the urging of Trump campaign officials, the Republican Party Platform Committee changed language in the draft platform, deleting an endorsement of sending lethal weapons to Ukraine to help it resist Russia's intervention there.[7] If that was Kislyak's goal, it was ultimately unsuccessful. In 2018, the Trump administration supplied Ukraine with more than 200 anti-tank rockets.[8]

More success was had by Turkey's president Recep Tayyip Erdogan, who was able to get his way with President Trump on Syria policy. At the 2018 G20 Summit in Buenos Aires, Erdogan unsuccessfully pressed Trump to stop US aid to Kurdish fighters in Syria who were part of the US-supported anti-Assad coalition. Erdogan couldn't see why the United States would be helping militias he saw as terrorists. A few weeks later in a subsequent phone conversation, Erdogan pressed Trump again, saying if ISIS had been defeated as Trump said, why did the United States need 2,000 troops in Syria? The response: "You know what? It's yours," Trump said of Syria. "I'm leaving."[9]

One of the best at "working" the US foreign policy system was Israeli prime minister Benjamin Netanyahu. After living in the United States as a teenager and with both an undergraduate and a master's degree from the Massachusetts Institute of Technology (MIT), Netanyahu understood US politics and culture well. As prime minister, he never hesitated to go to the White House to ask for what Israel wanted from the United States. Sometimes presidents did what he wanted, but often they did not. When he was unsuccessful in the White House, he routinely went straight to Capitol Hill to ask Congress, where he often got a much more favorable response. Both elected party leaders in Congress—including Republican House Speakers Newt Gingrich, John Boehner, and Paul Ryan, and Democratic House Speaker Nancy Pelosi—and rank-and-file members of Congress alike often publicly professed their support for Israel and its policy stances in the Middle East. Their unwavering support for Israel at times compromised the efforts of US administrations to use diplomatic pressures or threats of economic retaliation to force Israel to stop constructing Israeli settlements in the occupied territory of the West Bank, to push Israeli officials into meaningful peace negotiations with the Palestinians, or to back away from other policy initiatives the United States opposed.

Oddly enough, the unwavering pro-Israel stance of many members of Congress so complicated US outreach to Arabs that in at least one case, the Obama administration turned to Netanyahu to serve as a lobbyist. In 2011, both the Obama administration and Netanyahu's Israeli regime favored a $50-million aid package from the United States to the Palestinian Authority (PA), led by President Mahmoud Abbas. The aid was intended to strengthen the Palestinian Authority's ability to provide needed governmental services to Palestinians in the West Bank and to professionalize Palestinian security forces. Both the US and Israeli regimes strongly supported this strengthening of the PA's capability to govern effectively as a way to undercut the appeal of the PA's rival, Hamas. Yet opposition by Republican members of Congress to *any* foreign aid to the Palestinian side threatened the aid package. At the request of both President Obama and Secretary of State Clinton, Netanyahu met with dozens of congressional Republicans when they visited Israel in August, and he urged them not to block the funding, as it was essential to Israel's security. On this issue at least, congressional Republicans trusted Prime Minister Netanyahu more than they trusted President Obama.[10]

For President Trump, Iran policy was one of the issues on which he and Prime Minister Netanyahu were in complete agreement. Both men had long castigated the Iran nuclear deal and vowed to resist it. Less than a month after Trump was inaugurated, Netanyahu made an official visit to Washington, where Trump welcomed him warmly.[11] Netanyahu encouraged and reinforced Trump's opposition to the nuclear deal, and in 2018, Trump withdrew the United States from the deal and reimposed US sanctions on Iran.

Prime Minister Netanyahu has another important link to the inner circle of the Trump administration—Trump's son-in-law and senior adviser Jared Kushner. Netanyahu is an old friend of the Kushner family and may have helped connect Jared Kushner to Crown Prince Muhammad bin Salman. The question of how much influence the young Saudi crown prince has in the Trump administration is explored in Box 9.2.

Box 9.2 How Much Influence Does Muhammad bin Salman Have in the Trump Administration?

Close ties between the United States and Saudi Arabia are nothing new. President Franklin Roosevelt and King Abdul Aziz ibn Saud struck up a friendship in 1945, and the result was a tacit agreement: Saudi oil would come to the United States in return for US arms and security guarantees. Despite occasional rifts, such as US support for Israel and the 1973 Arab oil embargo, the relationship has survived. As noted earlier, Saudi prince Bandar bin Sultan was a close friend and confidant of both Presidents George H. W. and George W. Bush.

Such connections have been maintained through a new generation of leaders. Before Trump was inaugurated, his son-in-law Jared Kushner identified Muhammad bin Salman, the soon-to-be crown prince, as a rising force within the royal family. Kushner saw MBS (as the crown prince is often called in the press) as a visionary new leader who would modernize Saudi Arabia and diversify its oil-based economy. After the inauguration, Trump made Saudi Arabia the destination for his first foreign trip as president. Reportedly, Kushner and MBS have become personal friends, chatting often by phone, and this friendship has facilitated the intersection of Trump administration policies with those of Saudi Arabia.

Since coming into power as the de facto leader in place of his aging father King Salman, MBS has revved up the cold war between Saudi Arabia and Iran, unsuccessfully tried to force the resignation of Lebanon's prime minister, pushed the Trump administration to reject the Iran nuclear deal, initiated a naval embargo of Qatar (where 11,000 US troops are based), launched a war with the Iranian-backed Houthi rebels in Yemen, and allegedly targeted journalist Jamal Khashoggi for death after Khashoggi criticized MBS by name. In return, the Trump administration has pulled out of the Iran nuclear deal and reimposed US sanctions on Iran, sold Saudi Arabia the weapons it used against Yemenis, turned a blind eye to apparent crimes against humanity committed by the Saudi forces against Yemeni civilians, refused to pressure the Saudis to let

(continues)

Box 9.2 Continued

humanitarian relief reach starving Yemeni men, women, and children, and pointedly defended MBS against reports that he must have known about the killing of Khashoggi, if not personally authorized it.

What did the US administration receive in return for these friendly policies? The Saudis reaffirmed their commitment (made earlier during the Obama administration) to a multibillion-dollar arms purchase from US contractors, and in March 2018, the Saudi Public Investment Fund made multibillion-dollar commitments to a number of Silicon Valley firms. These included $45 billion to SoftBank, $3.5 billion to Uber, $2 billion to Tesla, and $1 billion to the space component of Virgin Group. When he returned home from a US trip, MBS told friends he "had Kushner in his pocket." According to the *Washington Post,* after Khashoggi's death, Trump told US officials that the close relationship Kushner had with MBS had become a liability, but Trump continued to reject the CIA's conclusion—which it made with high confidence—that MBS had to be complicit in the assassination of Jamal Khashoggi.

Does Saudi Arabia—and Muhammad bin Salman in particular—have too much influence in US foreign policy–making circles, or have US national interests been advanced by a close embrace of Saudi Arabia?

Sources:

Peter Bergen, "Kushner and MBS: A Tale of Two Princes," CNN, March 19, 2018, https://www.cnn.com/2018/03/19/opinions/trump-kushner-MBS-meeting-opinion-bergen/index.html; Julian Borger, "A Tale of Two Houses: How Jared Kushner Fuelled the Trump-Saudi Love-In," *Guardian,* October 16, 2018, https://www.theguardian.com/us-news/2018/oct/16/jared-kushner-trump-saudi-khashoggi-mbs; Josh Dawsey, John Hudson, and Anne Gearan, "Trump Doubts Saudi Account of Journalist's Death: 'There's Been Deception, and There's Been Lies,'" *Washington Post,* October 20, 2018, https://www.washingtonpost.com/world/national-security/white-house-privately-doubts-saudi-account-of-journalists-death/2018/10/20/4c459c07-eceb-4600-91ea-95228128e7ec_story.html?noredirect=on&utm_term=.195cf180f360; Ron Kampeas, "Five Key Moments in the Jared Kushner–Saudi Prince

Mohammed Bromance," *Jewish Telegraphic Agency,* October 12, 2018, https://www.jta.org/2018/10/12/news-opinion/5-key-moments-in-the -jared-kushner-saudi-prince-mohammed-bromance; Lesley Kennedy, "How FDR Charmed a Saudi King and Won U.S. Access to Oil," *History,* October 18, 2018, https://www.history.com/news/fdr-saudi-arabia -king-oil.

Thus, while many individuals representing their respective foreign governments have sought to influence and shape US foreign policy, individuals representing other entities have done so as well. Religious leaders have at times prominently pressed US foreign policy makers to change US foreign policy. A good example was Pope John Paul II. The leader of the Roman Catholic Church and President Ronald Reagan collaborated in their efforts to weaken the Soviet Union and its hold on Eastern Europe—and particularly on the pope's Polish homeland. In private messages to the president, Pope John Paul II strongly encouraged US pressure on the Communist regime in Poland because of its crackdown on the Solidarity movement there, and both President Reagan and White House staffers found the pope's support and encouragement inspirational. In turn, the White House carefully coordinated its actions with those of the pope to put maximum pressure on both the Polish and Soviet governments to liberalize their rule over the people of Poland and Eastern Europe.[12]

Similarly, South African Anglican bishop Desmond Tutu was instrumental in pushing US policy makers to press for the end of apartheid. Unable to bring down South Africa's policy of racial segregation from the inside by working within the system, Tutu sought out US senator Edward Kennedy (D-MA) and told him: "The world will not pay attention until someone like you comes to South Africa and brings the cameras and spotlights with you."[13] Kennedy thereafter went to South Africa, the cameras followed, and as soon as he returned to Washington, Kennedy introduced and pushed through Congress legislation that became the Comprehensive Anti-Apartheid Act of 1986. When President Ronald Reagan vetoed the bill, Kennedy led the successful effort to override the president's veto.

During the Obama administration, the reopening of diplomatic relations between the United States and Cuba was the result of a letter from Pope Francis to both Obama and Cuban president Raúl Castro. Pope Francis implored them to find a way to improve relations between the two countries and hosted a secret meeting at the Vatican to help facilitate the negotiations. Both leaders later credited the pope with the successful policy shift.[14]

However, not every foreign individual who tries to shape US foreign policy is well known. Sometimes the individuals are policy experts virtually unknown to the mass public. Agnes Klingshirn of the German aid agency GTZ is such a person. In her view, if the global community really wanted to improve the lives of women and families in developing countries in a meaningful way, someone would invent a cleaner, safer, and more efficient cookstove. In many countries, women and children spend much of their days hunting for firewood for their cookstoves. Moreover, both wood and kerosene cookstoves are highly dangerous; they often explode and always emit toxic fumes that often sicken family members. Three billion people are exposed to these toxic fumes and smoke, and 2 million premature deaths globally are linked to cookstove fumes—or one death every sixteen seconds. Klingshirn's ideas found the ear of then secretary of state Hillary Clinton, who announced in September 2010 the formation of a new public-private alliance called the Global Alliance for Clean Cookstoves. The goal of the alliance was to produce and distribute 100 million clean cookstoves by 2020, and the Obama administration's pledge to the effort was almost $51 million over a five-year period.[15] Founding partners in the alliance were the US Departments of State, Health and Human Services, and Energy, as well as the US Environmental Protection Agency and the US Agency for International Development. Other founding partners included the governments of Germany, Norway, and Peru, and NGOs such as Shell, the Shell Foundation, Morgan Stanley, and the Netherlands Development Organization. A number of UN agencies were the implementing partners.[16] After one year, the United States pointed to meaningful progress for the alliance: identifying over twenty country partners; distributing over 2.4 million clean cookstoves, thereby improving the indoor air for 14 million people; and raising over $80 million more to support the alliance's work.[17] Beyond those accomplishments is the goodwill such an initiative generates for the United States.

Far more often, however, individuals who influence foreign policy from the outside are celebrities who use their fame to focus attention on global problems. Princess Diana of Britain was an obvious example. Although the International Campaign to Ban Landmines was already active, public knowledge and awareness of the issue dramatically increased when Princess Diana lent her name and public endorsement to it. President Clinton was very enthusiastic about the effort to ban land mines, but politically he would not go any further than his military experts would support. He made it clear that he would support the treaty if an exception to the ban were made for the demilitarized zone separating North and South Korea, which is strewn with millions of land mines to slow down any future North Korean invasion. When that exception was not forthcoming, he could not commit to the treaty. However, he did issue Presidential Decision Directive 64 that would end the US use of land mines anywhere other than Korea, and the favorable publicity generated by Princess Diana's support made it easier for him to back away from the use of land mines.[18]

An example of a foreign individual who was even more successful in influencing US foreign policy is Paul David Hewson, better known as Bono, from the Irish rock band U2. Appalled that millions of Africans died of AIDS-related diseases when medicines existed that could prolong and improve the quality of their lives, Bono sought a US commitment to do more for African AIDS relief. To accomplish this, he communicated with the George W. Bush White House, met with President Bush personally, and participated with other entertainers in the Heart of America tour to raise public awareness about the AIDS crisis in Africa.[19]

Following President Bush's proposal for a $15-billion commitment over five years to combat AIDS in Africa, Bono kept in contact with the president, as he knew Bush would have to press Congress to approve the money. Knowing that many in Congress were skeptical about the benefits of foreign aid programs, Bono also put personal pressure on members of Congress to ensure that the money was appropriated. Not only did Bono appear on multiple television news programs to get his message across, but he also engaged in personal lobbying on Capitol Hill. He identified specific members of Congress on the relevant appropriations subcommittees for US foreign aid, met with them personally, and provided them with specific information on the scope of the need in Africa, the benefits the US aid would provide there, and *any relevant connections that might exist with the members' local constituents back home.* Because of his sustained efforts and those of President George W. Bush, Congress came through and appropriated the largest commitment of US economic assistance ever to sub-Saharan Africa.

Shaping Foreign Policy

International actors and other external groups seek to shape favorable outcomes by actively engaging in US foreign policy making when possible. Representatives of international governmental organizations, NGOs, foreign states, and individual opinion leaders continually make their desires known to US foreign policy makers through appeals via the mass media, personal communications, and face-to-face meetings with top policy makers. They bargain, persuade, cajole, and at times even threaten policy makers in trying to get their way, and they enter into alliances with domestic groups that share their concerns. In a foreign policy–making process very open to outside influence, these external actors engage actively to lobby administrative officials such as the president, the vice president, National Security Council members, and other top officials in the White House, relevant cabinet departments, and the Intelligence Community. They also actively seek out key members of Congress for their support. It is commonplace for top foreign officials to visit the United States, meet with the president and/or other top administrative officials, and then head directly to Capitol Hill to visit with the elected party leaders of each congressional chamber, the key members of the Senate Foreign Relations Committee and the House Foreign Affairs Committee, and at times, the Committees on Appropriations, Armed Services, Intelligence, Homeland Security, and Commerce. These foreign actors use many, if not most, of the same techniques to shape US foreign policy as do the societal actors described in Chapter 8. But how successful are they at influencing policy?

Influencing Foreign Policy

In an interdependent, globalized world, it is hard to argue that external influences do not matter in making US foreign policy. However, determining how much they matter may depend on one's theoretical point of view. As noted in Chapter 3, political realists and neorealists interpret international politics to be primarily the actions of states behaving as unitary actors that make rational choices in reaction to events or opportunities in an international system marked by anarchy. Thus, from this point of view, external influences are very important. They are the impetus for foreign policy actions in the first place, as states adapt to their external environment. As stimuli, they provide the starting point for foreign policy. Moreover, their subsequent inputs become vital feedback to determine how effective the US governmental output has been, and perhaps how it might be improved for the future.

Like realists and neorealists, idealists tend to see international actors as very important to US foreign policy. External events and the actions of international actors and opinion leaders shape the way things are, and idealists then react based on how they think things should be. To the extent they share normative values with other international actors, idealists will view those international actors as legitimate participants in the US process of foreign policy making. They will coordinate their domestic actions with those of external actors with similar views, use the presence of those international actors as leverage to push their preferred policy options, and then seek to engage those international actors to help implement the types of foreign policy outputs they prefer. Thus, when such normative values about how things should be are shared, domestic and international actors will work hand in glove to achieve their goals.

For their part, liberals believe foreign policy is primarily a product of the actions of key subnational actors such as elected and appointed officials, political parties, organized interest groups, experts, opinion leaders, public opinion, and both the news media and social media. From this theoretical point of view, external factors and actors may be quite important in some cases, but on a day-to-day basis, they are normally less important in shaping US foreign policy than domestic factors and the perceptions, needs, and desires of domestic policy makers. From this theoretical standpoint, foreign policy is primarily the product of domestic processes and actors and, once formed, is then projected outward. Therefore, liberals may see external actors as notable, but not necessarily determinative, actors in shaping US foreign policy outputs.

However, neoliberals may have a slightly greater appreciation of some external inputs. Neoliberals typically stress the need for creating, and then using, international organizations and other entities to create an international architecture that supports and promotes global cooperation. To the extent that they do so, they must be open to the inputs of representatives of these entities—the international organizations, NGOs, and other groups and individuals involved. Given this position, neoliberals are quite open to viewing external actors as more significant shapers of US foreign policy.

For constructivists, these external actors have only the importance assigned to them in the minds of domestic policy makers. If US foreign policy makers socially construct a reality in which external actors are thought to be important, then policy makers will act on the basis of that constructed reality, and those foreign actors will vie with domestic factors and actors as influential shapers of US foreign policy. Conversely, if policy makers socially construct a reality that says foreign actors should have little or no say in the formulation of US foreign policy, then such foreign actors will be unsuccessful.

Thus, one could argue that at times the George W. Bush administration, backed up by a Republican-controlled Congress from 2001 to 2005, acted in a realist fashion by stressing the idea that concerns about US sovereignty overrode the inputs of external audiences in making US foreign policy. Therefore, international critiques of the US effort to invade Iraq or to oppose mandatory fossil fuel emission reductions, for example, could be ignored as illegitimate factors in the decision-making process. Conversely, the election of Barack Obama to the presidency in 2008 ushered in a new group of foreign policy makers who continually reaffirmed each other's belief that foreign concerns were legitimate. Of course the United States did not necessarily have to do what foreign actors wanted, but Obama administration officials believed that the views of others deserved a respectful hearing and careful consideration. In 2016, the election of Donald Trump swung the pendulum back in the other direction. His America First agenda largely rejected the inputs of external actors, seeing such inputs as illegitimate considerations that wasted US resources pursuing the agendas of others. Yet at times, the external influences brought to bear by leaders he admired—such as Russian president Putin, Turkish president Erdogan, or Israeli prime minister Netanyahu—were welcomed in the Trump White House.

Conclusion

There are only a few societies in which foreign influences and the views of external actors seem to matter very little. North Korea—the so-called hermit kingdom—comes to mind, as does Myanmar (Burma), where until recently a military regime long ignored foreign attitudes regarding its policies. Yet in most countries, foreign policy makers cannot avoid being influenced to some degree by those outside the country, and that is certainly the case in the United States. The open and fragmented nature of the US foreign policy process provides many opportunities for access by external actors, just as it does for domestic actors. Further, many of those international actors understand well the intricacies of US foreign policy making and know where, when, and how to press to get their views considered. In that way, the pluralist process of groups and individuals vying for influence over US foreign policy applies just as much for international actors as for domestic ones.

Suggested Reading

Avant, Deborah D., Martha Fennimore, and Susan K. Sell, eds. *Who Governs the Globe?* New York: Cambridge University Press, 2010.

Gutner, Tamar. *International Organizations in World Politics.* Rev. ed. Thousand Oaks, CA: Sage/CQ Press, 2016.

Haass, Richard. *A World in Disarray: American Foreign Policy and the Crisis of the Old Order.* New York: Penguin Books, 2017.

Stoddard, Abby. *Humanitarian Alert: NGO Information and Its Impact on U.S. Foreign Policy.* Boulder: Kumarian Press, 2006.

Walt, Stephen M. *Taming American Power: The Global Response to U.S. Primacy.* New York: W. W. Norton, 2005.

Notes

1. Akin Gump, "Clients (436)," Law 360, https://www.law360.com/firms/akin-gump/clients

2. Ruth May, "GOP Campaigns Took $7.35 Million from Oligarch Linked to Russia," *Dallas Morning News,* August 3, 2017, https://www.dallasnews.com/opinion/commentary/2017/08/03/tangled-web-connects-russian-oligarch-money-gop-campaigns.

3. Stephanie Kirchgaessner, "Trump's Commerce Secretary Oversaw Russia Deal While at Bank of Cyprus," *Guardian,* March 23, 2017, https://www.theguardian.com/us-news/2017/mar/23/wilbur-ross-russian-deal-bank-of-cyprus-donald-trump-commerce-secretary.

4. Tom Porter, "Did the NRA Channel Russian Money to Trump?" *Newsweek,* January 29, 2018, https://www.newsweek.com/did-nra-channel-russian-money-trump-793487.

5. Matthew Mosk and Pete Madden, "Alexander Torshin, Russian Who Courted NRA Leaders, Sanctioned by U.S. Treasury," *ABC News,* April 6, 2018, https://abcnews.go.com/Politics/alexander-torshin-russian-courted-nra-leaders-sanctioned-us/story?id=54295231.

6. Bob Woodward, *State of Denial* (New York: Simon and Schuster, 2006), 3–4.

7. Steve Reilly, "Exclusive: Two Other Trump Advisers Also Spoke with Russian Envoy During GOP Convention," *USA Today,* March 2, 2017, https://www.usatoday.com/story/news/2017/03/02/exclusive-two-other-trump-advisers-also-spoke-russian-envoy-during-gop-convention/98648190/.

8. Yuras Karmanau, "Envoy: US Willing to Consider Further Lethal Aid to Ukraine," *Associated Press News,* October 15, 2018, https://apnews.com/3ae337d117ff483daa81d7a2f0d426e3.

9. Karen DeYoung, Missy Ryan, Josh Dawsey, and Greg Jaffe, "A Tumultuous Week Began with a Phone Call Between Trump and the Turkish President," *Washington Post,* December 21, 2018.

10. Jennifer Steinhauer and Steven Lee Myers, "House G.O.P. Finds a Growing Bond with Netanyahu," *New York Times,* September 21, 2011.

11. The White House, "Remarks by President Trump and Prime Minister Netanyahu of Israel in Joint Press Conference," February 15, 2017, https://www.whitehouse.gov/briefings-statements/remarks-president-trump-prime-minister-netanyahu-israel-joint-press-conference/.

12. Mark Riebling, "Freedom's Men: The Cold War Team of Pope John Paul II and Ronald Reagan," *National Review Online,* April 4, 2005, https://www.nationalreview.com/2005/04/freedoms-men-mark-riebling/.

13. Adam Clymer, *Edward M. Kennedy: A Biography* (New York: William Morrow, 1999), 363.

14. Dan Roberts and Rory Carroll, "Obama and Raúl Castro Thank Pope for Breakthrough in US-Cuba Relations," *Guardian,* December 17, 2014, https://www.theguardian.com/world/2014/dec/17/us-cuba-diplomatic-relations-obama-raul-castro.

15. "Global Alliance for Clean Cookstoves" Department of State Archived Content, https://2009-2017.state.gov/s/partnerships/cleancook stoves/index.htm.

16. "Foreign Policy's Second Annual List of the Top 100 Global Thinkers," https://foreignpolicy.com/2010/11/23/the-fp-top-100-global -thinkers-5; and The Global Alliance for Clean Cookstoves, https://www .who.int/life-course/partners/clean-cookstoves/en.

17. " Global Alliance for Clean Cookstoves," Department of State Archived Content, https://2009-2017.state.gov/s/partnerships/cleancook stoves/index.htm.

18. Doug Tuttle, "ICBL Releases New Annual Landmine Report," Project on Government Oversight, January 15, 2009, https://www.pogo .org/analysis/2009/01/icbl-releases-new-annual-landmine-report.

19. Tom Bonfield, "Rock Star Bono Praises Bush for AIDS Plans," *Cincinnati Enquirer,* July 10, 2003, https://www.u2france.com/actu/The -Cincinnati-Enquirer-Rock-star,49952.html.

10

Foreign Policy Outputs

Learning Objectives

- Define power in international politics.
- Differentiate between hard power, soft power, and smart power policy outputs.
- Explain when hard power, soft power, and smart power outputs seem most appropriate.

It was noted in Chapter 1 that foreign policy involves adapting to changes in the external environment. Some changes are welcome; others are not. Some represent challenges to be faced, whereas others represent opportunities to be seized and exploited. However, the outputs of the foreign policy decision-making process may involve a myriad array of policy instruments. It would be a start to talk about diplomacy, signaling behaviors, military statecraft, economic statecraft, and so on, but it would be *impossible* to identify every possible foreign policy instrument, behavior, or combination of instruments or behaviors that might be the product of foreign policy processes. Yet there is one commonality here. All such influence attempts involve some use of power.

Power is the ability to get others to do what one wants. The most basic means of doing so involve coercion, payments, and attraction. A useful way to differentiate foreign policy outputs is to identify how they reflect those three means: coercion, payments, and attraction. To examine such means, it is useful to consider hard power, soft power, and smart power policy outputs.[1]

Hard Power

Hard power involves getting others to do what one wants when they otherwise prefer not to do so. Such efforts can be either negative or positive. Negative approaches involve coercion, and either threatening to punish another international actor if it does not do what the United States desires or actually going through with that punishment. Positive approaches use some form of payment to reward others for doing what the United States wants.

Negative Approaches

The most obvious coercive foreign policy output would be the threat or use of military force. Such threats have been used many times. For example, during World War II when the United States and the Soviet Union were allies in the fight against Hitler's Germany, the Soviets occupied part of Iran to keep the oil reserves there from falling into Germany's hands. After the war ended, the Soviets did not want to leave Iran. In 1946, President Truman demanded that Soviet forces leave Iran, and he ordered a US naval task force to move into the eastern Mediterranean Sea, thereby sending a signal that could not be missed. Soviet forces departed. In the 1973 October War in the Middle East, when Israeli troops surrounded Egyptian troops in the Sinai Desert in violation of a UN-sponsored cease-fire agreement, the Soviets threatened to intervene militarily to save the Egyptian troops. The Nixon administration warned the Soviets not to intervene and conspicuously put US military forces on worldwide alert. The Soviets backed down, and a diplomatic solution to save the Egyptian troops was reached.

Such military threats did not occur just during the Cold War era. When the Chinese made threatening statements and conducted missile tests in the Taiwan Straits prior to the 1996 presidential election in Taiwan in an effort to derail the pro-independence candidate's chances, the Clinton administration sent a naval task force into the contested waters. The Chinese stopped their provocative actions. In 2005–2006, rumors abounded in Washington that plans were under way in the Pentagon for a military strike on Iran to destroy its uranium enrichment program. When specifically asked by reporters about such rumors, President George W. Bush replied that *all* options regarding Iran were on the table for consideration. Perhaps as a result of such threats, Iranian representatives sent personal letters to President Bush inviting him to meet and talk with them at the UN and other international conferences. The tension between the two regimes, which had been building, began to recede somewhat as a result.

Yet threats do not mean much if they are not credible, and to be credible they need to be carried out occasionally. The most obvious form of negative hard policy outputs involves the use of military force, which can result in general wars, limited wars, unconventional wars, and asymmetric conflicts.[2] A **general war** would be one like World War I or World War II, involving the United States in a conflict in which the geographic scope of the conflict would not be limited, all the conventional weaponry in the US arsenal would be available for use, and weapons of mass destruction could potentially be used. Given the horrific death and destruction caused by the world wars of the twentieth century, the possibility of a general war in the future seems unlikely in the post–Cold War international system.

After the destruction wrought by World War II, **limited wars** have been much more common. These are conflicts that are limited by geographic scope, the amount and types of weaponry used, and the goals for which the war is fought. In such cases, US foreign policy makers would not want a war to expand beyond its current political borders, weapons of mass destruction would not be used, some limits on conventional force would probably be in play, and the goals of the conflict would be restricted. The limits on the use of force could include caps on the number of military personnel committed to the conflict and some types of targets being ruled out of bounds (e.g., targets near heavily populated urban areas or religious shrines). The goals of limited wars are typically to react to a threat or take advantage of an opportunity but generally do not include the total defeat of an enemy society. Both the Korean and Vietnam Wars illustrate this limited-war option.

Unconventional war involving US forces against nonuniformed enemy forces have also become more common since the end of World War II. Much of the fighting in the Vietnam War prior to 1968 was unconventional, in that it involved US uniformed forces fighting against insurgent Viet Cong units that attacked and then melted back into the civilian population. In the case of the Iraq War, after the initial defeat of the Iraqi uniformed military in 2003, the war continued as informal Iraqi militia forces attacked US troops. As to Afghanistan, beginning in 2001, all of the fighting there was against nonuniformed Taliban and warlord militia forces. These cases illustrate that limited wars can be conventional or unconventional or both.

Finally, asymmetric conflicts have also marked the post–Cold War and post-9/11 environments. **Asymmetric conflict** pits two forces of vastly different size and apparent power against each other. Thus, the US responses to the 1998 terrorist bombings of US embassies in Kenya and Tanzania, as well as the US responses to terrorism after the attacks on September 11, 2001, involve asymmetric warfare. Small groups of terrorists—often numbering merely in the dozens—became the focus of the US military.

In pursuing terrorists, US foreign policy makers rely increasingly on covert operations and air strikes—either manned or unmanned. Each option punishes the enemy target while putting relatively few US military personnel at risk. In 2011, such a covert operation took the life of Osama bin Laden at his compound in Abbottabad, Pakistan. In this case, an operation involving a strike team numbering approximately seventy personnel and multiple helicopters took place in a military town deep inside Pakistan—without detection by the Pakistani military. The result of this policy output not only killed the person most associated with the 2001 terror attacks but also sent a clear message to the Pakistani military: if you don't take out terrorists living in your country, we will.

Air strikes are a very popular option for employing hard power as well, whether against terrorists or other enemy targets. The obvious military advantage of air strikes is that they bring death and destruction to the target while risking the lives of relatively few US military personnel. During the Cold War, the use of air strikes against a Soviet ally might risk a Soviet retaliation, but after the Soviet Union fragmented, air strikes became increasingly popular with US foreign policy makers. They were used in the former Yugoslavia in the 1990s, both in a limited way during the 1992–1995 Bosnian War and more heavily during the Kosovo War of 1999. In 2011, air strikes were the option of choice for NATO members seeking to protect Libyan dissidents from attacks by the Libyan military. Air strikes were also heavily featured in the US intervention in the Syrian civil war.

Arguably the most popular form of air strikes in 2020 involves the use of unmanned drone aircraft. Piloted remotely by US personnel often very far away from the battle scene, these aircraft can launch air-to-ground missiles without putting any US military personnel at risk in the attack. Air strikes launched from unmanned drone aircraft have been widely utilized against a number of targets, including terrorist cells primarily in Afghanistan, Pakistan, Somalia, Yemen, and Syria by recent administrations. Moreover, the numbers of these strikes have generally increased over time across the George W. Bush, Obama, and Trump administrations.

As the world's greatest military power, the United States will continue to rely on military instruments of policy in the future. An interesting question is whether the United States relies on the military too much or too often. Has the nation become too militaristic? Have US policy makers and the public fallen in love with the use of force as the ultimate form of statecraft? Box 10.1 examines this question.

Box 10.1 Is the United States a Militaristic Power?

In a provocative book, retired US Army colonel Andrew Bacevich calls out the United States, saying its public and leaders have fallen prey to militarism. He defines militarism as the assumption that greatness as a nation is defined in military terms, in a willingness to use force as a first rather than a last resort, and in the eagerness to give the military whatever it wants. This twenty-three-year military veteran and West Point

(continues)

Box 10.1 Continued

graduate makes the argument that it is hard to blame the military for trying to professionalize itself after the debacle of the loss in Vietnam. But that is not the real problem.

In Bacevich's eyes, the real problem began with the willingness of elected political leaders—starting with President Ronald Reagan in the 1980s and continuing through the present—to lavish praise on the military and the men and women who choose to serve in the armed forces. At some point, unrelenting praise created negative side effects. As the all-volunteer force members continued to hear that they represented the best of American values, the psychological gulf between those who chose to volunteer and the public they were vowed to protect grew, until an "us versus them" dynamic developed, which was reinforced by the fact that military service was routine in some families but unheard of in most others. This gulf was augmented by a post-Vietnam generation of movies that glorified either the military (*Top Gun*) or its fundamental values (*First Blood,* the original movie of the Rambo franchise) or its redemptive qualities (*An Officer and a Gentleman*), leading the public to embrace this militarism as well.

So, Americans rarely questioned how much was spent on defense and whether it was really needed. After the Cold War ended, the United States continued to maintain a global system of overseas bases and spent almost as much on defense as the rest of the world combined—even though the United States had no compelling military rivals. Worse, from Bacevich's point of view, was the fact that the public did not challenge the George W. Bush administration's decision to go to war with Iraq, a war that Bacevich saw as a war of choice and not of necessity.

In the end, Bacevich offers a series of corrective steps to deal with this problem that he sees as corrosive to the fundamental values of US society. These include using US military force for national defense only, not to try to remake the world in the US image; using force only as a last resort when all other options have failed; limiting US dependence on foreign resources so the United States will not have to go to war to defend its access to foreign oil; pegging US defense expenditures to what others actually spend on defense; finding ways to encourage more Americans to serve in the military so that later on, more civilians (and elected officials) will be military veterans who know what war looks like before they embrace it as a policy option; and remaking the military academies into graduate schools only, which military officers would attend only after having gone to civilian universities like everyone else.

In his first two years in office, President Trump may have continued this militaristic pattern. Chemical weapons attacks by Syria on its own citizens resulted in US airstrikes against President Assad's forces, which should not be a particular surprise. However, Trump's inability to get funding for a border wall with Mexico led to his sending US troops to the southern border, which surprised many in both the military and the public. Also, he initially relied on current or former generals and admirals in key advisory roles. His first two national security advisers were the retired general Michael Flynn and the active-duty general H. R. McMaster. His secretary of defense was retired general James Mattis, and his homeland security secretary was retired general John Kelly, who later became White House chief of staff. Interestingly, all left the administration within its first two years. Flynn, McMaster, and Kelly were fired by the president, and Mattis resigned his position in protest of Trump's policies. After Mattis announced his resignation publicly, Trump fired him.

So, what do you think of this argument? Is America in love with its military and war making, or are current US military policies reasonable and prudent, given global geopolitical realities?

Sources:

Andrew J. Bacevich, *The New American Militarism: How Americans Are Seduced by War* (New York: Oxford University Press, 2005); Matthew Schofield, "All-Volunteer Military May Desensitize U.S. to War, Some Fear," *McClatchy Newspapers,* December 31, 2012, https://www.mcclatchydc.com/news/politics-government/article24742384.html.

Although the threat or use of force is the most obvious form of negative hard power, a more common form of such policy outputs is the threat or use of **economic sanctions**.[3] In these cases, economic means are employed to punish another state or important individuals in it, most commonly in the form of trade sanctions. These typically involve retaliatory actions for another party's trade behavior. For example, in 2009 the Obama administration raised tariffs on imports of Chinese tires for a period of three years after US tire manufacturers complained that Chinese tires were being sold in the United States at less than fair market value. China appealed to the World Trade Organization, and in 2011, the WTO ruled in favor of the United States. In 2018, the Trump administration imposed billions of dollars in trade sanctions against China in an effort to push the Chinese to change their trade and monetary practices. Time will tell if this strategy works.

However, sanctions can also be used to seek broader political goals. Comprehensive trade sanctions involve refusing both to buy another country's goods or services and to sell US goods and services to that country. For decades, Cuba represented an obvious example of comprehensive US sanctions. After Fidel Castro's Communist regime nationalized foreign-owned properties in 1960, the United States responded with an embargo that by 1962 included prohibiting all US trade with and travel to Cuba. The goal was to bring down the Cuban regime. However, Cuba had the Soviet Union as an ideological patron, and though the Cuban economy was surely hurt by the total embargo, Soviet assistance kept the economy afloat. After the demise of the Soviet Union, the Cuban economy suffered, Fidel Castro stepped down, and his brother, Raúl, allowed limited private-property rights to be exercised in Cuba. Perhaps after fifty years, the embargo has begun to show some political results. Another example can be found in Iran. During the Islamic Revolution in Iran in 1979, Iranian students stormed the US embassy in Tehran, holding fifty-two diplomats hostage for over a year. The United States responded with comprehensive sanctions against Iran.

A major problem with both the Cuban and the Iranian sanctions is that they were unilateral in nature. The United States was sanctioning these regimes, but others were not. Therefore, other markets were available for Cuban and Iranian goods and services and as sources of the imports Cuba and Iran desired. Critics of such unilateral sanctions argue that the only ones who end up suffering as a result are the US businesses that are prevented from buying from or selling to those target countries. Demonstrating the limits of unilateral sanctions, the Iranian government only agreed to negotiations regarding its nuclear program once the EU added its own economic sanctions to the long-standing unilateral ones imposed by the United States. When the EU got involved, Iran lost both significant oil revenues and access to the global electronic banking network.

When comprehensive sanctions are multilateral in nature and imposed by most trading states in the international system, they are thus far more significant and can have devastating effects on the target. The classic example is Iraq after the 1991 Persian Gulf War. When the war ended, the Iraqi government agreed to accept all UN Security Council resolutions that would follow. When the UN later demanded that Iraq open its weapons-of-mass-destruction programs up for international inspection, the Saddam Hussein regime at first dragged its feet and then later expelled international weapons inspectors from the country. The UN Security Council then passed comprehensive sanctions against Iraq. While regime leaders continued to live in luxury, Iraqi civilians bore the brunt of the economic pain, as the country's infrastructure deteriorated from a lack of maintenance (thereby collapsing the electric grid and many sanitary water systems), food supplies ran short, and medical supplies virtually ran out. As thousands of Iraqis began to die as a result, the UN chose to allow limited sales of Iraqi oil so the Iraqi government would have the funds to buy food and other humanitarian supplies. Unfortunately, much of this money simply got skimmed by Iraqi officials (and some officials in the UN itself), so the Iraqi people continued to suffer.

The suffering of the Iraqi people led to an effort to find better ways to use economic sanctions. Now US policy makers prefer the use of **targeted or smart sanctions**. These are meant to punish the specific individuals who actually make the policies that are contrary to US interests rather than the people of the target country as a whole. Such sanctions can include freezing the international bank accounts of regime leaders and supporters, limiting their ability to travel internationally by denying visas, and restricting electronic money transfers to or from the targeted country. Such actions were taken in the 1990s against Haitian military leaders who had toppled a democratically elected government there; reportedly, their wives were particularly annoyed that they could no longer go on shopping trips to Miami. Targeted or smart sanctions were also used to punish specific high officials of the Iranian regime. After the Syrian government essentially went to war against its own citizens following the Arab Spring of 2011, such targeted sanctions have also been applied to specific individuals who compose part of Syria's governing elite. Most recently, smart sanctions have been applied to Russian elites and businesses as punishment for Russia's intervention in the 2016 US presidential elections and Russia's aggressive use of assassination against Russian exiles living in the United Kingdom, as well as to some Saudis linked to Jamal Khashoggi's murder.

Yet, as noted at the beginning of the chapter, not all hard power is employed negatively. There are positive ways to get others to do what the United States wants when the target would prefer not to do so.

Positive Approaches

Positive inducements in the form of rewards can also often persuade others to do what the United States wants. Depending on the other party involved, those inducements could involve an array of tangible or intangible rewards. For instance, in 2011 the former military government of Myanmar (Burma) did what the United States had long requested: it passed electoral reforms and allowed formerly imprisoned Nobel Peace Prize–winner Aung San Suu Kyi to participate in electoral politics. In return, the United States did what Myanmar wanted; it sent a high-ranking official—in this case Secretary of State Hillary Clinton—on a highly visible official visit to the country. The Burmese regime hoped that such a visit would help open Myanmar up to additional foreign direct investment, which its economy desperately needed. In response to the regime's ethnic cleansing policies targeting its minority Rohingya population, the Trump administration imposed economic sanctions against the Burmese regime in 2018, a move that will seriously compromise the regime's efforts to attract more foreign investment. Thus, in this case a positive approach was replaced with a negative one.

Although there may be many different ways to reward regimes for doing what the United States desires, two common types of rewards come in the form of economic or military assistance. Perhaps the best example of economic aid being used as a reward came in 1979 when President Jimmy Carter promised to grant Israel and Egypt economic assistance in return for their signing a peace treaty. Every administration since then has kept that commitment, making Israel and Egypt typically among the top five recipients of US assistance each year. When he was once criticized for having "purchased" this peace agreement, Carter defended the action by asking, "What's peace worth to you?"

Another example came during the George W. Bush administration. In the context of the UN's Millennium Development Goals that sought to improve human security dramatically in developing countries (by reducing poverty, improving access to education and health care, and so on), President Bush made it clear that regimes that embraced free market economic principles, governed justly, and invested in their people would get more US economic aid. The result has been an increase in US economic aid to many of the poorest countries of the world and an insistence that they meet measurable targets in improving the lives of their citizenry. The Obama administration continued this effort, but the Trump administration has yet to demonstrate a commitment to the successor to the Millennium Development Goals—the Sustainable Development Goals. Yet if US administrations can use economic assistance as leverage to get others to do what the United States wants, is it any wonder that most presidents tend to fall in love with foreign aid as a tool once they reach the Oval Office?

However, economic assistance is not the only currency for rewarding others. Military assistance is often used in this way as well. For years, the United States provided military assistance to Saudi Arabia, despite the fact that it shares neither the US commitment to democracy nor a commitment to human rights. Yet as long as the Saudis were willing to sell the United States oil and serve as a bastion of anticommunist and anti-Iranian stability in the region, they would be rewarded with significant US military aid. US military aid to Saudi Arabia continues, as the United States is a major supplier of the weapons and ordnance that Saudi Arabia is using in its controversial intervention in the Yemeni civil war. It would appear that as long as the Saudis are seen as a counterweight to Iran's influence in the Middle East, the Saudi regime will continue to receive US military support.

In an African example, in 2011 the United States rewarded the Ugandan government for its willingness to go after the Lord's Resistance Army (the LRA), a warlord militia operating in the Great Lakes region of Africa (which includes countries such as Uganda, Rwanda, Burundi, Kenya, and the eastern portion of the Democratic Republic of the Congo). Not only did the Lord's Resistance Army threaten to destabilize this part of eastern Africa but some of its former leaders faced trial before the International Criminal Court on charges of war crimes and crimes against humanity. Over time, the Lord's Resistance Army seemed to disappear, and in 2017 the Ugandan military ended its hunt for the LRA rebels and their leader, Joseph Kony. However, US military aid continued to flow to Uganda as the regime contributed forces to the fight against terrorist groups in Somalia and kept its mineral wealth open to Western investment.

Hard power options can therefore include both negative punishments to coerce others and positive rewards to induce them to meet US desires. Yet what is even better than pushing or pulling others to do what the United States wants is to get them to want what the United States wants. And getting others to want what you want is the very essence of soft power.

Soft Power

There are a variety of ways to induce others to want what you want, but two major and mutually reinforcing clusters of means can be identified: the advocacy of American values, and governmental agenda-setting at the global and regional levels. Each of these clusters deserves some attention.

Value Advocacy

A fundamental way for others to want what you want is for them to share your values. Thus, one way of using soft power is by projecting a set of values that are attractive to most people. Values such as liberty, democracy, and human rights are commitments to empowering individuals and showing them respect, and these are far easier values to "sell" to others than the values of authoritarian regimes, such as ruling through fear or doing what the government tells you to do. The United States stakes out its values in its Declaration of Independence, the Constitution, its laws, and in the organization of the government that flows from all of these sources. However, for these values to resonate with others, they must be shown to be more than mere words. How can this be done?

Certainly the US government can promote these values in a variety of ways. A traditional way in the past for such value transmission was the creation of a library in many US embassies abroad where foreign citizens could learn more about the United States, its society, and its governance. Unfortunately, in the era after the 2001 terror attacks, security concerns and the need to harden embassies against the threat of terrorist attack have severely eroded the ability of US diplomatic installations abroad to serve this type of role, as foreign nationals face more and more obstacles in just trying to enter these facilities.

That educational role now falls largely on entities such as the Voice of America (VOA). Funded by Congress, the VOA broadcasts 1,500 hours of programming each week in forty-three languages and in a variety of media outlets. Through the use of radio, television, the internet, mobile media, and social media, an estimated global audience of over 140 million per week is reached. In order to avoid the temptation to become simply a propaganda outlet of the US government, the entity's charter requires it to broadcast the news accurately and objectively. Although it seeks to effectively communicate US policies and actions, it is also required by law to include responsible, critical discussions about those policies and actions. Thus, VOA broadcasts can become a window into the United States, letting others know who Americans are and what they value.

Beyond the activities of the VOA, presidents, secretaries of state and defense, ambassadors, and other US officials can and do routinely stress US values and try to emulate them through their actions when meeting with foreign audiences. Whenever President Obama addressed a Muslim audience at Cairo University, or when officials such as Secretary of State Hillary Clinton and US Trade Representative Ron Kirk met with Kenyan economic officials, or when Ambassador Nikki Haley regularly addressed the UN Security

Council or Defense Secretary James Mattis met with his counterparts in Egypt and Israel, these officials were both discussing and
modeling US values by presenting who they were and how they
operated. There is another way such values are modeled as well.
Did you know the United States often sends female ambassadors to
Middle East states? Do you think the gender of these personnel
choices is a coincidence? Are values again being modeled?

Another way the government can advocate its values is
through the Fulbright Program. Sponsored by the State Department and funded by Congress, this program provides grants for
US students and scholars to study abroad and for foreign students
and scholars to study in the United States. Thus, US citizens
studying abroad can serve as pseudo-ambassadors, telling others
about life in the United States, and foreign citizens can come to
the United States and see for themselves how America operates.
They may often take those values back to their native lands.

Yet it is not just the government that participates in transmit-
ting American values. The US educational system does so as well.
The United States has an outstanding reputation in higher education, and thousands of foreign students are welcomed to US col-
leges and universities each year. Many of them will later rise to
the ranks of elite decision makers in their home societies. As
noted in Chapter 9, Israeli prime minister Benjamin Netanyahu
has two degrees from MIT. Former Liberian president and Nobel
Peace Prize–recipient Ellen Johnson Sirleaf is a graduate of Harvard's Kennedy School of Government, King Abdullah II of Jor-
dan attended Georgetown University's School of Foreign Service,
former UN secretary general Boutros Boutros-Ghali was a Fulbright Scholar at Columbia University, former Bolivian president
Gonzalo Sánchez de Lozada went to the University of Chicago,
Prince Bandar bin Sultan of Saudi Arabia went to Johns Hopkins
University School of Advanced International Studies, and so on.
While these foreign students are studying subjects such as Eng-
lish, business, political science, or engineering, they often also
pick up American values to take back home. So too do high
school students who come to the United States in exchange programs and live with American families. When those individuals
rise to positions of influence in their home countries, American
values may get represented there.

Yet perhaps the greatest transmitter of American values is in the private, not the public, sector. It is the media. US news and entertainment programming can be viewed by almost anyone in the world with a satellite dish, a cable connection, an internet link, or a smartphone. US movies are globally marketed, with many US films routinely selling more tickets outside the United States than domestically. To the extent that the media illustrates American values, much of the rest of the world can see and judge them. For many abroad, American values are seductive; they regret that their society does not value and respect individual freedoms and opportunities in the same way the United States does. To the extent such values make others look favorably on the United States and begin to see things as Americans see them, soft power is at work.

To be fair, the opposite can happen, too. Learning more about America may make others with very conservative values view the United States less favorably. That happened with Egyptian writer Sayyid Qutb, a leading member of the Muslim Brotherhood and considered by most to be the inspiration for later al-Qaeda leaders such as Osama bin Laden and Ayman al-Zawahiri. Qutb spent two years in the United States in the late 1940s and subsequently wrote that he was appalled by the consumerism, superficiality, and moral decay of American political culture. Years later, Yemeni American Anwar al-Awlaki similarly used his American experience to critique Western lifestyles and to urge Muslims to rise up against the United States.

Besides sharing values, there are other ways to get others to want what you want. One of those involves setting the international agenda.

Agenda Setting

As anyone who has ever presided over a meeting knows, one way to maximize your chances of getting what you want is to set the meeting's agenda. The same holds true in foreign policy. The United States did a masterful job of setting the international agenda for the post–World War II era by supporting the creation of a series of international institutions that, by meeting the needs of others, also met US needs.[4] This was done at both the global and the regional level.

On the global level, consider institutions such as the World Bank and the International Monetary Fund. These lending institutions sought to bring order and stability to the global economy after World War II. They established structures to address economic situations ranging from routine economic challenges or opportunities to full-blown crises, as well as the rules by which these structures would operate. Yet it took money to bring these institutions to life, and the United States provided more money to them than any other state. Moreover, the rules were generally written so that those that contributed the most money to these organizations had the most influence on the decisions they made. This meant the United States could largely shape the decisions being made, as it had more voting shares than any other state. States facing economic challenges got help, and the United States got to steer that help in the directions it preferred—typically toward capitalist, free market–based solutions. From the US perspective, this was a "win-win" scenario.

After the Cuban Missile Crisis scared the world with the possibility of a nuclear war, the US, British, and Soviet governments sought to back away from the nuclear brink of disaster. That effort began with the Nuclear Test-Ban Treaty. Moreover, the nuclear weapons powers had no desire to see others gain such weaponry, but other countries wanted the benefits and/or status of nuclear power. So, in 1964 the United States offered a proposal to the UN that later led to the drafting and signing of the Nonproliferation Treaty and the creation of the nonproliferation regime. Thus, US foreign policy makers found a way to get others to want what they wanted: a world in which there are established rules and procedures that safeguard countries' rights to develop peaceful nuclear power without risking a world filled with nuclear weapons states.

At the regional level as well, agenda setting can be an important form of soft power. In the Western Hemisphere, the United States has encouraged the development of organizations such as the Organization of American States (OAS), which promotes democracy, human rights, security from harm, economic development, and the rule of law. The fact that the headquarters of the OAS is in Washington, DC, tells us something important. When dealing with regional issues such as economic integration, immigration, or combating narcotrafficking rings, the United States was long able to set agendas so that the question was not whether the countries of the Americas would cooperate but how they would do so.

To be fair, we should note that US ability to determine the agenda in the Americas has been diminished in recent years by the relative neglect of the region by most US administrations and by the rise and vocal challenge of such leaders as Hugo Chàvez and Nicolàs Maduro in Venezuela and Bolivia's Evo Morales. Groups such as the Union of South American Nations seek to coordinate the political and economic policies of the region *without* the guidance of the United States.

Regional agenda setting and shaping can be found in Europe as well. In the 1990s, the United States began articulating a theme within the NATO community. If NATO members (and other Europeans more generally) did not like the United States acting as a military superpower, then what military roles were they willing to step up and take on themselves? Again, meetings became more about "what will you do and how will you do it," and less about "will you do anything?" As a result, other NATO members contributed to military missions in the former Yugoslavia and later in Afghanistan and Libya.

When discussing hard power and soft power policy outputs, we need to keep in mind that the world is a complicated place, and there are far more than two ways to get things done. Hard and soft power policy outputs can be pursued simultaneously. When combined together, they can be thought of as smart power options.

Smart Power

When correctly applied, hard power policy options may work, if enough coercive force is applied or sufficient incentives are offered. However, such policies may breed resentment on the part of the recipients, as those policies were not something the recipients initially wanted to adopt on their own. The targets of hard power policy options may thus interpret their subsequent actions as expedient or necessary, but not necessarily as legitimate choices. **Smart power** represents the combination of both hard and soft power options. Adding soft power elements can make a hard power option easier to accept by the target, because there is some degree of attraction or shared values involved. Sometimes the addition of soft power elements may make more coercive elements less necessary, as the result may be seen as more legitimate in the eyes of the target.

How might smart power work? Consider Islamic-based terrorism, for example. One way to deal with it is to try to kill every terrorist identified. That's hard power. But it seems an impossible task. Every terrorist killed has family and friends who may turn to terrorism because the United States killed their loved one. The "whack-a-mole" analogy applies; dealing with the problem in one place just makes it pop up in another. In addition to taking hard-core jihadists out of action whenever and wherever possible, what if other potential terrorists and their co-religionists learned that the United States did not hate Islam, was not at war with Islam, that several million Muslims openly practice their faith in the United States, that Muslims were elected to Congress and took their oath of office with their hand on the Quran, or that the Quran did not support the taking of innocent lives? Would the number of potential terrorists drop? For those whose terrorism is rooted in economic misery and lack of opportunity, what if the economy in their society grew, more jobs were available, and the quality of their lives materially improved? Would they turn to terrorism then?

Although the term was not in vogue then, a good example of smart power policy options at work can be found in the US expulsion of Iraqi forces from Kuwait in 1991. Certainly, hard power options were used. Over half a million US troops were moved to the Kuwait theater of operations, and the subsequent invasion routed the Iraqi troops in Kuwait and drove them in disarray out of the country. However, what made that operation so politically successful was the other policy options that were also employed. Every major step taken by the United States was approved in advance by the UN Security Council, so the actions were seen as legitimate in world eyes. After the initial Iraqi invasion of Kuwait in 1990, Secretary of State James Baker and other US diplomats traveled extensively throughout the region as well as the world, lining up support from other countries. The fact that more than two dozen other countries were willing to contribute military personnel to the effort to liberate Kuwait—including Arab states such as Egypt, Syria, Morocco, Oman, the United

Arab Emirates, and Qatar, as well as Saudi Arabia and Kuwait—
made it clear that they, too, felt the Iraqi occupation of Kuwait
was illegitimate and should not stand. In short, others wanted
what the United States wanted. Had the United States simply
gone to war against the Iraqi forces, Iraqi president Saddam Hussein would have been better able to sell his idea that this conflict
was between an Arab state and the United States or between him
and George H. W. Bush, thereby gaining some sympathy from
anti-US sentiments in the region.

Although complementing hard power options with soft power
options is nothing new, the idea of smart power gained considerable traction in the Obama administration. As the State Department's website said, "Military force may sometimes be necessary
to protect our people and our interests. But diplomacy and development are equally important in creating conditions for a peaceful, stable and prosperous world. That is the essence of smart
power—using all the tools at our disposal."[5]

One might expect the State Department to champion smart
power approaches to foreign policy problems, but former secretary of defense Robert Gates was also a very highly visible and
vocal proponent of a greater reliance on smart power policy outputs. During the Obama administration, he testified before Congress that the State Department needed more money, not less, to
serve US interests better. He pointed out that military successes
alone could not win the wars in Iraq and Afghanistan; it would
also take more diplomatic initiatives, better US outreach to potentially hostile groups, and far more economic aid to accomplish US
goals in those countries. That would require more US funding for
the State Department. At one point in his congressional testimony,
Gates referenced the final scene in the movie *Charlie Wilson's
War,* in which the Congress was willing to spend $1 billion to
defeat the Soviets in Afghanistan but not willing to spend $1
million to build the schools there, which might have prevented the
Taliban from coming to power.[6] In another comparison, Gates
pointed out that there are more US personnel in *one* aircraft carrier task force than in the entire US diplomatic corps, and he said
that if the State Department had more money to conduct more
civilian programs, then the Defense Department might be called
upon less and would need less money in the long run. In 2017 testimony before the Senate Defense Appropriations Subcommittee,

Secretary of Defense James Mattis agreed, calling soft power assets as essential to national security as hard power assets.

For his part, Secretary Gates did not just talk up this idea of relying more on smart power; he acted on it. For example, he appointed Admiral James Stavridis of the US Navy to head the US European Command, citing his prior successes as head of US military operations in Latin America. In his Latin American role, Stavridis combined soft power options (e.g., providing health care services and sponsoring soccer teams) with hard power options to take on the challenges of combating narcotrafficking and corruption and to create a more favorable image of the United States in the region. In Gates's view, such a cooperative approach was also appropriate for dealing with European allies, which often needed coaxing to act in what he saw as the US and European shared interests.[7] Even more impressive, Gates supported the creation of a new Africa Command that blended hard and soft power in its mission statement and personnel choices, as Box 10.2 demonstrates. Smart power policy options thus seem to be increasingly the "new normal" when it comes to US foreign policy outputs.

Box 10.2 What's So Different About AFRICOM?

For US foreign policy makers, Africa represents a multitude of current and future challenges. A billion people, one-seventh of the world's population, live there, and the population is growing rapidly. Africa's population could double by the middle of the twenty-first century. Not only is Africa the world's poorest continent, but it is also plagued by poor governance, corruption, and violent conflicts that killed 3 million to 5 million people between 1998 and 2003. Both traditional and nontraditional security challenges abound there. As a result, the United States created a new military unified command in 2007 to deal with protecting US interests in Africa: the United States Africa Command, or **AFRICOM**.

From the start, AFRICOM was different. Its website mission statement includes explicit reference to promoting good governance and development:

Africa Command protects and defends the national security interests of the United States by strengthening the defense capabilities of African states and regional organizations and, when directed, conducts military operations, in order to deter and defeat transnational threats and to provide a security environment conducive to good governance and development.

Moreover, AFRICOM is the first US regional military command to include civilian officials from other branches of government. More than thirty people from thirteen other government agencies or departments can be found in key leadership, staff, and administrative roles. Four senior foreign service officers are in key leadership positions, including one filling the role of deputy to the commander for civil-military activities—a position just one step removed from the top of the organizational chart. These interagency appointees help AFRICOM provide humanitarian assistance, crisis relief, and long-term economic development and good governance assistance for African states.

Yet over time, the hard power roles of AFRICOM seemed to grow. In 2014, approximately 700 US military personnel deployed in Africa were special operations troops who trained militaries in central and west Africa to hunt local insurgents. By 2018, the number of US special operators in Africa grew to approximately 1,200. The presence of that many special operators was generally unknown by the public until four of them were killed in an ambush in Niger in 2018. Not long after, the Pentagon announced plans to slash the number of special operators in Africa and to redeploy them to assist against higher-priority threats such as Russia and China. That change suggests that AFRICOM's role will swing back more in the direction of soft power or smart power options.

What do you think? Is AFRICOM's emphasis on combining hard and soft power options into smart power options the right way to go? If so, are such policy options appropriate just for Africa, or do they resonate elsewhere as well? On the other hand, is the military's role, as President George W. Bush once stated, to fight and win wars?

(continues)

Box 10.2 Continued

Sources:

"Advanced Questions for General William E. 'Kip' Ward, U.S. Army, Nominee for Commander, U.S. Africa Command," Senate Armed Services Committee, September 2007, https://www.armed-services.senate.gov /imo/media/doc/Ward%2009-27-07.pdf; "DR Congo War Deaths 'Exaggerated,'" *BBC News,* January 20, 2010, https://web.archive.org/web /20100121025213/http://news.bbc.co.uk/2/hi/africa/8471147.stm; "Population Dynamics of Africa," World Population Awareness, December 17, 2011, http://www.overpopulation.org/Africa.html; Kyle Rempfer, "Report: AFRICOM Looks to Cut Special Ops Missions, Pull Out Hundreds of Troops from Africa," *Military Times,* August 2, 2018, https://www .militarytimes.com/news/your-military/2018/08/02/report-africom-looks -to-cut-special-ops-missions-pull-out-hundreds-of-troops-from-africa/; US Africa Command website, http://www.africom.mil/; "World Population," Population Reference Bureau, UN Population Division, September 2011, http://www.nationsonline.org/oneworld/world_population.htm.

Conclusion

As the United States moves deeper into the twenty-first century, foreign policy challenges that are increasingly global and transnational in nature will call for a variety of foreign policy outputs. Hard power outputs—the ability to get others to do what you want—will always have a role. The power to coerce—through the threat or use of force—or to reward—through incentives like foreign aid and other side payments—will be used where appropriate.

However, as someone once said, you cannot nuke global warming. Numerous other foreign policy challenges and opportunities will call for soft power outputs—emphasizing shared values and common concerns so that others want the same things that the United States wants. For example, improving the quality of life elsewhere—through outputs like targeted foreign assistance or democratization assistance—can serve US interests in a variety of ways. Societies can become more stable and less violence prone. As other societies improve their economies, they have the ability to purchase more US goods and services and have a greater stake in preserving an increasingly beneficial international order.

The coupling of hard and soft power policy outputs into smart power approaches seems to be the wave of the future. The United States is not a hegemonic military power that can impose its will on others with impunity. That was evident in the first decade of the twenty-first century, as the ability to fight two wars at the same time seriously stressed the US military and gave countries such as Iran the breathing room to more actively pursue their national interests at the expense of US interests. When the George W. Bush administration threatened Iran with the use of force over its support for terrorist groups and its nuclear weapons program, Iranian supreme leader Ayatollah Sayyid Ali Khamenei called the US bluff, publicly stating that the US military was stretched so thin that it could do nothing to Iran. At the time, he was largely correct. Further, as the United States continues to recover from the Great Recession of 2008–2010 and faces a "fiscal cliff" of mounting debt, the need to find lower-cost options than the use of military force will be paramount.

Thus, the United States now pursues a range of foreign policy outputs to deal with ongoing issues. The first step is normally soft power—diplomatic outreach and engagement—which tends to be more successful to whatever degree the United States has been able to share its values with the target state. Should those means prove insufficient, hard power outputs in the form of rewards offered or threats made may be next. Should those fail to suffice, US foreign policy makers have to decide if the issue is significant enough to justify the use of force. If so, in the twenty-first century, that use of force—to be most effective—will probably be accompanied by other soft power elements to form a smart power response so that the matter is seen as a more legitimate step by the international community.

Suggested Reading

Nye Jr., Joseph S. "Get Smart: Combining Hard and Soft Power." *Foreign Affairs* 88 (July–August 2009): 160–163.
———. *The Paradox of American Power: Why the World's Only Superpower Can't Go It Alone.* New York: Oxford University Press, 2003.

Viotti, Paul. *The Dollar and National Security: The Monetary Compo-nents of Hard Power.* Stanford: Stanford University Press, 2014.
Walker, Christopher, and Jessica Ludwig. "The Meaning of Sharp Power: How Authoritarian States Project Power." *Foreign Affairs,* November 16, 2017, https://www.foreignaffairs.com/articles/china/2017-11-16/meaning-sharp-power.
Wilson, Ernest J. "Hard Power, Soft Power, Smart Power." *Annals of the American Academy of Political and Social Science* 616 (2008): 110–124.

Notes

1. I borrow heavily in this chapter from the work of Joseph S. Nye Jr.: *The Paradox of American Power: Why the World's Only Superpower Can't Go It Alone* (New York: Oxford University Press, 2002); "Get Smart," *Foreign Affairs* 88 (July–August 2009): 160–163; and his book with Robert O. Keohane, *Power and Interdependence,* 4th ed. (Boston: Longman, 2012).

2. In this section, I draw on Chapter 5 of James M. Scott, Ralph G. Carter, and A. Cooper Drury, *IR: International, Economic, and Human Security in a Changing World,* 3rd ed. (Thousand Oaks, CA: Sage/CQ Press, 2019).

3. In this section, I draw on Chapter 9 in ibid.

4. For more on this idea, see G. John Ikenberry, *After Victory: Institutions, Strategic Restraint, and the Rebuilding of Order After Major Wars* (Princeton: Princeton University Press, 2000).

5. "American 'Smart Power': Diplomacy and Development Are the Vanguard," Department of State Factsheet, May 4, 2009, https://2009-2017.state.gov/r/pa/scp/fs/2009/122579.htm.

6. Lisa Daniel, "State Department Needs Iraq Funding," *American Forces Press Service,* February 17, 2011, http://terrorism-online.blogspot.com/2011/02/state-department-needs-iraq-funding.html.

7. Gordon Lubold, "Pentagon to Show Softer Side to the World," *Christian Science Monitor,* March 25, 2009, http://www.csmonitor.com/USA/Military/2009/0325/p03s03-usmi.html.

11
Looking to the Future

As someone once said, the one great constant is change. After World War II, expectations that the Allied Powers would continue to cooperate, reflected in the creation and structure of the new United Nations in 1945, were dashed by the swift arrival of the Cold War. The rivalry between the United States and the Soviet Union dwarfed all other foreign policy issues and caused most issues to be perceived through the prism of national security interests. When the Cold War ended, the decade of the 1990s offered the expectation of a new era of peace and cooperation. As Francis Fukuyama suggested,

237

"We're all liberals now."[1] However, long-pent-up national, tribal, clan, and sectarian rivalries exploded in multiple parts of the world. The result was a messy, violent political order, famously characterized as "a clash of civilizations" by Samuel Huntington.[2] Thus, the Clinton administration spent far more time than it anticipated dealing with humanitarian threats and regional security crises. Then came the terrorist attacks of September 11, 2001. Not surprisingly, the George W. Bush administration launched its War on Terror, which again dwarfed most other issues.

The election of Barack Obama promised a change in US foreign policy, and in some stylistic ways, that change was realized. The phrase "War on Terror" no longer escaped the lips of US foreign policy makers. Instead, "change" and "engagement" were the mantras of the new administration. Based primarily on a different mindset by officials of the new administration, many of the challenges—events and situations that the previous administration had defined as national security inputs to be met with largely unilateral or only selectively multilateral policy outputs—were now socially constructed as opportunities impacting the international system as a whole. Motivated by liberal and neoliberal interpretations, these challenges were to be met with multilateral responses. Most significant, President Obama and his team tried to shift US policy away from participation in Middle East wars to confront challenges in Asia, most of them personified by the rise of China as a rival and potential threat. Diplomatic, economic, and military options were explored to preserve the United States as the dominant power in the Asia/Pacific region.

Then Donald Trump got elected. In his first two years, it seemed President Trump reflexively opposed anything the former administration endorsed. US military commitments to NATO and the Middle East were questioned, and a military pullout from Syria was announced. Diplomatically, significant outreach efforts were undertaken via summit conferences with President Putin of Russia, President Xi of China, and North Korean leader Kim Jong-un. President Trump seemed to have more respect and appreciation for authoritarian rulers than for longtime democratic allies. Arguably, the most notable changes in US policy were transactional approaches to trade policy and efforts to restrict immigration. The North American Free Trade Agreement (NAFTA) was replaced by the United States-Mexico-Canada Agreement, although not without significant friction along the way. Tariffs were raised on imported steel and aluminum, primarily hurting longtime allies rather than rivals, and a trade war was started with China. As for immigration, a travel ban was imposed on a number of mostly Muslim states, and troops were sent to the southern border to stop migrants and asylum seekers from entering the country illegally— or perhaps even legally.

Given such changing priorities, what types of inputs, processes, and outputs can we expect in the early part of the twenty-first century?

Policy Inputs

As indicated in Chapter 2, foreign policy makers rely on their understandings of the way the international system works—in other words, the theories that explain behavior—to cut through the noise of the international system and decide which threats and opportunities to respond to and how to respond. Most American administrations are largely composed of realists and neorealists, officials who try to address national interests expressed in power terms. The George W. Bush administration had its share of such realists and neorealists, but it also had idealists. President Bush, Vice President Cheney, Defense Secretary Rumsfeld, and others were, to varying degrees, idealists who wanted to use American power to impact the world for the better, while relying on US military power to defend the nation against the scourge of terrorism. For their part, the officials at the top of the Obama administration were largely neoliberals. Led by President Obama, Secretaries of State Hillary Clinton and John Kerry, and Defense Secretaries Robert Gates, Leon Panetta, Chuck Hagel, and Ash Carter, they sought to use cooperation as a means to advance US national interests.

As I write this, based on its first two years, the Trump administration seems harder to categorize. In many ways, President Trump seems to prefer conflict with longtime allies rather than cooperation with them. Again, he shows a preference for cooperation with authoritarian leaders. Given his transactional approach to foreign policy, which measures success in zero-sum terms, it may be that his worldview values power and leans more toward realism than neoliberalism. Then the question remains as to his campaign mantra: Make America Great Again. The theoretical approach that best explains this foreign policy goal depends on how *great* is defined. Is America great if it is feared (realism) more than liked or respected (liberalism)? Does American need to be "great" again to be able to act unilaterally on its interests without the cooperation of others? Answers to such questions may lie in the eye of the beholder.

Yet whatever their basic understandings of how the international system works, future administrations surely will face events that, as foreign policy inputs, are understood in terms of security interests: national security, economic security, and human security.[3] Each of these merits discussion.

National Security Inputs

Although it is impossible to note all potential national security threats facing the United States, a few deserve special mention. First, the national security situation has evolved significantly following the decade marked by the War on Terror. Although sectarian-based terrorism has not ended, it has fundamentally changed. Al-Qaeda as a monolithic entity has been defanged—through the drying up of its ability to easily move money across international borders and the targeted killing or capturing of its top leaders and field operatives. Now terrorist activity is more locally based, whether within the United States by homegrown terrorists inspired by groups such as ISIS or by terrorist cells that have the ability to strike near their own locations—for instance, al-Shabaab in Somalia and Kenya; al-Qaeda in the Arabian Peninsula in Yemen; al-Qaeda in the Islamic Maghreb in northwestern Africa; or Boko Haram in Nigeria.

Second, the Iranian agreement to suspend its enrichment of nuclear fuel, reduce its supply of enriched fuel, and allow international inspections of many of its nuclear facilities for a trial period of six months was welcomed by the five permanent members of the UN Security Council, Germany, and many other states in the international system. However, the deal did not reassure the Israelis or other Sunni regimes in the region that continued to insist that the Iranians were developing the missile and nuclear fuel–enrichment technologies needed for nuclear weapons. Who would be the targets of such a potential weapon? The Israelis? The Saudis? Further, Iran continued to play an assertive role in the region by supporting the Shi'a or Shi'a-friendly forces elsewhere. These include the Shi'a militia and political party Hezbollah in Lebanon, the Shi'a-based Iraqi regime, and the Alawite-dominated regime of Bashar al-Assad in Syria. In short, Iran's role in the region kept both Israeli and Sunni Muslim populations on edge. Would Israel launch a preventive strike on Iran? Was sectarian war within Islam a looming possibility within the region, with Shi'a Iran and its allies challenging Sunni Saudi Arabia and its allies?

Third, other national security risks plagued the Middle East. The Arab Spring of 2011 sputtered to a halt, with only Tunisia democratizing to a greater extent. Other authoritarian regimes managed to remain in power, and Libya and Syria collapsed into civil wars. Further, Turkey continued to flex its regional military muscle. Its pursuit of Kurdish insurgents across the border into Syria risked the threat of border clashes and territorial incursions that could easily escalate with attacks on Russian military personnel deployed in Syria.

Fourth, the Obama administration began moving more military personnel to Asia to offset provocative Chinese activities there. Particularly troubling were Chinese efforts to assert their control over the South China Sea, the resources surrounding the Senkaku/Diaoyu Islands jointly claimed by China and Japan, and the resources surrounding the Spratly Islands, which China, Vietnam, and the Philippines all claimed. Both the Obama and Trump administrations undertook "freedom of navigation" operations, to sail through and fly over the disputed territories claimed by China.

North Korea could not be ignored in this list. As a nuclear power with a large standing army, a questionable economy, an impoverished civilian population, and an uncertain leader in young Kim Jong-un, the possibilities for national security crises were manifold. Under Kim's father, Kim Jong-il, North Korea often undertook provocative actions, such as firing missiles near and over Japan. To deal with North Korea, President Trump did what no other US president has done; he attended a one-day summit meeting with the North Korean leader. The result was one-sided. The North Koreans closed one missile test site thought by many to be obsolete, while in return President Trump suspended regularly scheduled US–South Korean military exercises without consulting the South Koreans in advance. Thereafter, satellite photos showed what appeared to be new locations for missile and possible warhead testing in North Korea that had not been acknowledged by the regime. Although it appeared President Trump got "played" by Kim Jong-un at this Singapore summit, in early 2019 the two leaders met again in Hanoi, Vietnam. This time their summit conference ended early and abruptly. Before a scheduled luncheon on the second day of the meeting, President Trump walked away from the conference and flew home. He later explained that Kim wanted all US sanctions on North Korea lifted in return for the closing of one North Korean nuclear facility. Trump wanted all North Korean nuclear facilities either closed or opened to international inspection. Kim said no, and Trump walked away. While both leaders said their personal relationship remained fine and they continued to communicate with each other, the two sides seem deadlocked with irreconcilable policy differences. So at the time of this writing, the threat of a nuclear exchange between the United States and North Korea cannot be totally dismissed.

Some national security opportunities deserve mention as well. After the end of the Cold War, the United States was relatively successful in getting NATO members to shoulder more military burdens in places such as Bosnia and Afghanistan. Arguably, it was the EU embargo on purchasing Iranian oil and denial of the use of the global electronic banking network that finally pushed Iran to the negotiating table for its nuclear deal. Also, NATO states participated with the United States in patrolling the waters of the western Indian Ocean to protect maritime traffic from Somalia-based pirates. As these examples show, there were precedents for more cooperation and burden sharing.

In a reversal of longtime practice, President Trump's stances toward NATO early in his administration created an obstacle to better US-NATO cooperation. By suggesting the United States might not uphold its Article 5 mutual-defense obligations if another NATO member was attacked and/or making such an obligation conditional on the defense-spending levels of that fellow NATO member, the credibility of the defense treaty was significantly damaged. President Macron of France suggested that Europeans might have to become more responsible for their own security, and Russian president Putin suggested Russia represented a more reliable military ally for European states than did the United States.

Economic Security Inputs

The effects of the Great Recession of 2008–2010 lingered for years. US economic growth was sluggish after the recession, and additional steps were taken to stimulate economic growth, to coordinate international responses to shared economic problems, and to regulate the practices that led to the recession.

The George W. Bush administration reacted to the Great Recession with selective bailouts of large financial institutions and corporate entities and with steps designed to stabilize the credit markets. Soon thereafter, the new Obama administration got two large stimulus packages passed, but neither of them had a transformative effect on the growth of jobs in the country. The administration also sought to convince other countries to initiate their own stimulus programs, so those countries' economies would be buying more US products as well. Of the major economic powers, only China responded with its own stimulus package. To avoid increasing the size of their national debt, many European countries responded with reduced government spending and other austerity measures, which made some of the weaker economies in Europe even more fragile.

The worry soon became potential bankruptcy for some member states of the Euro Zone (those using the shared euro currency). The possibility of countries such as Greece, Italy, or Spain going bankrupt threatened the economies of other Euro Zone members, as they had to decide whether—and how much—to bail out their poorer member states to preserve their shared currency's value. Those European threats also found their place on the US foreign policy agenda. US corporations are heavily invested in Europe, and US-European trade ties are extensive. Literally, anything that hurts the European economy also hurts the US economy. Anything that hurts the euro as a currency puts additional pressure on the US dollar, at a time when the Chinese and Russians have been calling for the replacement of the dollar as the global default currency. As Europe goes, so goes the global economy, and that includes the United States. US administrations might be called upon to coordinate economic policy to help European states more in the coming years, and that may be a hard sell with the voters back home.

Finally, others rose from the chaos of the Great Recession more quickly than the United States. Compared to the third quarter in 2012, China's annual GDP increased by 7.8 percent in the third quarter of 2013, while US annual GDP for the same period increased by only 1.8 percent.[4] For the same time period, South Korea's rising economic might was indicated not only by a 3.3 percent growth rate in annual GDP but also by the rising visibility of Hyundai and Kia automobiles, Samsung smartphones, and LG appliances in the American marketplace.[5] All the while, the US economy continued a pattern of slow growth.

Thus, the Trump administration inherited a national economy that, after increasing at an annual post-recession growth rate of roughly 2.0 percent, seemed ready to respond to any good news. President Trump's election, his business background, and his promises of tax reform and a rollback of many regulations on businesses combined to bring a spark to the economy. In 2017, the GDP growth rate increased into the 2–3 percent range and into the 3–4 percent range for much of 2018. However, an increase in tariffs on imported steel and aluminum, a Trump-initiated trade war with China, and the longest government shutdown on record caused economic output to drop into 2019. Thus, the economic situation facing US foreign policy makers continues to be unsettled, to say the least.

Human Security Inputs

Human security involves the ability of people around the world to live their lives with the expectation of having adequate food, shelter, health care, education, income, and safety from violence to ensure a reasonable quality of life. The challenges from this point of view are many. For example, how will sluggish economic growth and widespread societal violence in Central America impact the United States? Will the violence spread across the border, or is President Trump correct in saying that it has already done so? Will migrant caravans seeking asylum in the United States continue as the violence between narcotrafficking rings, gangs, and armed militias takes its toll on Central American cities and towns? The same questions can be posed for considerable portions of Mexico as well.

In South America, the poster child for such human misery was the Maduro regime in Venezuela. Its predecessor regime led by Hugo Chàvez set in motion a program of government spending that its economy could not sustain, and the policies of Nicolàs Maduro made the economic situation even worse. By the end of 2018, stratospheric inflation rates caused millions of working-age Venezuelans to flee to neighboring countries in search of jobs, leaving Venezuela essentially destitute. In early 2019, the leader of the National Assembly, Juan Guaidó, declared himself the acting president. President Trump and a number of South American leaders recognized Guaidó as the legitimate regime leader, but the Venezuelan military elite sided with Maduro, a response that seems likely to keep Maduro in power at least for the near future. However, the United States and some other European countries cut off the Maduro regime from Venezuela's financial accounts abroad, and in some cases made those financial assets available to Guaidó. Russia stepped up to purchase Venezuelan crude oil and may also have sent private military contractors to help prop up the Maduro regime. Meanwhile, most Venezuelans have struggled to survive economically.

However, as the example of AFRICOM suggested in Chapter 10, Africa may be the greatest problem in this regard. Despite impressive economic growth in some countries (Ghana, Ethiopia, and Côte d'Ivoire, for example), grinding poverty, corruption, mismanagement, and intrastate violence still plague many countries. Desperate people will do whatever it takes to survive. They will work in dangerous conditions, such as illegal gold and diamond mines, where their risk of injury or death is high. Some will sell their family members into slavery or push them into prostitution. Either willingly or unwillingly, others will join criminal groups or militias run by warlords. Some will become refugees and thus someone else's domestic problem.

These perilous human security situations may well pose national security threats for US interests at home and abroad, as do al-Shabaab in Somalia and Kenya, Boko Haram in Nigeria and Chad, and al-Qaeda in the Islamic Maghreb, for example. Yet they can present opportunities as well. The United States gained considerable respect in many African societies through its economic assistance to offset the scourge of HIV/AIDS. What other possibilities to create goodwill might be present in places such as Africa? Might carefully targeted foreign assistance programs help some African recipients, and could more foreign economic assistance slow the flow of migrants from Central America as well?

More broadly, though many around the world are hurting, women in poor societies suffer more than their male counterparts. Women employed outside the home are often the first fired, they tend to become victims of violence and oppression, and they often lack access to opportunities to change their circumstances. Much needs to be done to protect women's rights, and this creates an opportunity for the United States if its leaders choose to seize it.

Finally, in terms of human security, other transnational issues have risen in importance in recent years as well. Perhaps the best single example is the issue of global climate change. The UN and most national governments now accept the premise that human activity is influencing global climate change and producing more intense storms and weather phenomena. Some results linked to global climate change are easy to see. Record-setting floods, heat waves, increasing desertification, and more frequent and more severe hurricanes cause more people to die as a result. Dealing with such problems located in the "global commons" will pose real difficulties for US foreign policy makers. Whatever the types of inputs, the policy-making processes of the US government have the task of transforming them into outputs.

Policy-Making Processes

To get a good sense of likely directions for US policy making, we need to think about the types of actors likely to participate mean-ingfully in US foreign policy making, as well as about the ways policy making works.

Actors

At first glance, the actors who typically make US foreign policy have not changed. The president is still in a favored position to make foreign policy, with the help of personal advisers as well as numerous officials from the White House, the National Security Council, the major cabinet departments, the military, the Intelligence Community, and so on. Congress is still hardwired into the foreign policy process through such roles as the legislative authorization and appropriations processes, oversight and investigative processes, and senatorial approval of treaties and key personnel appointments. The courts may occasionally venture into the foreign policy realm, as they have regarding the rights of detainees in the War on Terror. Elected officials still listen to public opinion and interest groups, and many officials listen to experts, celebrities, cable television pundits, and foreign leaders, albeit to varying degrees.

However, changes seem apparent in the weight some actors may wield in shaping US foreign policy. In recent administrations, the national security–related actors took center stage, which did not seem surprising in light of the 9/11 terrorist attacks and the resulting US War on Terror. However, in hindsight it now seems clear that sound advice from civilian experts working for the State Department and the National Security Council and in other parts of the administration was at times overlooked by White House actors, and time has also shown that combating terrorism abroad requires all the tools of civilian statecraft—political, diplomatic, economic, and cultural—as well as military and paramilitary tools.

Beyond needing more across-the-board civilian help, the United States also needs more experts who focus on parts of the world relatively underrepresented among government employees—areas such as Africa, Asia, and the Middle East. Also needed is an expedited clearance procedure so US citizens whose families are relatively recent immigrants from such areas (and who can thus speak languages such as Arabic, Farsi, Dari, Pashto, Punjabi, Urdu, and Somali) can get security clearances more rapidly so they can bring their linguistic and cultural skills to the federal government. These shortages have been exacerbated by the Trump administration's cutbacks in State Department funding and its reluctance to fill the high numbers of vacant positions among ambassadorships and other senior State Department offices. The Trump administration prioritizes personal diplomacy by President Trump or, as needed, by Senior Adviser Jared Kushner or Secretary of State Mike Pompeo. The traditional expertise represented by career foreign service officers and State Department officials was neglected or ignored during the first two-plus years of the administration. The administration's approach seems counterproductive in light of the changing nature of foreign policy opportunities and challenges.

In the current economic setting, the influence of economic officials will probably continue to grow as well. The US trade representative may be an increasingly significant foreign policy actor, as trade relations either deteriorate into trade wars or improve into newly negotiated trade agreements. As globalization more tightly connects national and global economies, actors such as the National Economic Council, the Council of Economic Advisers, and the secretaries of the Treasury and Commerce Departments will find more of their time spent on activities formerly thought of as foreign policy.

On Capitol Hill, another change can be seen. The assertiveness of members of Congress to challenge the administration's requests has gradually increased over time.[6] Congressional assertiveness in foreign policy making dramatically increased during the Vietnam War, increased again after the Cold War ended, and then again after the 9/11 attacks.[7] Even in the arena long thought to be the president's sole preserve—use-of-force decisions—the partisan makeup of Congress now plays an important role in shaping whether, and how quickly, an administration will choose to go to war.[8] Thus, any idea that members of Congress will willingly take a backseat to the administration in formulating US foreign policy can probably be safely discarded. Even when Congress was controlled by Republicans during the first two years of the Trump presidency, this Republican president had difficulties getting other Republicans to share his foreign policy priorities. There was significant congressional pushback against President Trump's NATO policy, his orientation toward Russia, and his abrupt decision to withdraw US troops from Syria. The 2019 dispute between President Trump and congressional Democrats over funding to amp up border security and build a wall on the southern US border is a prime example of how funding decisions will give Congress a critical voice in foreign policy making into the future.

Processes

Within the executive branch, some things generally stay the same. Presidents and their close advisers have always struggled to keep effective lines of communication open within the administration, so they can know what they need to know when they need to know it. After all, knowledge is power. For their part, bureaucracies have generally tried to control the flow of information to increase their relative influence or to attain other bureaucratic goals, as bureaucrats often equate what is good for their agency or department with the broader national interest. Thus, within the executive branch, interagency communication, cooperation, and coordination are constant challenges, and structural adjustments cannot make such challenges go away.

A good example of this can be found in the Department of Homeland Security. It was created as a response to the fact that, prior to the 2001 terrorist attacks, different parts of the executive branch possessed different tidbits of information about the heightened threat of a terrorist attack or about the nineteen future terrorists who were already in the United States. After 9/11, the thought in Congress was that if many of these agencies were lumped together in the same department, they would talk to each other more readily and someone might be able to create a cohesive picture of potential threat from all this disparate information. However, since its formation in 2002, the various components of the administration responsible for homeland security still find it difficult to coordinate their efforts or even to communicate with each other. Thus, within the administration, more and more time is spent in meetings in an effort to produce a coordinated US response to foreign policy opportunities and challenges, and it takes a considerable investment of effort on the part of White House officials to try to get all relevant administration actors moving in the same direction in support of the president's foreign policy initiatives.

This situation is made even worse when presidents choose to rely on their personal instincts rather than on regularized processes that ensure that multiple voices are heard before a decision is announced. Both Presidents George W. Bush and Donald Trump have made foreign policy decisions based on their instincts (or their "gut," as both these presidents call it). President Trump carries this approach to an extreme when he frequently claims to know more than the experts in many foreign policy–related fields. Such a decision-making approach minimizes if not eliminates the normal roles for expert-based advice, increasing the chances of making poor decisions leading to suboptimal outcomes. Moreover, both these presidents rarely reviewed the quality of their prior decisions, and thus a feedback loop for future inputs could often not be found.

Although all administrations are conflicted by bureaucratic cleavages, Congress is beset by partisan ones. The idea that partisan politics stops at the water's edge has been an outdated assumption since the 1950s.[9] Partisan control of the presidency and Congress matters tremendously. Despite some exceptions, we can even speak of a Republican or Democratic foreign policy agenda. In recent years, Republican officials in Washington have generally stressed foreign policy themes that emphasize national security goals, a preference for hard over soft power, and a more unilateralist stance on protection of US sovereignty from international, multilateral, or supranational intrusions. Conversely, most Democratic officials in Washington have typically emphasized economic goals, soft or smart power over hard power alone, and greater multilateral engagement and cooperation to achieve US objectives. Thus, perhaps more than ever before, which party controls the presidency and Congress matters, in terms of both the issues seen as important and the preferred means by which to address those issues.

Within Congress, party polarization has grown because centrist Republicans and Democrats have increasingly chosen not to seek reelection or have not survived in party primaries against candidates supporting more extreme policy positions. Thus, as groups, congressional Republicans have generally become more conservative and congressional Democrats generally more liberal. As a consequence, presidents not only face difficulty wooing members of the opposition party to support their initiatives but also often have difficulty securing the support of their own party members in Congress. Because of their need to do what is best for the country as a whole, presidents may often propose somewhat more moderate or centrist policies that are neither conservative enough to satisfy Republicans nor liberal enough to satisfy progressive Democrats. In a telling example, in late 2018 President Trump suggested he was willing to sign a stopgap spending bill, one that did not include funding for a border wall, in order to keep all parts of the federal government running. Assailed immediately by conservative opinion leaders in the media such as Ann Coulter and Rush Limbaugh for capitulating to the Democrats, Trump reversed his decision the next day, and the longest government shutdown on record resulted.

Despite party polarization, the House is still capable of passing highly contentious foreign policy legislation, as all it takes is a simple majority vote. If the majority party in the House speaks with one voice, it can pass bills. On the other hand, Senate procedures greatly complicate getting things done that require votes. According to the Senate's cloture rule, sixty votes are normally needed to end floor debate on any issue, so unless the majority party leaders can identify sixty of the 100 senators willing to vote to end any possible filibuster, they will often avoid even scheduling contentious issues—such as passing a budget. Thus, structural gridlock is increasingly frequent in the Senate. In late 2013, Senate Democrats addressed one frustrating facet of this gridlock by changing the number of votes needed to end filibusters on most presidential appointment nominations from sixty to a bare majority of fifty-one. When Republicans recaptured control of the Senate, they went back to requiring sixty votes for passage. However, Senate majority leader Mitch McConnell's subsequent policy of not even scheduling floor debate or votes unless it was clear that President Trump would support the legislation meant that the Senate became a largely inactive legislative body.

The impacts of growing partisanship in both chambers have been seen in foreign policy making. The impact of congressional committees has diminished over time as the influence of elected party leaders in each chamber has grown. In essence, less legislation is being considered in committee and more considered on the chamber floors, thus making the floor leaders more important. More and more foreign policy issues get caught in partisan legislative battles, in which neither side wants to give in to the other, and the result is even fewer pieces of legislation passed than before. As suggested earlier, just passing the annual budgets for the foreign policy bureaucracy is increasingly difficult—even though funds have to be appropriated for the government to function. As a consequence (and often well after the new fiscal year begins on October 1), more and more different issues get lumped together in massive omnibus appropriations bills or continuing resolutions to keep the government running. The result is that individual budget items get less careful evaluation than before and legislators are forced to vote yes or no on large collections of greatly varying measures just to get the money needed for the few issues that are important to them.

Although it may seem counterintuitive, even as Congress is more hamstrung by partisan politics and passing legislation becomes more difficult, the influence of individual members of

Congress who care about foreign policy has not diminished. Congressional foreign policy entrepreneurs work with administrations to get their foreign policy agendas advanced, but when administrations do not cooperate, these entrepreneurs find a wide variety of ways to push the issues they care about anyway. Further, the number of congressional foreign policy entrepreneurs has steadily increased over time.[10] Future presidents will have to contend with multiple members of Congress who are quite willing to tell the administration what it should do and how it should do it, and members of Congress will be more than willing to penalize presidents who fail to go along with their wishes—often by saying no to the important items on the president's foreign and domestic policy agendas. Those foreign policy entrepreneurs who occupy elected party-leader positions in their chamber or sit on the appropriations, armed services, or foreign affairs committees in Congress will be even more able to use their negative power to hinder or kill administration requests if their policy wishes are ignored. Further, any member of Congress can have an impact if he or she can mobilize key interest groups to put pressures on other legislators or the president. Thus, if the president and Congress cannot agree on the broad outlines of US foreign policy, policy gridlock will continue.

Policy Outputs

As was explained in Chapter 10, there are differences between hard power, soft power, and smart power policy outputs. Some initial thoughts on each of these can be considered.

Hard Power Outputs

Almost twenty years after the 2001 terrorist attacks, US foreign policy priorities are shifting. The emphasis on combating terrorists is changing, as are the means for doing so. War-weariness on the part of the public and the political need to reduce the number of US combat casualties have led to the sharp reduction of US troops stationed in Iraq and Afghanistan, but not their total withdrawal. The result has been a lessening of the number of combat casualties, which then reduces the press coverage devoted to what was previously called the War on Terror and is now more often referred to as the fight against religious extremism. The US counterterrorism efforts of the Obama and Trump administrations increasingly relied on attacking suspected terrorist sites through the use of special operations forces, unmanned drone aircraft, other air strikes, willing allies, or some combination of all these means. Those terrorist sites thought to be of greatest threat are less frequently located in Iraq or Afghanistan and more often in places such as Syria, Pakistan, Yemen, Somalia, and Mali.

Not only did the political need to reduce combat casualties drive a change in military strategy but the rising financial costs of military operations did as well. For example, the Iraq War was the second-most-costly war in US history, trailing only World War II in inflation-adjusted terms. The direct costs of the war exceeded $800 billion (not the $50–$60 billion the George W. Bush administration initially predicted), and the indirect costs of medical care and disability compensation costs for wounded veterans over the next forty years could reach $1 trillion.[11] Given such rising costs and the need to cut nearly $500 billion from the defense budget over the next ten years, the Pentagon announced a shift in strategy in which the United States would no longer be able to fight two wars at once; instead, its goal would be the simultaneous capability to fight one war and respond to a "military situation" elsewhere. The defense spending cuts announced in early 2012 emphasized reductions in the numbers of personnel in the army and marine corps and a greater reliance on special operations forces that involve far fewer personnel, the use of unmanned drone aircraft, and cybersecurity initiatives. For these reasons, in the future the number of hard power options for US foreign policy makers may be fewer than they have been in the past.

Soft Power Outputs

Barring a major shift in thinking in Washington, a greater reliance on soft power policy outputs may be forthcoming. There are several reasons for this shift. First, the Obama administration moved in this direction, both because of the desire to differentiate itself from its predecessor, the George W. Bush administration, and because it saw soft power options such as enhanced diplomatic engagement to be the preferred way to address difficult twenty-first-century situations.

For example, shortly after assuming office, President Obama made his famous address at Cairo University to reach out to the Islamic world. Obama augmented this effort by appointing Farah Anwar Pandith to the newly created position of special representative to Muslim communities, a post that reports directly to the secretary of state. An American Muslim originally from the predominantly Muslim Kashmir region of India, Representative Pandith previously served in the George W. Bush administration as director of Middle East regional initiatives for the National Security Council and before that she was the chief of staff for the Bureau for Asia and the Near East of the US Agency for International Development.[12] Another step came in early 2012 when administration officials began meeting with representatives of Egypt's Muslim Brotherhood, trying to forge some form of relationship with the organization that won the largest share of seats in Egypt's parliamentary election in late 2011. Such outreach was a reversal of long-standing US policy, which saw the Muslim Brotherhood as an Islamic fundamentalist organization opposed to US interests in the region. Then after one year, the administration had to find common ground with Egypt's military after it ousted Egypt's Islamist president, Muhammad Morsi.

Whereas the Obama administration sought to elevate US soft power outputs, the Trump administration's approach has been harder to characterize. When it comes to relations with traditional US allies, President Trump seems to rely on hard power–based threats—such as not guaranteeing a US response to a threat against a fellow NATO member unless that member is meeting the 2 percent of GDP target in its defense spending, or in another example, by relying on missile strikes to send messages to the Syrian regime. The administration has also relied on hard power in the form of a trade war with China. On the other hand, soft power approaches have been taken by the Trump administration toward a number of populist or authoritarian regimes, such as Russia, Turkey, Hungary, Brazil, and others. Thus, after the first two years of the Trump presidency, a mix of hard and soft power outputs has been employed. However, as noted earlier, the US public seems increasingly war weary, so hard power policies may get less public support going forward.

Second, many of the difficult twenty-first-century situations are increasingly global in nature. Problems such as global climate change, pandemic diseases, and human rights concerns are extraordinarily difficult to resolve unless there is at least regional, if not global, cooperation. Such cooperation requires all the tools of multilateral diplomacy to be effective. Although the UN and its various components will continue to be important forums for diplomatic efforts, groups such as the G7 major industrial powers, the G20 major market countries, and regional groups such as Asia-Pacific Economic Cooperation will increasingly be the locations for negotiation over such regional and global issues.

Third, soft power outputs are attractive in terms of their costs. These outputs may take considerable time to bear fruit, but they often require fewer out-of-pocket expenses than hard power outputs do. As suggested in Chapter 10, the entire US diplomatic corps entails fewer employees than one aircraft carrier task force. A global architecture already exists to reach out to others to deal with mutual problems and challenges; it is the system of US embassies, consulates, and missions. Additional numbers of well-trained diplomats could take better advantage of this existing resource. To paraphrase former British prime minister Winston Churchill, to jaw-jaw is better than to war-war.

Smart Power Outputs

In an era in which the United States is not a hegemonic power that can impose its desires on the rest of the international system, using every combination of tools in the US foreign policy toolbox just seems to make sense to most observers. Smart power outputs thus appear to be increasingly likely in the future.

For example, consider the problem of improving the quality of lives of women and children in the Great Lakes region of eastern Africa. Informal militias in the region at times forcibly conscript children into their ranks, using death threats against them or their families if they do not comply. These militias (and at times national armies) in Uganda, Kenya, Somalia, Rwanda, Burundi, and eastern Democratic Republic of the Congo also prey on women, either simply because they can or to humiliate and shame their rivals. To this violence directed against women, add the problems of daily life that these women and children face: finding sufficient water, food, and cooking fuel to meet the needs of their families. The United States is addressing their needs in a variety of ways.

Hard power is used in the form of US military assistance. US military aid helps the Kenyan government's military offensive into Somalia to stop al-Shabaab raids in Kenya and Uganda, and both US military assistance and armed military advisers help the Ugandan government's military campaign against militias such as the Lord's Resistance Army, which preys on women and children. Unmanned drone aircraft are also now based in eastern Ethiopia and can be used in the Great Lakes region if needed. These efforts help local regimes protect their own citizens.

Soft power is used as well. As noted in Chapter 10, the US State Department, USAID, the US Department of Health and Human Services, the US Department of Energy, and the US Environmental Protection Agency formed an alliance with German, Norwegian, Dutch, and Peruvian governmental agencies and numerous nongovernmental organizations from the United States and abroad to create the Global Alliance for Clean Cookstoves. The alliance seeks to stop the shortening of women's and children's lives caused by breathing toxic fumes from cooking fuels. Among its other global locations, this effort to improve women's and children's health is active in Kenya, Rwanda, and Uganda. US economic assistance is also going to address long-standing women's and children's health problems, such as combating malaria and tuberculosis, providing safe drinking water, and assisting with family planning in both Kenya and Rwanda, among other places. Through this combination of hard and soft power, the United States is seeking to improve the lives of millions of women and children in eastern Africa.

Conclusion

The old French epigram reads: "The more things change, the more they stay the same." Both parts of that sentiment apply to US foreign policy making in the twenty-first century. To some degree, the inputs to policy making have changed. The global context is quite different from the scary days of the Cold War and the heady days of the post–Cold War period of the 1990s. The United States finds itself facing challenges from terrorists who would prey on US citizens and allies, global economic competitors, other major powers seeking to dominate their respective region of the world, and those who say the time of the United States as the world's leader has come and gone. In terms of foreign policy–making processes, this new environment for foreign policy making will almost certainly require some rebalancing of needs, interests, and means. Yet that rebalancing will be done by the same governmental and political actors and processes by which foreign policy has been made for decades. Can US foreign policy–making structures and entities designed for the Cold War effectively address the challenges of the twenty-first century? If not, can sufficient agreement be found among the relevant actors to make the institutional or structural changes needed to produce effective policy outcomes for this new environment? As has been the case in the past, people of goodwill can rise to this challenge. Reducing the ideological and partisan polarization in Washington, DC, in order to focus on pressing foreign policy needs would be a good start.

Suggested Reading

Bacevich, Andrew J. *Twilight of the American Century.* Notre Dame, IN: University of Notre Dame Press, 2018.
Gilpin, Robert. *War and Change in World Politics.* Cambridge: Cambridge University Press, 1981.
Stiglitz, Joseph E. *Globalization and Its Discontents Revisited: Anti-Globalization in the Era of Trump.* Oxford: Oxford University Press, 2018.
Weber, Steven, and Bruce W. Jentleson. *The End of Arrogance: America in the Global Competition of Ideas.* Cambridge, MA: Harvard University Press, 2010.
Zakaria, Fareed. *The Post-American World: Release 2.0.* New York: W. W. Norton, 2011.

Notes

1. Francis Fukuyama, "The End of History?" *National Interest* 16 (1989): 3–18.
2. Samuel P. Huntington, "The Clash of Civilizations?" *Foreign Affairs* 72 (1993): 22–49.
3. The emphasis on national, economic, and human security is based on the approach illustrated in James M. Scott, Ralph G. Carter, and A. Cooper Drury, *IR: International, Economic, and Human Security in a Changing World,* 3rd ed. (Thousand Oaks, CA: Sage/CQ Press, 2019).

4. "China GDP Annual Growth Rate," http://www.tradingeconomics .com/china/gdp-growth-annual; "United States GDP Annual Growth Rate," http://www.tradingeconomics.com/united-states/gdp-growth-annual.

5. "South Korea GDP Annual Growth Rate," http://www.trading economics.com/south-korea/gdp-growth-annual.

6. James M. Scott and Ralph G. Carter, "Acting on the Hill: Congressional Assertiveness in U.S. Foreign Policy," *Congress and the Presidency* 29 (2002): 151–179.

7. Ralph G. Carter and James M. Scott, *Choosing to Lead: Understanding Congressional Foreign Policy Entrepreneurs* (Durham, NC: Duke University Press, 2009).

8. William G. Howell and Jon C. Pevehouse, *While Dangers Gather: Congressional Checks on Presidential War Powers* (Princeton: Princeton University Press, 2007).

9. Ralph G. Carter, "Congressional Foreign Policy Behavior: Persistent Patterns of the Postwar Period," *Presidential Studies Quarterly* 16 (1986): 329–359.

10. Carter and Scott, *Choosing to Lead.*

11. Backgrounder, "The Cost of the Iraq War," Council on Foreign Relations, November 7, 2006, https://www.cfr.org/backgrounder/cost -iraq-war.

12. "Expert Bio: Farah Pandith," Council on Foreign Relations, https://www.cfr.org/expert/farah-anwar-pandith.

Glossary

Abu Ghraib. Prison in Iraq where detainees in the US invasion of Iraq were mistreated, degraded, and in some cases sexually humiliated by US military police.

AFRICOM. The Defense Department's United States Africa Command, which combines both military roles and humanitarian and development roles in its mission statement and which includes nonmilitary as well as military personnel.

al-Qaeda. "The base," in Arabic. The name for the group of Islamic militants dedicated to opposing the US military presence in the Middle East and US support for Israel. It was created by Saudi Arabian multimillionaire Osama bin Laden from a core group of Islamic freedom fighters who had battled the Soviet presence in Afghanistan in the 1980s.

Almond-Lippmann consensus. The idea that public opinion was too volatile and lacking in an underlying knowledge structure to be useful to foreign policy makers and hence it had little impact on foreign policy making in a democracy. The name was based on the works of scholar Gabriel Almond and newspaper columnist Walter Lippmann.

American exceptionalism. The idea that not only is the United States unique and thus different from other countries but also those differences make it better than other countries.

American Israel Public Affairs Committee (AIPAC). The leading interest group representing the pro-Israeli lobby in the United States.

American Service-Members' Protection Act. A law that prohibits US cooperation with the International Criminal Court. The law also threatens non-NATO countries with the loss of US military aid if they do not sign Status of Forces Agreements exempting US forces from being turned over to such a court, and it justifies the use of any means necessary to free any US military personnel arrested for trial before the International Criminal Court.

anarchy. The idea that no supranational governing entity controls what states may do, thus there is no cop on the corner. It doesn't mean "chaos," because the international system is surprisingly orderly in most of its operations.

apartheid. The policy of the Republic of South Africa of granting different levels of political and human rights to its citizens based on their skin color. Blacks had the fewest rights, whites had the most rights, and those considered "colored and Asians" fell in between the other two extremes. Although the roots of this policy can be found in the eighteenth century, it was enshrined in law from 1948 until the constitution was changed in 1994.

Asia-Pacific Economic Cooperation (APEC). Forum that includes twenty-one Asian/Pacific Rim economies that represent approximately 40 percent of the world's population, over half of the world's GDP, and nearly half of the world's trade.

asymmetric conflict. A conflict featuring two forces of vastly different size and apparent power.

Bush Doctrine. George W. Bush's idea of responding to imminent threats by striking enemies before they can attack the United States. See the *US National Security Strategy.*

capitalist peace. The idea that advanced capitalist societies do not choose to go to war against each other.

careerism. In a bureaucracy, being so concerned with one's individual career prospects (merit raises, promotions, etc.) that it gets in the way of the organization's broader goals; in essence, substituting what is good for the career official for what is good for the organization— or perhaps the country.

Central Intelligence Agency (CIA). Created by the *National Security Act of 1947,* this civilian agency engages in intelligence gathering and analysis, counterintelligence, and covert operations.

Cold War. A period of hostile competition between a Western bloc of anti-Communist states led by the United States and an Eastern bloc of Communist states led by the Soviet Union, which lasted forty-two years (1947–1989). Although the two bloc leaders never went to war directly against each other, members of their respective blocs did, and the risks of a global and nuclear World War III could not be discounted.

Committee on Foreign Investment in the United States (CFIUS). The administration actor (headed by the treasury secretary and composed of representatives of various cabinet departments and administration offices) charged with reviewing foreign investment in select US corporations where threats to national security might arise.

congressional foreign policy entrepreneurs. Members of Congress who choose to act on their own foreign policy agendas without waiting for the administration to do so.

Congressional Research Service (CRS). A nonpartisan staff agency that assists Congress in its policy-making roles by providing information and analysis.

constructivism. The theory based on the premise that reality is socially constructed by agents interacting with the structures in their environment. Thus, material facts are less important than how they are socially interpreted.

crisis. A foreign policy situation that represents a threat to core values or high-priority goals, requires a quick response, and comes as a surprise to decision makers.

cybernetic decision making. Mindlessly trying available options until an option produces a satisficing response or all available options have failed.

decision heuristics. Rules of thumb to make decision making easier and faster.

Defense Intelligence Agency (DIA). A multiservice agency responsible for intelligence functions in the Defense Department.

democratic peace. The idea that well-established liberal democracies do not typically go to war against each other. Also known as the *liberal peace.*

director of national intelligence (DNI). A position created in 2004 to coordinate the information gathered by the other sixteen members of the *Intelligence Community.*

economic sanctions. Economic means to punish a state or other international actor, such as by refusing to buy its products, sell it what it needs, or limit its financial transactions.

elitism. The idea that a single group dominates foreign policy making.

European Union (EU). If the United Kingdom completes its exit arrangements, the EU will become a group of twenty-seven democratic European states that are bound together economically and, to a slightly lesser extent, politically.

first-generation rights. Individual human rights such as the freedoms of speech, assembly, and religion.

foreign policy. The goals and actions of the US government in the international system.

Foreign Policy Initiative (FPI). A think tank founded in 2009 following the demise of the Project for the New American Century. Two of its four original directors were William Kristol and Robert Kagan.

G8. The Group of Eight major industrial nations (Canada, France, Germany, Italy, Japan, Russia, the United Kingdom, and the United States) that meet annually to coordinate their economic policies. Russia's expulsion in 2014 made it the G7.

G20. The Group of Twenty major industrial powers and key emerging markets formed in 1999 to coordinate economic policy. The twenty members are Argentina, Australia, Brazil, Canada, China, France, Germany, India, Indonesia, Italy, Japan, Mexico, Russia, Saudi Arabia, South Africa, South Korea, Turkey, the United Kingdom, the United States, and the European Union.

general war. A conflict in which all the conventional weaponry in the US arsenal would be available for use, the geographic scope of the conflict would not be limited, and weapons of mass destruction could potentially be used.

Government Accountability Office (GAO). A nonpartisan staff agency that assists Congress in its policy-making roles by providing financial information and analysis.

gross domestic product (GDP). The total value of goods and services a state actor produces within its borders.

groupthink. The phenomenon that occurs in a concurrence-seeking group when the desire by members to get along outweighs their willingness to challenge the dominant viewpoints of the group, resulting in assumptions not being examined, doubts not being expressed, and poor decisions often being made.

hard power. Getting others to do what you want when they otherwise do not want to do so, typically by using coercion or payments.

hegemon. An international actor so powerful it can basically do whatever it wants, even if all other major powers oppose it.

Homeland Security Council (HSC). The group charged with advising the president on homeland security matters and coordinating such policies across the various governmental actors involved.

human rights. Rights that societies assume should apply to all people.

idealism. The desire to make the world a better place by using US power and influence to spread a system of Western values throughout the world—primarily values such as the protection of individual rights and freedoms and the promotion of democracy and capitalism.

illiberal regimes. Those that fall short on at least one of liberalism's criteria: the protection of individual liberties, free-market capitalism, and democratic rule.

incrementalism. Making only minor changes from current policy or from what has been done before in similar circumstances.

inputs. The stimuli that cause potential foreign policy makers to act.

Intelligence Community (IC). Seventeen entities that participate in the collection and analysis of intelligence information, counterintelligence operations, and at times covert operations.

International Atomic Energy Agency (IAEA). The UN agency tasked with promoting the peaceful use of nuclear energy and its related technologies.

International Criminal Court (ICC). International court created by the Rome Statute of 1998. Its purpose is to act as a court of last resort for individuals accused of war crimes, crimes against humanity, genocide, and, more recently, aggression. It went into effect in 2002.

International Monetary Fund (IMF). Part of the UN family, this international organization of 186 member states acts as a global bank, providing short-term loans to protect the value of its members' currencies; it coordinated the global monetary response to the Great Recession of 2008–2009.

internationalism. The belief that US national interests are advanced by interacting with other countries and peoples and that such regular, ongoing contacts with others may also contribute to the greater good of all.

Iran nuclear deal (also called the **Joint Comprehensive Plan of Action**). Agreement negotiated by the United States, Russia, the United Kingdom, France, China, and Germany in 2015 in which Iran got access to over $100 billion of its financial assets frozen in Western banks since 1979 in return for exporting 98 percent of its enriched uranium, mothballing approximately 3,000 modern centrifuges, converting a plutonium-based reactor into a light-water one, and allowing international inspections to verify the above. This agreement was seen as significantly delaying the development of an Iranian nuclear weapon.

ISIS. The self-proclaimed Islamic State in Iraq and Syria (also known as ISIL—the Islamic State in Iraq and the Levant—or simply as Da'esch, the Arabic acronym for the group).

isolationism. The belief that the dangers of regular and ongoing engagement with the world beyond US borders outweigh the advantages.

jihadists. Muslims who seek to conduct a "holy war" (or jihad) against nonbelievers.

Kyoto Protocol. An amendment passed in 1997 to the International Convention on Climate Change specifying mandatory reductions in fossil fuel emissions by developed countries, but not by developing countries, in the international effort to slow down global warming.

liberal peace. The idea that well-established liberal democracies do not typically go to war against each other. Also known as the *democratic peace.*

liberalism. The theory of politics that emphasizes the importance of individual freedom from state control, free-market capitalism, and democracy.

limited war. A conflict that is limited by geographic scope, the amount and types of weaponry used, and the goals for which the war is fought.

lobbyists. Individuals who represent a group and who contact government officials to try to influence the decisions those officials make so the decisions reflect the group's policy wishes.

multiple advocacy. An approach to decision making in which an official is responsible for ensuring that all major options and considerations are examined and fairly presented to the president prior to a decision being made. The aim is to have vigorous advocates presenting their cases to the president to ensure that all relevant facts are considered before deciding.

mutual assured destruction (MAD). The idea that a direct military conflict between the United States and Soviet Union during the Cold War would inevitably escalate into a full-blown exchange of nuclear weapons, thereby destroying both societies. Based on this, mutual assured destruction became a nuclear strategy; if neither country would survive a nuclear war, then starting such a war would be irrational and thus unlikely.

National Economic Council (NEC). The group charged with advising the president on domestic and international economic policy and coordinating such policies across the various governmental actors involved.

National Security Act of 1947. Legislation that created the Department of Defense (uniting the air force, army, marines, and navy), the Central Intelligence Agency, the National Security Council, and the position of *national security adviser.*

national security adviser. This presidential appointee in national security affairs normally briefs the president daily on national security–related events. Created by the *National Security Act of 1947.*

National Security Agency (NSA). Agency that provides information assurance by preventing vital information from falling into the hands of other powers (often through the use of cryptography), collects signals intelligence (by eavesdropping on the communications of others), and conducts the research necessary for both information assurance and signals intelligence. It provides nearly 80 percent of the intelligence information used by the federal government.

National Security Council (NSC). Group charged with advising the president on issues of national security policy and coordinating such policies across the various governmental actors involved.

National Security Staff (NSS). The combined members of what previously had been the National Security Council Staff and the Homeland Security Council Staff.

neoliberalism. The idea that international institutions can be created to provide incentives for states to cooperate with each other. Thus, states cooperate not necessarily out of any inherent goodness on their part but rather because cooperation advances their national interests.

neorealism. The idea that the structure of the international system forces states to act as they do. The most important aspect of system structure is anarchy; there is no overarching coercive authority present to enforce system rules. In such an anarchical system, prudence forces states to seek to maintain and increase their power resources and to pursue their own national interests.

New START. A 2011 strategic arms reduction treaty between the United States and Russia that limited the deployment by each country to no more than 1,550 nuclear warheads and 700 heavy bombers and missiles.

9/11. Attacks by al-Qaeda on September 11, 2001, on the World Trade Towers and the Pentagon; another plane crashed in Pennsylvania. These attacks resulted in years of the US-led War on Terror.

normal trade status. Previously known as "most-favored-nation status," it means that any state having such status with the United States will get the same, best deal on a trade policy matter that any other state gets from the United States.

norms. Unwritten rules; expectations of appropriate behavior in international society.

North Atlantic Treaty Organization (NATO). Initially a military alliance linking the United States, Canada, and a number of Western European states to oppose Communist expansion in the 1950s; it evolved to include more Central and Eastern European members after the breakup of the Soviet Union.

NSC-68. A National Security Council paper formally entitled "United States Objectives and Programs for National Security," which recommended the massive rearmament of the US military in the face of the growing Soviet threat in 1950.

nuclear nonproliferation regime. A global set of rules and institutions (like the International Atomic Energy Agency) that seeks to limit the spread of nuclear weapons and to ensure their control by prudent governments.

operational code. A relatively fixed blueprint or set of beliefs decision makers use to specify what is important, what motivates others, and what tends to work best in solving foreign policy problems.

outcomes. The consequences of foreign policy outputs.

outputs. The actions taken by foreign policy makers in response to the inputs they receive.

parochialism. In a bureaucracy, the tendency to limit one's viewpoint to just the perspective of that particular organization and, in worst-case instances, to equate the broader national interest to that particular organization's narrower interests.

pluralist policy process. The idea that the public gets its sentiments injected into the process of foreign policy making through membership in organized groups, and these organized groups then compete to get their preferences enacted into policy.

poliheuristic. A two-step decision-making process in which as many options as possible are quickly eliminated in the first step, and then in the second step, whatever time is needed is devoted to carefully evaluating the few remaining options with the goal of maximizing benefits and minimizing risks.

presidential preeminence model. The idea that presidents dominate foreign policy making for the issues they care most about.

principal-agent model. The idea that bureaucrats are the agents who carry out the wishes of their principals, who tend to be elected officials.

Project for the New American Century (PNAC). A think tank founded in 1997 that advocated the use of American power to advance the spread of American ideals in the world; particularly associated with the 2003 US invasion of Iraq.

prospect theory. The idea that when things are going well, decision makers tend to act prudently and become more risk averse so as not to upset a status quo that is favorable. When things are not going well, decision makers become prone to risky strategies as they seek to change that unacceptable status quo.

public opinion. What Americans think about specific issues.

rally effect. A usually short-lived boost in presidential support or popularity by the public during a crisis or emergency.

rational actor model (RAM). A decision-making process that attempts to identify all possible options available, considers systematically each option's strengths and weaknesses, and then selects the optimal option. The optimal option is the one that promises the best overall result, the best result in light of the incurred costs, or the result that is least bad if all options are bad.

realism. The theory of international politics that sees states as the most important actors, with those states seeking to achieve their national interests primarily through the threat or use of military power. States are seen as unitary actors interacting in the international system. Sometimes called classical realism.

Responsibility to Protect (R2P). The idea that states have a responsibility to protect their population from gross abuses of human rights, such as genocide, war crimes, and crimes against humanity, at the very least.

second-generation rights. The material rights of societies, such as the right to food, shelter, education, and medical care.

security dilemma. How states protect their security in a system marked by anarchy without alarming other states and prompting them to enhance their own security measures as a result.

shifting constellations model. The idea that presidents and their White House advisers, elements of the foreign policy bureaucracies, and Congress compete for policy-making influence; as foreign-policy issues change, the one that dominates the process can change.

smart power. The combination of hard and soft power, in which targets are encouraged to do what they would otherwise choose not to do but are encouraged in such a way that the request seems more legitimate.

social Darwinism. The idea that, like species, societies evolve by the "survival of the fittest," and thus it is the natural order of things for the strong to prey on the weak.

soft power. Getting others to want what you want by co-opting rather than coercing them.

standard operating procedures (SOPs). Patterns of steps developed over time and followed by bureaucratic actors that have produced coordinated organizational responses to situations.

subgovernment. The combination of bureaucratic agencies, interest groups, and members of Congress who develop relationships over time and who share policy goals and reinforce each other's efforts to achieve them; sometimes referred to as iron triangles.

Sunni. The majority sect within Islam, composing 85–90 percent of all Muslims worldwide.

targeted or smart sanctions. Sanctions meant to punish the elites who actually make the policies that are contrary to US interests rather than the people of the target country as a whole.

theories. Sets of interrelated ideas that explain reality. Theories of international politics help us understand what international actors consider important and may prescribe the methods they employ to achieve their goals.

think tanks. Privately funded research organizations.

third-generation rights. Rights assigned to groups at risk within society, such as unpopular minorities, women, children, or the elderly.

unconventional war. A conflict in which one side employs uniformed troops and the other side does not.

United Nations (UN). A global organization of 193 member-states created after World War II to enhance peace and security.

UN Security Council Resolution 1674. The 2006 UN Security Council resolution reaffirming that states have a responsibility to protect their citizens from gross abuses of human rights, such as genocide, war crimes, and crimes against humanity, and that others have the right to intervene if states do not meet that responsibility.

US National Security Strategy. A 2002 statement that, because of the increasing availability of weapons of mass destruction and the hostility of nonstate actors less susceptible to conventional means of deterrence, the United States would not wait until its enemies struck first. Instead, it would strike preemptively at its opponents to eradicate threats before they could materialize. Also known as the *Bush Doctrine*.

War Powers Resolution. A 1973 law requiring presidents to inform Congress of use of force decisions and giving Congress the opportunity to authorize—or not authorize—that use of force.

World Trade Organization (WTO). The supranational organization that creates the rules for free trade, implements those rules, and adjudicates and enforces those rules.

Selected Bibliography

Adams, Gordon. *The Iron Triangle: The Politics of Defense Contracting.* Piscataway, NJ: Transaction, 1981.

Alden, Chris, and Amnon Aran. *Foreign Policy Analysis: New Approaches.* 2nd ed. London: Routledge, 2017.

Allison, Graham T., and Philip Zelikow. *Essence of Decision: Explaining the Cuban Missile Crisis.* 2nd ed. London: Pearson, 1999.

Almond, Gabriel. *The American People and Foreign Policy.* New York: Praeger, 1965.

Art, Robert J. "Bureaucratic Politics and American Foreign Policy: A Critique." *Policy Sciences* 4 (1973): 467–490.

Avant, Deborah D., Martha Fennimore, and Susan K. Sell, eds. *Who Governs the Globe?* New York: Cambridge University Press, 2010.

Bacevich, Andrew J. *The New American Militarism: How Americans Are Seduced by War.* New York: Oxford University Press, 2005.

———. *Twilight of the American Century.* Notre Dame, IN: University of Notre Dame Press, 2018.

Bamford, James. *Body of Secrets: Anatomy of the Ultra-Secret National Security Agency from the Cold War Through the Dawn of a New Century.* New York: Doubleday, 2001.

———. *The Shadow Factory: The Ultra-Secret NSA from 9/11 to the Eavesdropping on America.* New York: Anchor Books, 2009.

Baum, Matthew A., and Philip B. K. Potter. *War and Democratic Constraint: How the Public Influences Foreign Policy.* Princeton: Princeton University Press, 2015.

Carlsnaes, Walter. "The Agency-Structure Problem in Foreign Policy Analysis." *International Studies Quarterly* 36 (1992): 245–270.

Carr, Edward Hallett. *The Twenty Years' Crisis, 1919–1939: An Introduction to the Study of International Relations.* New York: St. Martin's, 1946.

Carter, Ralph G. "Congressional Foreign Policy Behavior: Persistent Patterns of the Postwar Period." *Presidential Studies Quarterly* 16 (1986): 329–359.

Carter, Ralph G., and James M. Scott. *Choosing to Lead: Understanding Congressional Foreign Policy Entrepreneurs.* Durham, NC: Duke University Press, 2009.

Checkel, Jeffrey T. "Constructivism and Foreign Policy." In *Foreign Policy: Theories, Actors, Cases,* ed. Steve Smith, Amelia Hadfield, and Tim Dunne, 71–82. New York: Oxford University Press, 2008.

Crile, George. *Charlie Wilson's War: The Extraordinary Story of the Largest Covert Operation in History.* New York: Atlantic Monthly Press, 2003.

Deudney, Daniel, and Jeffrey Meiser. "American Exceptionalism." In *US Foreign Policy,* ed. Michael Cox and Doug Stokes, 24–42. Oxford: Oxford University Press, 2008.

Diamond, John. *The CIA and the Culture of Failure: U.S. Intelligence from the End of the Cold War to the Invasion of Iraq.* Stanford: Stanford University Press, 2008.

Doyle, Michael W. *Ways of War and Peace.* New York: W. W. Norton, 1997.

Farnham, Barbara. "Impact of the Political Context on Foreign Policy Decision Making." *Political Psychology* 25 (3) (2004): 441–463.

Fenno, Richard F. *Congressmen in Committees.* Boston: Little, Brown, 1973.

Ferguson, Yale H., and Richard W. Mansbach. *The Elusive Quest Continues: Theory and Global Politics.* Upper Saddle River, NJ: Prentice Hall, 2003.

Fowler, Linda L. *Watchdogs on the Hill: The Decline of Congressional Oversight of U.S. Foreign Relations.* Princeton: Princeton University Press, 2015.

Fukuyama, Francis. "The End of History?" *National Interest* 16 (1989): 3–18.

Gartzke, Erik. "The Capitalist Peace." *American Journal of Political Science* 51 (2007): 166–191.

George, Alexander L. "The Case for Multiple Advocacy in Making Foreign Policy." *American Political Science Review* 66 (1972): 751–785.

———. "The 'Operational Code:' A Neglected Approach to the Study of Political Leaders and Decision-Making." *International Studies Quarterly* 13 (1969): 190–222.

———. *Presidential Decisionmaking in Foreign Policy: The Effective Use of Information and Advice.* Boulder: Westview, 1980.

Gilpin, Robert. *War and Change in World Politics.* Cambridge: Cambridge University Press, 1981.

Gries, Peter Hays. *The Politics of American Foreign Policy: How Ideology Divides Liberals and Conservatives over Foreign Affairs.* Stanford: Stanford University Press, 2014.

Gutner, Tamar. *International Organizations in World Politics.* Rev. ed. Thousand Oaks, CA: Sage/CQ Press, 2016.

Gvosdev, Nikolas K., Jessica D. Blankshain, and David A. Cooper. *Decision-Making in American Foreign Policy: Translating Theory into Practice.* Cambridge: Cambridge University Press, 2019.

Haass, Richard. *A World in Disarray: American Foreign Policy and the Crisis of the Old Order.* New York: Penguin Books, 2017.

Halberstam, David. *The Best and the Brightest.* New York: Random House, 1989.

Halperin, Morton H., and Priscilla A. Clapp, with Arnold Kanter. *Bureaucratic Politics and Foreign Policy.* 2nd ed. Washington, DC: Brookings Institution, 2006.

Harrison, Ewan, and Sara M. Mitchell. *The Triumph of Democracy and the Eclipse of the West.* New York: Palgrave Macmillan, 2014.

Hermann, Charles F. "Some Issues in the Study of International Crisis." In *International Crises: Insights from Behavioral Research,* ed. Charles F. Hermann, 3–17. New York: Free Press, 1972.

Hermann, Charles F., ed. *When Things Go Wrong: Foreign Policy Decision Making Under Adverse Impact.* New York: Routledge, 2012.

Hersman, Rebecca K. C. *Friends and Foes: How Congress and the President Really Make Foreign Policy.* Washington, DC: Brookings Institution Press, 2000.

Hilsman, Roger. *The Politics of Policy Making in Defense and Foreign Affairs: Conceptual Models and Bureaucratic Politics.* 3rd ed. Upper Saddle River, NJ: Prentice Hall, 1993.

Hinckley, Barbara. *Less Than Meets the Eye: Congress, the President, and Foreign Policy.* Chicago: University of Chicago Press, 1994.

Holsti, Ole R. "Public Opinion and Foreign Policy: Challenges to the Almond-Lippmann Consensus." *International Studies Quarterly* 36 (1992): 439–466.

Howell, William G., and Jon C. Pevehouse. *While Dangers Gather: Congressional Checks on Presidential War Powers.* Princeton: Princeton University Press, 2007.

Hudson, Valerie M. *Foreign Policy Analysis: Classic and Contemporary Theory.* 2nd ed. Lanham, MD: Rowman and Littlefield, 2013.

Hunt, Michael H. *Ideology and U.S. Foreign Policy.* 2nd ed. New Haven: Yale University Press, 2009.

Huntington, Samuel P. "The Clash of Civilizations?" *Foreign Affairs* 72 (1993): 22–49.

Ikenberry, G. John. *After Victory: Institutions, Strategic Restraint, and the Rebuilding of Order After Major Wars.* New ed. Princeton: Princeton University Press, 2019.

Janis, Irving L. *Groupthink.* 2nd ed. Boston: Wadsworth, Cengage Learning, 1982.

Jentleson, Bruce W. "The Pretty Prudent Public: Post Post-Vietnam American Opinion on the Use of Military Force." *International Studies Quarterly* 36 (1992): 49–73.

Jentleson, Bruce W., and Rebecca L. Britton. "Still Pretty Prudent: Post–Cold War American Public Opinion on the Use of Military Force." *Journal of Conflict Resolution* 42 (1998): 395–417.

Johnson, Chalmers. *The Sorrows of Empire: Militarism, Secrecy, and the End of the Republic.* New York: Holt Paperbacks, 2004.

Johnson, Loch K. *A Season of Inquiry: The Senate Intelligence Investigation.* Lexington: University Press of Kentucky, 1985.

Kahneman, Daniel, Amos Tversky, and Paul Slovic, eds. *Judgment Under Uncertainty: Heuristics and Biases.* Cambridge: Cambridge University Press, 1982.

Kaufman, Joyce P. *A Concise History of U.S. Foreign Policy.* 4th ed. Lanham, MD: Rowman and Littlefield, 2017.

Kay, Sean. *America's Search for Security: The Triumph of Idealism and the Return of Realism.* Lanham. MD: Rowman and Littlefield, 2014.

Keohane, Robert O., ed. *Neorealism and Its Critics.* New York: Columbia University Press, 1986.

Kingdon, John W. *Congressmen's Voting Decisions.* 3rd ed. Ann Arbor: University of Michigan Press, 1989.

Levering, Ralph B. *The Public and American Foreign Policy, 1918–1978.* New York: William Morrow, 1978.

Lindblom, Charles E. "The Science of 'Muddling Through.'" *Public Administration Review* 19 (1959): 79–88.

Lindsay, James M. *Congress and the Politics of U.S. Foreign Policy.* Baltimore: Johns Hopkins University Press, 1994.

Lipset, Seymour Martin. *American Exceptionalism: A Double-Edged Sword.* New York: W. W. Norton, 1996.

Mayhew, David R. *America's Congress: Actions in the Public Sphere, James Madison Through Newt Gingrich.* New Haven: Yale University Press, 2000.

McCormick, James M., ed. *The Domestic Sources of American Foreign Policy.* 7th ed. Lanham, MD: Rowman and Littlefield, 2017.

Milner, Helen V., and Dustin Tingley. *Sailing the Water's Edge: The Domestic Sources of American Foreign Policy.* Princeton: Princeton University Press, 2015.

Mintz, Alex, "How Do Leaders Make Decisions? A Poliheuristic Perspective." *Journal of Conflict Resolution* 48 (2004): 3–13.

Mintz, Alex, and Carly Wayne. *The Polythink Syndrome: U.S. Foreign Policy Decisions on 9/11, Afghanistan, Iraq, Iran, Syria, and ISIS.* Stanford: Stanford University Press, 2016.

Moravcsik, Andrew. "Taking Preferences Seriously: A Liberal Theory of International Politics." *International Organization* 51 (4) (1997): 513–553.

Morgenthau, Hans J., and Kenneth W. Thompson. *Politics Among Nations.* 7th ed. New York: McGraw-Hill Education, 2005.

Neack, Laura. *Studying Foreign Policy Comparatively: Cases and Analysis.* 4th ed. Lanham, MD: Rowman and Littlefield, 2018.

Niebuhr, Reinhold. *Moral Man and Immoral Society: A Study of Ethics and Politics.* Introduction by Landon Gilkey. Louisville, KY: Westminster John Knox Press, 2002.

Nye, Joseph S., Jr. "Get Smart," *Foreign Affairs* 88 (July–August 2009): 160–163.

———. *The Paradox of American Power: Why the World's Only Superpower Can't Go It Alone.* New York: Oxford University Press, 2003.

Organski, A. F. K., and Jacek Kugler. *The War Ledger.* Chicago: University of Chicago Press, 1980.

Oye, Kenneth, ed. *Cooperation Under Anarchy.* Princeton: Princeton University Press, 1986.

Page, Benjamin I., and Robert Y. Shapiro. *The Rational Public: Fifty Years of Trends in Americans' Policy Preferences.* Chicago: University of Chicago Press, 1992.

Perkins, Dexter. *The American Approach to Foreign Policy.* Rev. ed. Cambridge, MA: Harvard University Press, 1962.

Preston, Thomas. *The President and His Inner Circle: Leadership Style and the Advisory Process in Foreign Affairs.* New York: Columbia University Press, 2001.

Rudalevige, Andrew. *The New Imperial Presidency: Renewing Presidential Power After Watergate.* Ann Arbor: University of Michigan Press, 2005.

Russett, Bruce. *Grasping the Democratic Peace.* Princeton: Princeton University Press, 1994.

Schafer, Mark, and Stephen G. Walker, eds. *Beliefs and Leadership in World Politics: Methods and Applications of Operational Code Analysis.* New York: Palgrave Macmillan, 2006.

Scott, James M., and Ralph G. Carter. "Acting on the Hill: Congressional Assertiveness in U.S. Foreign Policy." *Congress and the Presidency* 29 (2002): 151–169.

Scott, James M., Ralph G. Carter, and A. Cooper Drury. *IR: International, Economic, and Human Security in a Changing World.* 3rd ed. Thousand Oaks, CA: Sage/CQ Press, 2019.

Silverstein, Gordon, *Imbalance of Powers: Constitutional Interpretation and the Making of American Foreign Policy.* New York: Oxford University Press, 1997.

Simon, Herbert A. "Theories of Decision-Making in Economics and Behavioral Science." *American Economic Review* 49 (1959): 253–283.

Snyder, Richard C., H. W. Bruck, Burton Sapin, Valerie M. Hudson, Derek H. Chollet, and James H. Goldgeier. *Foreign Policy Decision Making (Revisited).* New York: Palgrave Macmillan, 2002.

Sterling-Folker, Jennifer, ed. *Making Sense of International Relations Theory.* 2nd ed. Boulder: Lynne Rienner, 2013.

Stiglitz, Joseph E. *Globalization and Its Discontents Revisited: Anti-Globalization in the Era of Trump.* Oxford: Oxford University Press, 2018.

Stoddard, Abby. *Humanitarian Alert: NGO Information and Its Impact on U.S. Foreign Policy.* Boulder: Kumarian Press, 2006.

Terry, Janice J. *US Foreign Policy in the Middle East: The Role of Lobbies and Special Interest Groups.* Ann Arbor, MI: Pluto, 2005.

Trubowitz, Peter. *Defining the National Interest: Conflict and Change in American Foreign Policy.* Chicago: University of Chicago Press, 1998.

Truman, David B. *The Governmental Process.* New York: Knopf, 1951.

Viotti, Paul. *The Dollar and National Security: The Monetary Components of Hard Power.* Stanford: Stanford University Press, 2014.

Walker, Christopher, and Jessica Ludwig. "The Meaning of Sharp Power." *Foreign Affairs,* November 16, 2017. https://www.foreignaffairs.com /articles/china/2017-11-16/meaning-sharp-power.

Walt, Stephen M. *Taming American Power: The Global Response to U.S. Primacy.* New York: W. W. Norton, 2005.

Waltz, Kenneth. *Theory of International Politics.* Reading, MA: Addison Wesley, 1979.

Weber, Steven, and Bruce W. Jentleson. *The End of Arrogance: America in the Global Competition of Ideas.* Cambridge, MA: Harvard University Press, 2010.

Wendt, Alexander. *Social Theory of International Politics.* Cambridge: Cambridge University Press, 1999.

Wilson, Ernest J. "Hard Power, Soft Power, Smart Power." *Annals of the American Academy of Political and Social Science* 616 (2008): 110–124.

Wittkopf, Eugene R. "What Americans Really Think About Foreign Policy." *Washington Quarterly* 19 (1996): 91–106.

Zakaria, Fareed. *The Post-American World: Release 2.0.* New York: W. W. Norton, 2011.

Index

275

DNI. *See* Director of national intelligence
Dobriansky, Paula, 168
Dole, Bob, 129, 133
Donilon, Thomas, 95
Dulles, Allen, 196
Dulles, John Foster, 65, 196

Economic sanctions, 72, 142, 167, 220–222; on Iran, 50, 108, 165, 172, 200, 201; on North Korea, 242; on Russia, 6, 22, 36–37, 50, 129, 146, 152, 197; on South Africa, 41
Eikenberry, Karl, 95
Eisenhower, Dwight, 65, 86; Iran under, 172
Election, 2016. *See* Russian intervention in 2016 US Election
Elitism, 163
Emanuel, Rahm, 95
Erdogan, Recep Tayyip, 199
EU. *See* European Union
European Union (EU), 16; economies of, 35
ExComm, 100
Executive agreements, 5
Executive branch: cabinet officials in, 64–67; intelligence community in, 67–69; policy-making process from, 60–69, 248–249; president in, 60–61; presidential advisers in, 61–64
Exon-Florio Amendment, 70

Facebook, 140, 162, 177, 183
Falun Gong, 148
Family separations, 122–123
FAS. *See* Foreign Agricultural Service
Federal courts, policy-making process from, 77–80
First-generation rights, 33
Flynn, Michael, 197
Ford, Gerald, 16–17

Foreign Agricultural Service (FAS), 166–167
Foreign aid: conditional nature of, 139; Congress members immigrant roots with, 139–140; good business from, 139
Foreign investment, approval for, 70–71
Foreign Operations Subcommittee, 132
Foreign policy: actors in, 59–80; attitudinal clusters for, 181*fig*; bureaucratic role in, 105–125; concentric circles of making, 7*fig*; Congress role in, 127–157; decision-making phase of, 3–4, 8; defined, 2; Democratic party agendas for, 39–40; entrepreneurs, 75–76; five-stage process in making, 3, 4*fig*; inputs to, 3, 4*fig*, 8, 39, 179–185, 239–246; interbranch interactions with, 6–8; international actors role in, 206–209; making US, 1–10; outcomes from, 3, 4*fig*; outputs from, 3, 4*fig*, 9, 213–235, 252–256; overlapping powers with, 6; pluralist policy processes with, 162–164, 164*fig*; president appointed officials for, 5; presidents role in, 3–5; problematic, 2; process of making, 4*fig*; public participation in, 162–163; Republican party agendas for, 39–40; shift in, 11; societal actors role in, 185–186; theory for goals of, 12; US recent history in, 42–55
Fox and Friends, 175
Fox News Channel, 174–175, 198
Free trade, 20–21
Fukuyama, Francis, 237–238
Fulbright, William, 133
Fulbright Program, 226

Smart power, 229–233; future with, 255–256
Smith, Adam, 14
Smith, Christopher, 137
Social Darwinism, 32
Social media, 8, 23, 177, 207, 225
Societal actors: foreign policy influenced by, 185–186; individual opinion leaders, 164*fig*, 178–179; interest groups, 164–167, 164*fig*; mass media, 164*fig*, 171–177; motivations for, 179–185; political culture with, 179–180; public attitudes and opinion with, 180–185; role of, 161–187; social media, 8, 23, 177, 207, 225; think tanks, 164*fig*, 167–171
Soft power: agenda setting with, 227–229; future with, 253–255; value advocacy with, 224–227
Somalia, 245; militias in, 255; terrorist sites in, 217, 253
SOPs. *See* Standard operating procedures
South China Sea: Chinese claim to, 24–27, 241; Chinese military bulwark with, 25; constructivist view of, 27; fishery resources with, 25; idealist view of, 26–27; liberal view of, 26; realist view of, 25
Spain, economic aid to, 155
Speaker of the House, 128–129
Standard operating procedures (SOPs), 110, 113
State Department: budget of, 66; interagency vetting process of, 87; president consulting, 107; roles of, 64–65; Travel Advisories list of, 108
Status of Forces Agreements, 46
Stavridis, James, 232
Subgovernment, 166
Sultan, Bandar bin, 198–199
Summit conferences, 4

Sunni, 45
Symington, Stuart, 131
Syria: chemical weapons in, 48–49; terrorist sites in, 217, 253

Taft-Hartley Act, 77–78
Taliban: Afghanistan counterinsurgency campaign against, 44, 95–96, 109; contractors paying off, 112; Kabul regime of, 35
Theory: as cognitive maps, 12; constructivism in, 17–20; defined, 12; foreign policy goals with, 12; idealism in, 16–17; impact of, 11–28; liberalism in, 14–16; realism in, 12–14
Think tanks, 164*fig*, 167–171
Third-generation rights, 33
Thucydides, 12
Thune, John, 52
Tillerson, Rex, 65–66, 149
Torshin, Alexander, 52–53, 197
Tower, John, 148–149
TPP. *See* Trans-Pacific Partnership
Transactionalism, 90–91
Trans-Pacific Partnership (TPP), 26, 50, 146
Travel Advisories list, 108
Trudeau, Justin, 123
Truman, Harry, 65, 85, 92
Trump, Donald J.: authoritarian rulers respected by, 238; campaign slogan of, 55; Congress pushback to, 145–146; counterterrorism efforts under, 253; decision making by, 86, 87, 91, 249; economic growth rate under, 244; emoluments clause violation by, 145; family Separations under, 122–123; Global Magnitsky Act invoked by, 195; immigration rhetoric and policies of, 55; Iran policy of, 200; isolationism with, 41; Kurdish fighters aid by, 199; MBS influence on, 201–202;

About the Book

Whether your approach to teaching US foreign policy is thematic, historical, case-study oriented, regional, or perhaps a blend of several approaches, *Making US Foreign Policy: The Essentials* is likely to be a text that you will want to assign as required reading.

The text focuses on the most fundamental questions: Who makes foreign policy decisions? How? What accounts for particular decisions? At the same time, discussions of current examples—responses to Russian interference in US elections, the travel ban targeting Muslim-majority countries, the Trump administration's immigration policies, reactions to the murder of Saudi journalist and US resident Jamal Khashoggi, and many more—make the topic "real."

Clear, concise, and reasonably priced, this is the book that will provide your students with a solid understanding of, and interest in, the process by which foreign policy is made in the current environment and the full range of actors involved.

Ralph G. Carter is Piper Professor of 2014 and professor of political science at Texas Christian University.